Manifestos for History

'An engaging and stimulating collection that encourages and indeed provokes all of us to consider our futures with and even beyond history.'
Marnie ......-Warrington, *Macquarie University*

'A stimulating ... dialectic collection of observations by some of the best practitioners of the dev... volume is an optimistic call to arms for the next generation of historia... ing read.'
Philippa ...... *sity of Southern California*

Write ...... f the world's leading historians and theorists of history, *Ma...ory* draws together a series of manifestos that address the que ...... .inds of histories we ought to be considering and making in and ...... .iy-first century. With a foreword by Joanna Bourke and an a...... Hayden White, these manifestos – critical, innovative, reflex...... nal – are absolutely essential reading, not just for those emba...... study of history, but for all those who would think seriously abou ...... m ...f history' in its present and possible future forms. This coll...... .ish es a benchmark for all future considerations upon the disco...... story.

Keith Jenkins is r......essor of Historical Theory at the University of Chichester. He is ...... hor of six books on historical theory, including *Rethinking Hist...* ...... ge Classic, 1991/2003) and *Refiguring History* (2003).

Sue M. ...... .ader in Women's and Gender History at the University of Chi...... . the author of several works on the history of gender and relig...... .nist historiography. Her most recent book is *The Feminist Hi...* ...... (Routledge, 2006).

Alun Munslow is UK Editor of *Rethinking History: The Journal of Theory and Practice* and the author of several books on the nature of history. His most recent is *Narrative and History* (2007). He is Visiting Professor of History and Historical Theory at the University of Chichester.

Manifestos for History

Edited and Introduced by
Keith Jenkins, Sue Morgan
and Alun Munslow

Routledge
Taylor & Francis Group

LONDON AND NEW YORK

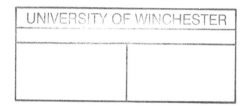

First published 2007
by Routledge
2 Park Square, Milton Park, Abingdon, Oxon OX14 4RN

Simultaneously published in the USA and Canada
by Routledge
711 Third Avenue, New York, NY 10017

Routledge is an imprint of the Taylor & Francis Group, an informa business

© 2007 Keith Jenkins, Sue Morgan and Alun Munslow

Typeset in Sabon
by Keystroke, 28 High Street, Tettenhall, Wolverhampton

British Library Cataloguing in Publication Data
A catalogue record for this book is available from the British Library

Library of Congress Cataloging in Publication Data
Manifestos for history / edited and introduced by Keith Jenkins,
Sue Morgan and Alun Munslow ; with a foreword by Joanna Bourke
and an afterword by Hayden White.
    p. cm.
Includes bibliographical references and index.
1. History–Philosophy. I. Jenkins, Keith, 1943– II. Morgan, Sue, 1957–
III. Munslow, Alun, 1947–
D16.8.M268 2007
901–dc22
2007006603

ISBN10: 0–415–37776–5 (hbk)
ISBN10: 0–415–37777–3 (pbk)
ISBN10: 0–203–96234–6 (ebk)

ISBN13: 978–0–415–37776–8 (hbk)
ISBN13: 978–0–415–37777–5 (pbk)
ISBN13: 978–0–203–96234–6 (ebk)

Contents

Contributors

Frank Ankersmit is Professor of Intellectual History and Historical Theory at Groningen University. He has published some fifteen books and many articles on the philosophy of history, aesthetics and political philosophy. His latest book was *Sublime Historical Experience* (Stanford, 2005).

Joanna Bourke is Professor of History at Birkbeck College, University of London. She has published seven books on Irish history, gender and 'the body', the history of psychological thought, modern warfare and the emotions. Her books have been translated into Chinese, Italian, Portuguese, Spanish, Catalan and Turkish. *An Intimate History of Killing: Face-to-Face Killing in Twentieth Century Warfare* (Granta) won the Frankael Prize in Contemporary History for 1998 and the Wolfson History Prize for 2000. Her latest book entitled *Fear: A Cultural History* was published by Virago in 2005. She is currently writing a history of rapists in the nineteenth and twentieth centuries.

Dipesh Chakrabarty is the Lawrence A. Kimpton Distinguished Service Professor of History and South Asian Studies at the University of Chicago. He is a founding member of the editorial collective of *Subaltern Studies*, a co-editor of *Critical Inquiry*, and a founding editor of *Postcolonial Studies*. His books include *Provincializing Europe: Postcolonial Thought and Historical Difference* (2000; second edition forthcoming). He was elected a fellow of the American Academy of Arts and Sciences in 2004. He is currently working on a book entitled *The Public Life of History*.

Elizabeth Deeds Ermarth writes on the construction and eventual deconstruction of a humanist culture of representation, and on the paradigmatic changes involved in moving out of modernity into what she calls the 'Discursive Condition'. She has published many essays and five books: *Realism and Consensus* (1998; 1983), *George Eliot* (1987), *Sequel to History* (1992), *The English Novel in History 1840–1895* (1997); her forthcoming *Re-writing Democracy* (2007) is a collection of essays by scholars and political activists addressing the political implications of the critique of modernity. She is Emerita Saintsbury Professor at the

University of Edinburgh and works on the renewal of democratic process and of higher education in the United States.

Greg Dening, after twenty-one years as the Max Crawford Professor of History at the University of Melbourne, is currently Adjunct Professor at the Centre for Cross-Cultural Research, Australian National University, where he conducts workshops for doctoral students of all disciplines and professions on the Creative Imagination in the Presentation of Scholarly Knowledge. His own latest creations are: *Beach Crossings: Voyaging across Times, Cultures and Self* (Melbourne University Publishing, 2004) and *Church Alive! Pilgrimages in Faith, 1956–2006* (University of NSW Press, 2006).

Ewa Domanska is Assistant Professor of Theory and History of Historiography in the Department of History, Adam Mickiewicz University, Poznan, Poland, and since 2002 Visiting Assistant Professor at the Department of Social and Cultural Anthropology, Stanford University. She is author of *Microhistories: Encounters in-between worlds* (1999, in Polish); *Unconventional Histories: Reflections on the Past in the New Humanities* (2006, in Polish); and editor of *History: A World too Far?* (1997, in Polish); *Encounters: Philosophy of History after Postmodernism* (1998); *History, Memory, Ethics* (2002, in Polish); and collections of essays by Hayden White and Frank Ankersmit (in Polish).

David Harlan teaches in the History Department at California State University, San Luis Obispo. He is co-editor of the journal *Rethinking History* and the author of *The Degradation of American History* (1997).

Patrick Joyce is Professor of Modern History, Manchester University, and Visiting Professor of Sociology at the London School of Economics, 2006–9. He has published widely in the history of class, work, politics and the city, his most recent books being *The Social in Question* (Routledge, 2002) and *The Rule of Freedom* (Verso, 2003). He is also interested in questions of historiography, history and theory, and social theory. His current work is a book on the nature of the British state, with the working title *The Soul of Leviathan: Making the British Technostate*. He is a research convener with the Centre for the Study of Sociocultural Change (CRESC/ESRC).

Wulf Kansteiner is an Associate Professor of History and Judaic Studies at Binghamton University (SUNY) where he teaches German history, Holocaust studies and historical theory. He has published essays on collective memory, trauma theory, and German intellectual and media history in *History and Theory, German Politics and Society, New German Critique, History of the Human Sciences* and the *Journal of Contemporary History*. He is author of *In Pursuit of German Memory: History, Television, and Politics after Auschwitz* (2006) and, with Ned Lebow and Claudio Fogu, is co-editor of *The Politics of Memory in Postwar Europe* (2006).

Dominick LaCapra teaches at Cornell University, where he is Professor of History and Comparative Literature, the Bryce and Edith M. Bowmar Professor of Humanistic Studies, and director of the School of Criticism and Theory. He is the author of twelve books, the most recent of which are *History and Reading: Tocqueville, Foucault, French Studies, Writing History, Writing Trauma* and *History in Transit: Experience, Identity, Critical Theory*. He has also edited or co-edited two other books.

David Lowenthal, Emeritus Professor of Geography and Honorary Research Fellow at University College London, has taught at some forty universities in Britain, the United States, Australia, Jamaica and continental Europe. His books include *West Indian Societies, Geographies of the Mind, Our Past before Us: Why Do We Save It?, The Past Is a Foreign Country, Landscape Meanings and Values, Possessed by the Past: The Heritage Crusade and the Spoils of History, George Perkins Marsh: Prophet of Conservation* and *The Nature of Cultural Heritage and the Culture of Natural Heritage*.

Mark Poster is Chair of the Department of Film and Media Studies and a member of the History Department at the University of California, Irvine. He has courtesy appointments in the Department of Information and Computer Science and the Department of Comparative Literature. He is a member of the Critical Theory Institute. His recent books are: *Information Please: Culture and Politics in a Digital Age* (Duke University Press, 2006); *What's the Matter with the Internet?: A Critical Theory of Cyberspace* (University of Minnesota Press, 2001); *The Information Subject* in Critical Voices Series (Gordon and Breach Arts International, 2001); *Cultural History and Postmodernity* (Columbia University Press, 1997); *The Second Media Age* (Polity and Blackwell, 1995); and *The Mode of Information* (Blackwell and University of Chicago Press, 1990).

Ann Rigney is Professor of Comparative Literature at Utrecht University. She has published widely in the field of philosophy of history, narratology and cultural memory, and is author of *The Rhetoric of Historical Representation: Three Narrative Histories of the French Revolution* (Cambridge University Press, 1990) and *Imperfect Histories: The Elusive Past and the Legacy of Romantic Historicism* (Cornell University Press, 2001). She directs a research programme on the Dynamics of Cultural Remembrance and is currently writing a book on the cultural afterlife of Walter Scott.

Robert A. Rosenstone, Professor of History at the California Institute of Technology, is an author of works of history, memoir and fiction. His scholarly books include *Crusade of the Left: The Lincoln Battalion in the Spanish Civil War* (1969), *Romantic Revolutionary: A Biography of John Reed* (1975), *Mirror in the Shrine: American Encounters with Meiji Japan* (1988), *Visions of the Past: The Challenge of Film to Our Idea of History* (1995), and *History on Film/Film on History* (2006). He has published a historical novel, *King of Odessa* (2003), and a memoir entitled *The Man who Swam into History* (2005). He has edited several collections of essays, including *Revisioning History: Film and the Construction of a New Past* (1995) and *Experiments in Rethinking History* (2004), and has served as a contributing editor of the *American Historical Review*, associate editor of *Film Historia*, and is founding editor of *Rethinking History: The Journal of Theory and Practice*.

Joan W. Scott is Harold F. Linder Professor of Social Science at the Institute for Advanced Study. She works in the fields of French history, women's and gender history, feminist theory and intellectual history. Her books include *Gender and the Politics of History* (1988), *Only Paradoxes to Offer: French Feminists and the Rights of Man* (1996), *Parite: Sexual Equality and the Crisis of French Universalism* (2005) and, most recently, *The Politics of the Veil*.

Beverley Southgate is Reader Emeritus in History of Ideas at the University of Hertfordshire and Visiting Fellow in History at the University of Chichester. His publications include *Postmodernism in History: Fear of Freedom?* (Routledge, 2003) and *What is History for?* (Routledge, 2005). He is currently pondering the relative merits of contentment and aspiration.

Hayden White is Emeritus Professor of the History of Consciousness, University of California, and teaches comparative literature at Stanford University. He is currently working on a book on *The Philosophy of the Preposition*.

Foreword

Joanna Bourke

The joy that comes from writing history infuses this book. Pleasure and passion, ethics and engagement, are at the heart of the historical endeavour, allowing these essays to celebrate the historical sublime, with its relentless search for meaning in the midst of a radically unknowable past and its aesthetic yearnings despite recognising the unrepresentability of history. A historical consciousness is 'an indispensable dimension of a human being's ontology', the editors of *Manifestos for History* tell us. The composition of history becomes the ultimate act of creation, making us human through critical dialogic exchange.

Of course, I think there are hints of anxiety. And why not? *Manifestos for History* is being published at a time of ubiquitous state-sponsored terror, torture and tyranny. Inhumanity seems to be on the rise. The question 'What does it mean to be human?' is being met with looks of bewilderment. Natural law is moribund. The edifices assembled by the greatest manifesto of the nineteenth century, *The Manifesto of the Communist Party* (1848), have come tumbling down. International law – with its hallowed spectre, human rights – has been variously co-opted and used to justify abuse. The obligations of public intellectuals have rarely been so urgent, yet many conventional historians are too timid to exploit their potential political and cultural acumen effectively. Religious and political censorship is set to invade the classroom, surveillance technologies and an auditing culture attempt to limit the range of cultural exploration, and the pernicious impact of rhetorics of certainty (whether this is evolutionary psychology or the endorsement of an ethics of objectivity) all suggest that history has lost its way. This is why we need manifestos like these.

While much history in the mass media wallows in *fin de siècle* sentimentality, lauding a nostalgic world of community, stability and certainty, the historical profession has attempted to remain true to the more brittle narratives and images emanating from a thoroughly complex and perplexing past. They have sought to do this in numerous ways. After all, there was never any static or elemental conception of history; historicisations of the past have always come about by way of a series of heartily contested versions and modes of action. The dominant forms of historiography in any one period are nothing other than the consequences of previous struggles.

These manifestos attempt to speak to the future of 'doing history'. Their gift to this future is less a party platform than a solidarity of perspective. Some authors boldly set forth a series of rules, with 'thou shalts' outnumbering 'thou shalt nots'. Most, however, proffer more open-ended suggestions, nudging readers to a widening appreciation of potentialities. Methodological pluralism is urged. Forms of history that devolve into accountancy – a totting up of footnotes judiciously weighted to favour manuscript over printed material and secondary sources – are snubbed. Twenty-first-century technologies, with their capacity for fashioning new cultural forms and their scope for engaging with wider publics, are eulogised. Self-reflexivity is commended. All reject universalist precepts, reminding readers that there is no single discourse of history. After all, the pursuit of the past is an unending cultural process, permeated with competing politics relating to social action. It is always in the process of evolution, devolution, revolution. Contrary to certain vulgar attacks on recent theoretical interventions, the 'truth' word is discussed without flinching, as are the beauties of journeying through archives. Discourses of dissent and subversion coexist with languages of conformity; the manifesto authors remain loyal to certain conceptions of historical composition while also celebrating the fervent glossolalia that always accompanies the exploration of new ways of imagining the real.

The ethics of writing history are highlighted in these manifestos. Discourses – *all* discourses – are exercises in power. Historians have an obligation to people who lived in the past: we strive to be true to their lives. Through exposing seemingly universal modes of being as necessarily situated in time and place and embedded in humdrum practices and everyday knowledges, historians reveal the specificities of the past. This enables us to imagine more emancipatory futures. Critical history/critiques of history leave the present open to the future. They open up possibilities of resistance in times of tyranny. Being steeped in notions of trauma and seduced by apocalyptic fantasies, it is easy to forget that regimes of suffering are always contested. 'Why are *you* doing this to *me*?' the suffering subject asks, insisting on historical specificities, instead of any ahistorical narrative based on supposedly biological, psychological or transhistorical (particularly religious and ideological) constants. Terror is always local. To universalise it is to remove the specificities of an individual's history; it is to situate suffering in the realm of moral edification. Critical history enables us to make manifest diverse constructions of the human, making ways of creating the self and sociality imaginatively accessible and contestable. As such, as in other manifestos, a utopian vision can be discerned in many of these essays. They speak to a hope for a better future through a commitment to the dignity of each unique, singular person within specific times and geographical places. They are manifestos that endeavour to do more than merely persuade; they aim to mobilise.

Introduction

On fidelity and diversity

Keith Jenkins, Sue Morgan and
Alun Munslow

If, at the beginning of the twenty-first century, we can assume that history is constituted as a complex series of narratives – representations – of the past, then we have the foundations upon which we can build our visions of its future. The important point to make here, of course, is that there are always multiple visions rather than one vision of what history is or what it may become. Just as there can never be one authorised version of the past, so there can be no single methodological way of bringing that past to us as history. To sustain a commitment to the 'time before now' therefore suggests that we must continually develop our relationship with it and that part of that process of commitment is to dissent from orthodoxies. All historians have, in effect, a duty of discontent.[1] Happily, the notion of history as a narrative that can never be merely revised but has, rather, to be constantly rewritten and reimagined is its greatest strength and safeguard against the 'corruption' of contentment. To be a historian means at some point to make a break; to make something anew. Historians must be disloyal to some degree precisely to have a *larger* loyalty to a tradition or a belief system or a theory: up to a certain (radically undecidable) point, to be loyal means *not* being loyal; to be truly faithful involves a degree of infidelity. Jacques Derrida encapsulates this paradox in a single phrase: 'to be true to what you follow you have to interrupt the following'.[2] There is thus, perhaps, a 'deeper' understanding of fidelity at play here: to be a follower of Marx, Nietzsche or Freud, for example, or of the 'historical' methods of, say, *Annales*, empiricism, phenomenology, post-structuralism, hermeneutics and so on, we have to repeat, but always repeat differently. We are all, therefore (in certain degrees), simultaneously acolytes of history and revisionists, followers and rebels, believers in old things and celebrators of the new, conformists and dissenters; each of us full of both reiterations and innovations.

The contributors to this volume have offered perspectives that can be regarded as being both loyal to history and dissenting from it in varying degrees. Accordingly, the idea of history writing as an act of both fidelity and rebellion seemed to us to be a useful device around which to organise this collection of *Manifestos for History*. How, in more detail, might that be the case? Well, let us try to explain by putting this book into just some of what might be called its 'current circumstances'.

When we first conceived of the idea for this volume, despite having our own very singular readings of its significance, we thought more generally that the time was probably ripe for a further injection of ideas with regard to ways of refiguring and refashioning what arguably *ought* best to go on today and tomorrow under the name of history. Originally a historian of ideas and political theory, one of the editors (Keith Jenkins) has developed over the last twenty-five years or so a 'postmodern' position on history which, expressed in a series of texts, has argued that history should now be read as a post-empirical, post-epistemological *aesthetic* discourse bringing to an end epistemologically striving histories/historians because they seemed to be: a) intellectually and logically confused and confusing *vis-à-vis* the ways histories actually seem to be *made*; and b) predominantly expressive of an ideological conservatism variously construable.[3] According to Jenkins, historicisations of 'the past' (the 'before now') always have been and always necessarily will be, as histories, aesthetic phenomena. And this could open up the 'before now' to the possibility of infinite refigurings and multiple meanings which, while taking 'into account' epistemological (knowledge) elements, were seen as but one technical aspect of histories *per se*. What have been proposed by Jenkins are histories of a postmodern type which, he hoped, might be useful for those who had not yet had histories in their own right/write. There is still a kind of faithfulness to historicisations here, but to historicisations going well beyond old histories: 'histories after the end of history', as it were. Here there is a kind of reworking of the idea of one who is loyal to the 'before now' and to the idea of dissent and disobedience – loyal to histories that just don't follow; loyal to the voices of others who have yet to speak.

As a historian of gender, religion and sexuality, one of us (Sue Morgan) has, in her commitment to feminism and a feminist appropriation and historicisation of the past, expressed another version of the acolyte/dissenter paradox. In the introduction to her book *The Feminist History Reader*, for example, Morgan traces the recent production of a richly theorised and reflexive feminist historiography, understood as a critical rethinking of historical discourse more generally. Feminists have never united around a single theoretical position or methodological framework, she argues, as is evident from the multiplicity of positions that continue to disturb and enrich the field. Such an absence of feminist unanimity is no cause for concern, however, nor for the dismissal of the integrity of the discourse itself; rather, it is a source of tremendous optimism, creativity and analytical momentum. 'Feminist history in the twenty first century can never inhabit the historical mainstream in any epistemological sense,' argues Morgan, 'for that would be a disavowal of its fundamentally subversive practice. What characterises feminism's history and its perpetual interrogation of dominant categories is, as Joan Scott notes, its "radical refusal to settle down" and to call anywhere "home".' This is the radical openness of a discourse which accepts in its rewriting and retheorising of history that it must look to its own transformations and its own reimaginings, aware that the very best we produce will, in the future, always be seen as 'not having been good enough'.[4]

Originally a socio-economic, empirical historian with a specialism in nineteenth-century America, Alun Munslow has made an intellectual journey away from that 'original' position to one which, today, puts him in a theoretical place adjacent to that occupied by Jenkins. A writer of numerous texts and a founding editor of the international journal of 'theory and practice', *Rethinking History: The Journal of Theory and Practice*, Munslow has increasingly experimented with ways of presenting/representing the 'before now' as the acts of the imagination they so obviously are at the expense of empirical/epistemological fashionings. Certainly more loyal than Jenkins to the continuation of history in the belief that a historical consciousness remains an *indispensable* dimension of human beings' ontology, Munslow's loyalty to historicisation has, nevertheless, led him to articulate that fidelity in dissent from the practices he sees traditional historians employing insofar as they remain (know it or not . . .) epistemological-strivers. His distinction between reconstructionist, constructionist and deconstructionist historians has been useful in pointing to the epistemological choices all historians make in orientating themselves *vis-à-vis* the past. He has consistently argued that the epistemological choice is always prior to 'doing history'.[5]

Though by no means speaking with a unified voice, then, each of us as the editors of this volume were in agreement that, while we may well have our own singular agendas such that had we been asked to write manifestos of our own we would certainly have written very different ones, nevertheless, we all thought that, at the beginning of the twenty-first century, the ambivalent attitudes we variously held about our *acolyte–rebellious* takes on history were probably fairly typical (indexical even) of many historians' predicaments as they wrestled with the problematics of 'history today'. And so, as we've said, we thought it a good time to put before students of history a series of perspectives from a number of important and well-known historians which embody what they now most desired for history in general and for that history closest to their own interests. Accordingly, the question which we asked them to address (and to which we return a little later) was along the lines of what sort of historical consciousness would they like students of history to have in order to do the kinds of things they thought students *ought* to be doing – and thinking – in the best of all possible worlds, taking into account the circumstances of today?

Having made several references to the 'circumstances of today', what, one might ask, might these be, and how do they affect history? This short introduction offers us neither the time nor the place (nor the space) to go into great detail as to why it might *still* be useful to categorise – despite detractors who variously consider the whole idea/phenomenon as tired and passé – the times in which we live as the time of *postmodernity*, and that our all-pervasive intellectual *habitus* is that of *postmodernism*. Not that we are saying, of course, that the contributors to this volume would necessarily sign up to this portrayal. But, for us, in various ways, the arguments as to why we live *after* modernity and the consequences of doing so are persuasive at least as a *proposal* which might help us to situate the manifestos which constitute this collection. And so follows a brief discussion of our (possible) circumstances.

The relationship of modernity to postmodernity is a difficult one to pin down, signalling, as it does, a range of social and economic transformations across local, national and transnational locations that defy easy analyses and which ripple out culturally and ideologically in ways which even the finest-grained examination cannot fully grasp; there is always an indeterminacy, an affecting excess. But that's fine. For these indeterminacies and failed representations can themselves be seen as expressions of that epistemological shortfall that characterises postmodernism itself and to which it draws attention – and it was, of course, ever thus! That said, it is perhaps useful on this occasion to go along with the *proposal* that we can at least take it as an axiom that we do indeed live *after* modernity; that we have come to the end of the 'experiment of modernity' and that those post-Enlightenment experiments of attempting to establish, in both bourgeois and proletarian forms, 'human rights communities' have now failed on their own terms amid the genocides, the gulags and the death camps of the twentieth century. Post-modernity is therefore, to borrow Elizabeth Ermarth's brilliant phrase, 'the whatever it is'[6] that comes *after* the breakdown of that experiment, with postmodernism being that condition of postmodernity raised to the level of consciousness more generally and, more specifically, to theoretical levels.

Again, who and what constitute these theoretical levels is complex. They bring together both proper and common names including, *inter alia*, Roland Barthes, Michel Foucault, Judith Butler, Gilles Deleuze, Jean-François Lyotard, Jean Baudrillard, Helene Cixous, Ernesto Laclau, Alain Badiou, Jacques Derrida and Richard Rorty; they hybridise poststructuralism, post-Marxism, post-colonialism, post-feminism, neo-pragmatism and so on. They are indeed complicated – as is assessing their impact. But, arguably, such theorists and critical interrogations have in the space of the last forty years deconstructed the whole of the Western tradition, especially the Western tradition in its late modernist forms in favour of what might be called a second, very different 'Enlightenment to come', in the name of a different emancipatory future, yet an Enlightenment nevertheless. In that sense postmodernism can be seen as a clearing of the decks of those modernist assumptions that, once so vital and energising 'first time around', might now actually prevent a new emancipatory project. Postmodern theories so considered thus acted as a kind of critical retrospective of the Western tradition, a sifting out of its constitutive elements to see whether, amid the clutter, anything could be retained as useful for new social livings. Very little was.

At which point it might be possible to stipulate a working definition of postmodernism which captures both its deconstructive retrospection of modernity and the way in which it sees such critiques as clearing the ground for new building work, albeit, this time around, without sure and certain, total foundations. In a nutshell, then, it goes like this: postmodernism is the era of the raising to consciousness of the *aporia* for, perhaps, future emancipatory needs. This is an era, in other words, when all the decisions we take – political, ethical, moral, interpretive, representational, figural, etc. – are ultimately undecidable (*aporetic*); a time when our chosen ways of reading things lack solid, universal foundations. Thus, as far as historical discourses are concerned, if there are no objective or foundational truths out there waiting to be discovered, if all historical discourses are instead of an aesthetic kind, intentional processes of shaping and meaning-making, if history is a verb and not a noun, if we are all engaged in 'historying' (as Greg Dening describes it), then this is potentially a massively liberating thing. As the contributors to this volume bear witness, the postmodern condition (or something akin to it) does not necessarily lead to nihilism, as so many of its critics would claim, but can point to new creations and new ways of thinking about the past.

Which brings us directly to history. For the attempt to know the past 'modernistically' with all the epistemological certainty, confidence and self-assurance of empirical historians did not escape the critical attention of 'postist' deconstructors. The first and most obvious casualties of such interrogations, of course, were those grand metanarrative (empirical and extra-empirical/abstract) edifices (Hegelianised Marxisms, for example) which presumed that they could find an essential meaning unfolding teleologically within them: today, towards them, we can only express that attitude of 'incredulity towards metanarratives' that Lyotard famously essayed. But professional, academic history has not escaped unscathed, either. Born and sired in the exigencies of modernity, the fate of academic history (a 'recent, relatively local European invention' as Ermarth puts it) has also been bound up with the fortunes of its host body. Consequently, the arguable coming-to-the-end-of modernity included the problematicising of all of its 'historical', constitutive parts as well: history's empirical/epistemological rug has thus been pulled from under its feet; 'history' *per se* now wobbles.

And it is this condition, we think, that has been responsible for the massive contemporary growth in probing the very 'idea' of history. This probing has been expressed in many ways: in the recent upsurge in historical theory and the philosophy of history; in the reshaping of older historiographical lineages; in linguistic, hermeneutic and aesthetic 'turns'; in new methodological developments – neo-dialogism and neo-empiricism – and all those other currents prefixed by 'post' and 'neo'. These interventions stand behind a plethora of new historical ventures, some of which have been easily incorporated into older areas and others which have been variously radicalising: thus the new social histories and the new cultural histories with their new subjects of enquiry and/or their refiguring of older ones, of feminist and gender, black and diaspora studies; of collective memory, of witnessings, of trauma, and so on. Such developments have led to the breakdown of many of the older, fixed disciplinary boundaries, encouraging a discursive cross-fertilisation that several of the contributors to this volume endorse and wish to see extended (see especially Rigney, Southgate, LaCapra, Harlan, Ankersmit and Ermarth). Accordingly, historical studies is, as a consequence, now much changed and deeply contested, resulting in even its *raison d'être* being raised to the level of the questionable: what, now, *is* history? What might – what *should* – histories be for? What is the connection between past, present and future, history-wise? What are the conditions of possibility for historical figurations? What kind of histories, what kind of historying – if we can justify their 'need' – might be of the best kind? And what is 'the best'? The manifestos in this book begin to address these and other critical questions which are much debated today right across the field.

A book of manifestos then. A manifesto – an old, modernist form indeed – inherent in which is a strong utopian strain: a politics of perfection, the expression of a dream, the promise of *the* good to come. A legislative form. And those of us who have lived through the twentieth century, who have seen or can variously recall some of its most noble dreams become night-mares, well, we are more sensitive now to panaceas and fittingly shy of proposing definitive blueprints. Yet, if postmodernism can be seen as both a retrospective and the beginnings of a renewal of hope (and Derrida urged us never to give up on that great dream of emancipation; of an enlightenment still to come, of democracies still to come . . .), if we have learned the lessons of total, totalising and totalitarian dangers so that they are now tempered by a relativism that does not imply licence but ethical injunctions that though foundationless are none the worse for that (for 'bad guys', as Richard Rorty has put it, 'like absolutes'), then it may be essential to keep the dreams coming and a sense of passion for an open-ended, critical spirit which indeed thrives, as Joan Scott has observed, 'on the pursuit of the not-yet-known'.[7] Thus a critical historical consciousness may still have a part to play here.

So, it was in this vein, against this 'background', and for these kinds of reasons, that we conceived of the idea of asking a group of thoughtful and eminent historians to write their own manifestos for history. We decided not to go for representatives of different periods or approaches in order to achieve some kind of general coverage, but instead to ask historians who were considered not only as brilliant practitioners in their various specialist areas but who had expressed a range of views on 'the nature of history' in thoughtful, provocative and informed ways. We wanted historians who were, as it were, both historians and intellectuals, both experts and yet overtly concerned with wider issues, including the future of their discourse: we wanted acolytes and dissenters. And we wanted strong views and individual opinions. Consequently, in our letter of invitation we provided no detailed template for the contributors to write to so as to encourage an open-ended reflection upon 'the kind of history and the kind of historical consciousness [they] would like to see developed in the twenty-first century in, as it were, the best of all possible worlds'. Contributors were invited to be 'as idealistic and imaginative' as they wished so that, as a possible corollary, 'the boundaries of what currently constitutes historical studies (as widely construed as deemed necessary) might be examined, questioned and gone beyond'. This was, we said, the opportunity for them to test out the elasticity of the word 'history', to sketch out the kind of history they might desire for themselves and for students, but have not yet got. Manifestos, we added, tend to be not only challenging declarations of interest, but usually direct, polemical and to the point, and we hoped, with that in mind, that they would try to write accordingly, and in as 'accessible and student-friendly a manner' as possible.

As a result of this unfettered advice, the wide range of responses we received back reflected, in all their radical singularities, the diversity, vibrancy and, indeed, the fractured nature of history at the beginning of the twenty-first century. This diversity (regarded by us as wholly to the good in its stimulus for new directions in historicising the past) is manifested not only in the content of the papers, but in the different registers, styles and length of referencing formats which we have deliberately not standardised. The manifestos you have before you, therefore, are the ways in which the writers wished to express their views (discursively, polemically, idealistically, inspirationally) and thus the degrees to which they wanted to see their manifestos variously liberated from, or inserted within, the genres of historical discourses within which they work. Moreover, this diversity of expression and intention has also been extended to the order in which the manifestos appear in this volume. We have resisted the temptation to group contributions into named parts or sections, nor have we opted for alphabetical ordering in order to avoid 'leading' readers in any way. Rather, we have tried to juxtapose the manifestos in such a way that, read in order (which is by no means compulsory!), the range of viewpoints, approaches, styles, address, desires and so on bounce off each other to build into a medley of perspectives which keeps any notion of a singular history unsettled; which calls upon the reader to remain open to what is to come and to do any ordering they wish as they think through fidelity and diversity; which puts things in order for them – for you.

We think that the final list of contributors is impressive and wide ranging: Professors Frank Ankersmit (Groningen), Dipesh Chakrabarty (Chicago), Greg Dening (Australian National University), Ewa Domanska (Stanford and Warsaw), Elizabeth Ermarth (Connecticut), David Harlan (California), Patrick Joyce (Manchester), Wulf Kansteiner (State University, New York), Dominic LaCapra (Cornell), David Lowenthal (University College London), Mark Poster (California), Ann Rigney (Utrecht), Robert Rosenstone (California), Joan Scott (Institute for Advanced Studies) and Beverley Southgate (Hertfordshire). In the event, they have risen to the challenge in exceptional ways. Their manifestos range from multimedia challenges to historical consciousness to leaving room for birds to fly (Kansteiner and Rosenstone); from classical figures to radical deconstructions, from feminist agendas to giving voices to people(s) without voices their own place in the sun, from Holocaust traumas to emancipatory dreams, from eclectic overviews (Lowenthal) to rigorously argued polemics and from interdisciplinary vantage points to new starting places under construction (Poster). As a further appetiser they include considerations of new political histories (Ankersmit), the somatic qualities of writing imaginative history (Dening), greater acknowledgement and working of the Discursive Condition by historians (Ermarth), a renewed emphasis upon the category of experience as commodity-form and the way in which globalisation and the attendant logic of placelessness may affect future history-writing (Chakrabarty), a recognition of the prophetic elements of history-writing (Domanska), history as an ongoing quest for what it means to be 'human' (Southgate), the interface between academic and popular forms of history and historians as *bricoleurs* (Harlan), the role of literature, film and museum exhibitions and the cultural authority of the historian in such a 'do-it yourself, perform-it-yourself approach to the past' (Harlan and Rigney), the practice of history as critique (Joyce and Scott) and the reconceptualisation of research, theory and practice in working through trauma (LaCapra). Together, they put before readers anxieties and hopes, generalisations and details that ought to give all students of history pause for thought before they begin, perhaps anew, to work and rework past historicisations into historicisations of/for the future. None of them suggest that, in being 'loyal to history', we can stand still.

In order to 'top and tail' the text, we asked Professor Joanna Bourke (Birkbeck, London) and Professor Hayden White (Stanford) to write a foreword and an afterword, respectively. The collection you have before you therefore brings together some seventeen papers. As previously mentioned, we accepted the papers in the form and the length that they came in; these are our contributors' manifestos and 'comments', not ours. Our editorial work has been primarily facilitative. And finally, we decided against writing short summaries of each of the manifestos or of providing thematic overviews of them, not least because we had in mind Lyotard's observation that, in a society that never stops rushing, that takes all manner of short cuts, that always wants – because it is money – to 'save time', summaries/précis can be counter-productive. They inevitably cast a shadow over the chapters to be read; they direct attention and emphasise areas that may well not be to the point; they often second guess the (never attainable) author's intentions; and they often, ironically, substitute themselves for the 'text' to which they seek to introduce readers. They may 'save time', they may be useful to newcomers, but we want readers to read these manifestos for themselves and not read our opinions of them. These are singular, individual sets of ideas and thoughts and we wish to respect their differences and autonomy. Besides, as editors, we have already possibly said more than enough; we have, no doubt, already set up a way of thinking about this text and perhaps raised (false) expectations about it that may variously affect or 'limit' it. And so, at the risk of doing even more damage, we will at this point just stop . . . The manifestos which follow are here for themselves and for you: we hope you variously benefit from them.

Read them slowly!

Notes

1 'The Duty of Discontent' is the title of a lecture given by the Chartist and poet Thomas Cooper in 1853. The title was used for a collection of essays in honour of Dorothy Thompson who, as a historian, confronted much orthodoxy in labour history. See Owen Ashton, Robert Fyson and Stephen Roberts, *The Duty of Discontent: Essays for Dorothy Thompson* (London: Mansell, 1995).

2 The point made in our first paragraph, that the historian must be disloyal, that a constant process of renewal is not just necessary but inevitable, rests not least on the back of a remark by Jacques Derrida. In a round-table discussion with Nicholas Royle *et al.* in 2001, Derrida draws an initial distinction between the idea of the 'acolyte' and the notion of 'anacoluthon'. These concepts appear opposite in meaning, at least linguistically. To be an acolyte (from the Greek *akolouthos*) is to be a dedicated follower; whereas *anacoluthon* refers to its direct opposite – that which is lacking in sequence, a grammatical break which 'does not follow on'. For Derrida these are not oppositional concepts at all, however, but the terms of an unavoidable creative tension in which to be an acolyte in the fullest and most faithful of ways involves precisely a 'not following'. Thus, if in the twenty-first century you want to be a revolutionary Marxist, for example, then obviously you have to be loyal to the revolutionary Marx, but not in a literal sense. For simply to repeat an allegiance to the texts of Marx (the only Marx we have), texts written around 150 years ago in particular circumstances that infused them *then* with particular revolutionary ideals, is not to be loyal to the way Marx must now be reread if he is still to be relevant to today's very different conditions. To be an acolyte of Marx, therefore, requires that you perform an anacoluthic act, a *break* with Marx. You must be disloyal to some degree precisely to have a larger loyalty to the Marx(ist) tradition as you read it: up to a certain (radically undecidable) point, to be loyal means *not* being loyal; to be truly faithful involves a degree of infidelity. It is in *this* context that we have used Derrida's phrase that 'to be true to what you follow you have to interrupt the following'. For this discussion, see M. Payne and J. Schad (eds), *life. after.theory* (London: Continuum, 2003), pp. 1–52, *passim.* Marx himself, of course, knew how things to be loyal to have to change. Thus, in 1846 when the idea of a book on 'capital' was already being developed, he wrote to his German publisher: 'I shall not have it published without revising it yet again, both as regards matter and style. It goes without saying that a writer who works continuously cannot, at the end of six months, publish word for word what he wrote six months earlier' (cited in Francis Wheen, 'The Poet of Dialectics', *Guardian*, 8 July 2006.

3 See Keith Jenkins, *Rethinking History* (London: Routledge, classic edition, 2003); *On 'What Is History?'* (London: Routledge, 1995); *The Postmodern History Reader* (London: Routledge, 1997); *Why History?* (London: Routledge, 1999); *Refiguring History* (London: Routledge, 2003); and *The Nature of the New History Reader*, co-edited with Alun Munslow (London: Routledge, 2004).

4 Sue Morgan, *The Feminist History Reader* (London: Routledge, 2006), p. 37.

5 See Alun Munslow, *Deconstructing History* (London: Routledge, 2006 [1997]);

The New History (London: Pearson, 2003); *The Routledge Companion to Historical Studies* (London: Routledge, 2000 [2006]); *Experiments in Rethinking History*, co-edited with Robert A. Rosenstone (London: Routledge, 2004).

6   Elizabeth Deeds Ermarth, 'Ethics and Method', *History and Theory*, 43, 4 (2004): p. 68.

7   Joan Scott, 'Feminism's History', *Journal of Women's History* 16, 4 (2004): p. 25.

1 Space for the bird to fly

Robert A. Rosenstone

> Spectres are haunting the world of history. Flickering images on screens, large and small, that tell us everything we need to know about the world – including the world of the past. In the post-literate age, there will be no more need for journals and books. Historians will use film, video and the internet to create a new historical imaginary that will show us all, at last, that history is a matter of personal and emotional connection with what has gone before. Historians of the world unite! You have nothing to lose but your footnotes.

Manifestos by historians? Come on Jenkins, Morgan and Munslow, you've got to be kidding! It's one thing for you, Sue, to produce a major critical feminist reader, for you, Keith, to write a book called *Rethinking History*, and for you, Alun, to found a journal with that same title, but asking a bunch of historians, we who march through the world looking backwards, to write manifestos about the future? I once subtitled an essay on postmodern history films 'the Future of the Past', a phrase which I have seen used by several other historians now in various contexts, not, I think, as plagiarism, but perhaps as an idea whose time has come, a reflection of a moment (as possible is this collection) when (a few or ever more?) historians have turned from the past to the future, concerned with what will happen to their professional calling in the decades and centuries to come, fearful that in this age of instant communication and gratification, when an era as recent as the sixties can seem to our students as remote as the Wars of the Roses was to us in our college days, that history is going the way of the dodo.

If you are going to write a manifesto, what better model than the original, the first great party manifesto (Marx's *The Manifesto of the Communist Party*, 1848), the one that aimed to turn the world upside down, and pretty much helped to do so. That was the idea that led to my initial proposal, now the epigraph that heads this chapter . . . er, manifesto. Not that any of us can hope to have the tiniest smidgeon of the influence that the original manifesto writer had. Imagine: 160 years of influence over hundreds of millions of people, labour unions, political parties, belief systems, works

of art, revolutions, wars across all the continents of the world save for Antarctica, and maybe if penguins could read . . . And not just influence, but be the actual cause of major changes in empires and regimes, not to mention deaths by the tens of millions, and gulags named and unnamed in countless countries. There was brilliant writing in that original manifesto, but perhaps too brilliant, too forward looking, too terrifying in its results. Maybe it creates a cautionary note. Maybe we historians should keep our faces turned towards the past and let the future take care of itself? It will anyway, despite what we write.

Nevertheless, after a life of nosing into archives and writing countless footnotes and long bibliographic essays to support one's narratives, you can't help but be curious: what will happen to this realm to which we have devoted so (too?) many of our days, this realm or practice we call history, our attempt to tell the past truly and make meaning of it for our peers in the present. Of course, it hardly seems to be the same realm we entered on leaving graduate school four decades ago. Or at least the realm we imagined it to be in those days when our professors wore neckties and herringbone tweed jackets with leather elbow patches and delivered judgements on the past (and on our seminar papers) that had the weight and importance of ideas carved onto stone tablets. Now such certainty seems absurd. We know too much about framing images and stories, too much about narrative, too much about the problematics of causality, too much about the subjectivity of perception, too much about our own cultural imperatives and biases, too much about the disjuncture between language and the world it purports to describe to believe we can actually capture the world of the past on the page.

REPORTER: Mr Godard, surely you agree that a story must have a beginning, a middle and an end.
JEAN-LUC GODARD: Yes, of course. But not necessarily in that order.

One reason why it's difficult to write a new manifesto for historians is that, as far as I am concerned, we already have the one we need, one that says all that has to be said and said it forty years ago. Not that it was framed as a manifesto. Nobody in academia in the sixties would have been bold enough to propose such a thing. Instead, it was a plain, scholarly article, written by Hayden White, the closest thing we historians have to a Karl Marx. Entitled 'The Burden of History', this essay (perhaps best remembered for its depiction of historians as shifty folks who, if questioned by scientists, claim that history is an art, but, if questioned by artists, claim it is a science) pointed to the fact that historians in their work fail wholly to identify with the art of their own time (the sixties), with 'action painters, kinetic sculptors, existentialist novels, imagist poets, or *nouvelle vague* cinematographers', but instead follow the forms of the realists of the nineteenth century, primarily novelists such as Sir Walter Scott and William Makepeace Thackeray. By highlighting their absence, the essay becomes in essence a manifesto calling for experiments and innovation, for 'surrealistic, expressionistic, or existentialist historiography'.

The world has changed a great deal since the nineteenth century, as we historians above all should know. When we attempt to tell stories about the past or present these days – in words on the page, or in photos, or on the motion picture or television screen, or in a museum display, or on a website – we as a culture are no longer so firmly wedded to the notions of literal reality that pervaded the nineteenth century. The impact of the visual media themselves (if we include among them the internet) are certainly the chief carriers of messages in our twenty-first-century world, and this alone assures a major alteration in our sensibilities, the way we see the past. The continual revolutions in artistic visions over the last century – the movements or tendencies we may label cubism, constructivism, expressionism, surrealism, abstraction, the New Wave, modernism, postmodernism, hip hop – have helped to alter our ways of seeing, telling and understanding our realities. The quotation by the great Swiss-French *avant garde* filmmaker which heads this section puts it succinctly by saying, 'not necessarily in that order', an idea which would have been incomprehensible to our professors in graduate school as well as to our younger selves.

The point is this: we need to liberate history from its own history and to create forms of historical telling for today and tomorrow, forms of history suited to the sensibility of the times.

> In his late Cubist period, Picasso was asked to paint the portrait of a woman. One afternoon, the husband of the woman came by the artist's studio to take her home. He asked Picasso to see the painting of his wife and Picasso showed it to him. The husband looked at it with a horrified expression and said, 'It doesn't look at all like my wife.' Picasso considered this, then asked, 'What does your wife look like?' The husband reached into his pocket and brought out his wallet. From it, he took out a snapshot of his wife and handed it to the painter, who studied it for a while, then turned to the husband and said, 'I didn't realise she was so small.'

Not necessarily in that order. Not necessarily of that size. Not necessarily in that frame. Not necessarily in that medium. Not necessarily in the way we have been taught. What we need is history that surprises and startles us. That lets us see things we haven't seen. Hear things we haven't heard. Feel things we haven't felt about some particular period, person, moment or movement in the past. Learn things from the seeing, hearing and feeling we haven't learned before. What we need are historians brave enough to experiment with the past in the spirit of scientists who investigate the unknown in the micro- and the macrocosmic. What we need are historians who are brave enough to experiment with language, image, sound, colour and any other elements of presentation that will make the past live and vibrate and terrify us once again. What we need are forms of history that make us deeply care about people and moments we never cared about, history that tries to make us understand not only our own past and ourselves but the past and selves of those others whom we never before knew or wished to know.

> We are the other people, we are the other people, we are the
>   other people
> You're the other people too!
> Found a way to get to you.
>
> Frank Zappa

I am not talking research here. Not talking about extracting new traces of the past in all those brilliant ways historians have devised during what might be called the research revolution of the last half century-plus. I am not talking about the smart and difficult work of investigating parish registries from fifteenth-century Languedoc, finding wills or amassing statistics on longevity, property, literacy and stature from medieval Japan or China, learning the dietary habits of hunters and gatherers in East Africa and of factory workers in Manchester during the early Industrial Revolution, or uncovering the patterns of landownership and inheritance among pre-contact Tahitians. I trust that the sleuths among us will continue to devise new and ingenious ways to extract data from the silence of the past. Those who do so have been hailed for their accomplishments and been given grants and promotions by an academia which would like to turn professors into movie or rock stars if only they (we?) had more hair or shaved skulls.

What I am talking about is presentation, telling the past, creating the story of what happened – only it need not be a story in the usual sense, as Godard suggests. Perhaps it could be a collage, a comic book, a dance, a rap-song cycle, a series of emails sent to everyone online, or a combination of expressive forms we have not yet seen, forms which go beyond White's notion of 'surrealistic, expressionistic, or existentialist historiography' to encompass the shifts in artistic moods, modes, styles and forms that have developed since he wrote his path-breaking essay in the sixties.

Such innovative forms of history have already been produced – but rarely by historians. Art Spiegelman in *Maus* and *Maus II* created an intimate history of the Holocaust, the tale of his father's experiences in concentration and death camps as told to his son who can barely comprehend events, and all this through the medium of a comic book (or *graphic novel*, to give the form the dignity it now wants to claim); and Marjane Satrapi has done the same in *Persepolis*, with her own, personal experience of the Iranian Revolution. Filmmakers from many countries have (and continue to) put the history and biography on screens big and small, in popular dramatic forms (e.g., *Gandhi*, *Schindler's List*, *The Return of Martin Guerre*, *Born on the Fourth of July, Capote, Frida*), in innovative works of collage and pastiche (*32 Short Films about Glenn Gould, Far from Poland, Surname Viet, Given Name Nam*), and in unusual (by Hollywood standards) works that deal with Third World situations and mix both traditional and contemporary aesthetics (*Quilombo, Sarraounia, Ceddo*).

> Step out of line
> The man come and take you away.
> Bob Dylan

For professional historians, those of us who have gone through graduate school and become professors, those of us who want our books to be published, our careers to thrive, our grant and fellowship proposals to be rewarded so that we can have precious time off to research and write, it's a real problem, a huge problem. For all of us in the culture have been brainwashed (even yours truly, even while writing this, four decades into a career as a historian, now mostly behind me, and a voice somewhere inside, call it the internalised values of the discipline, call it the professional superego, says, 'You can't be saying this, it's too far out, too off the wall, nobody will take such a manifesto seriously') into thinking we know what is 'History', and it's always something with a *capital* letter, always something linear and sober, something on the page and stuffed full of facts and footnotes that make us feel virtuous and informed when we finish reading it (and even if we don't finish). The gatekeepers know, too – the publishers, the editors, and now, by God, the agents – all of them know exactly what history is and it isn't any of the things I have been calling for here.

Let me cite chapter, book and verse. Almost twenty years ago I produced a manuscript about three American sojourners in nineteenth-century Japan, a work motivated by and framed within my own experiences of teaching on a Fulbright Fellowship at Kyushu University for a year. The men whose tales I chose to recount – a missionary, a scientist and a writer – were, in one sense, emblems of cultural interaction, but they were also individuals whose exposure to Japan had turned them from firm believers in the superiority of Western civilisation into what we might call premature cultural relativists, folks who understood that this Asian nation had its own values that were not inferior to, but in some cases were superior to, those of the world from which they came. To render their lives, to get close to them, to suggest the interactions and moments, the sights, smells, tastes and feelings that underlay the shift in their perceptions and values, I found the traditional third-person narrative I had used in previous works to be too distanced, too lacking in immediacy and intensity. In order to convey the rich and personal encounters and experiences of their lives in this alien world I began to search for a more suitable and more evocative way of writing. What I produced, after much trial and error, was a work of history written in the present tense, recounted in several voices and told from several different perspectives, a work whose words occasionally speak directly to the reader or the historical characters, a work in which the historian is an occasional walk-on character who comments on the problems involved in producing the work being read. What I produced, in short, was a work of history which indulged in some of the techniques of the contemporary novel, a work which some reviewers labelled with the dreaded 'P' word: *postmodern*.

'This is not the proper way to write history!' said my editor at Knopf as he turned down the manuscript on which the publisher had an option. He was hardly alone in this opinion. Other editors said the same thing. Agents, too. Agents! I would snap back: 'But everything is footnoted. It has a huge bibliography. Nothing is invented. It just tells the story a different way.' No matter. Over and over again I heard: 'You can't write history like this!' But nobody could answer my question: 'Why not?' They could, however, refuse to publish the work, as many publishers did, before a brave editor at Harvard University Press named Aida Donald decided to take a chance on something different – and the result was *Mirror in the Shrine* (1988).

Let me skip over my fictional biography of Russian writer Isaac Babel, *King of Odessa* (2003), which I would maintain renders the man's life as more complex and truer than all the prior but more factual accounts, as well as my multi-voiced, *mostly true* story of three generations in my own family, *The Man who Swam into History* (2005), which has two of my grandparents talking from the grave – few will consider these history, even though I would be happy to make the case for both of them. For the problem is hardly mine alone. The most stunning piece of combined research scholarship and literary innovation that I have encountered, John Walker's *Pistols! Treason! Murder! The Rise and Fall of Gerolamo Vano, Venetian General of Spies*, is a work which utilises a dazzling display of contemporary literary and graphic techniques yet has footnotes galore and a bibliography that goes on for ever, both of which show years of work in the archives – yet this book went begging for a publisher for years, to the despair of the author, until finally the University of Melbourne Press took a chance on it. No offence to this Australian university, but to me Walker's work (in press as I write) should have been published by a major press and featured as a breakthrough in the realm of historical discourse.

I am talking scholarship here. I am talking Ph.D.s and professors. I am talking archives, footnotes, bibliography – none of this matters because we and they, the gatekeepers, claim to know precisely what history is and is not. To them, it is not innovation on the page, as produced by John Walker, and it certainly is not a series of songs, or paintings, or video installations. History is those books we keep producing that not many people want to read. (A thousand books is a very good sale for an academic work in the United States, with a population of 220 million. Doesn't anyone think there's something wrong with that, something not just in the public but in us?) Or it's those bestsellers that lots of people want to own because there has been an accompanying TV series (*The West, The Search for Troy, Aristocrats*). Or perhaps they are on a topic that makes us feel good about ourselves – works on the Great Generation, which saved the world from the Nazis in the forties, or biographies of presidents who, at this distance in time, seem to have lived calmer lives, which usually means a work about John Adams. What history is not is anything different, unusual or provocative in its telling. Isn't that one reason why it bores everyone? Isn't that why, when someone asks you at a cocktail party what you do, and you answer that you are a historian, they say either, 'History was my least favorite subject in school' or 'How interesting', and then turn quickly away to refresh their drink?

> Our concern with history . . . is a concern with preformed images already imprinted on our brains, images at which we keep staring while the truth lies elsewhere, away from it all, somewhere as yet undiscovered.
>
> W. G. Sebald, *Austerlitz*

People are hungry for the past, as various studies tell us and the responses to certain films, TV series and museums indicate. They want to touch, feel and experience the worlds of their forebears, but that hunger is not being well fed by professional historians. I share that hunger. The traditional work of history, be it monograph or synthetic study, has its own strengths, its own contributions to make, but they are not the strengths of compelling an interest in some aspect of the past. Works of history are written as if to cater only to those who already want to know about a particular subject and they write off the rest of the public. In the way they hang on to outmoded kinds of narrative and analysis, they seem to assume that you should care about what they have to say, but they don't justify that assumption. History is good for you, they imply – but they never say why. And if they don't answer that question, why would anyone else?

The time has come for historians to answer the question. Not just to tell the past, but to incorporate in that telling the reasons why the past can talk meaningfully to us today. This must be done in a language (oral, written, visual, aural) that people care about and can understand, in forms that appeal to contemporary tastes. We historians must do this as some outside the profession have been doing it – on screen, in graphics, in books written perhaps like detective stories or romances, in media yet unknown and forms yet to be invented. We must tell stories about the past that matter not just to us; we must make them matter to the larger culture. We must paint, write, film, dance, hip hop and rap the past in a way that makes the tragedies and joys of the human voyage meaningful to the contemporary world.

> A Japanese artist was commissioned by an American to do a painting. The completed work had, in the lower corner, the branch of a cherry tree with a few blossoms and a bird perched upon it. The entire upper half of the painting was white. Unhappy, the American asked the artist to put something else in the painting because it looked, well, so

bare. The Japanese refused the request. When pressed for an explanation, the artist said that if he did fill up the painting, there would be no space for the bird to fly.

Traditional story

This manifesto is not meant as an attack on books or traditional works of history. The tradition of such scholarship is a great tradition and one that will, no doubt, continue of its own inertia. This is an attack (if attack it is) on those preformed images imprinted on our brain, on the images that keep us from seeing or creating those undiscovered truths we need to discover in the past. It is an attack on a single notion of truth that disguises itself as 'The Truth'; that insists that once we have excavated the remains of the past, once we have studied its traces, there is but a single way of conveying their meaning to our culture, and that other ways are off limits, *verboten*, simply wrong. This is a call for opening our eyes and our imaginations to other ways of telling, showing, representing, making meaning out of the stories of humanity's past, our deep laboratory for understanding who we are and who we may become. This is a call for us to use imagination in our rendering of our relationship to the past – and when I say 'us', I mean those trained in history, for the deeper the knowledge, the more confident one can be that innovations in historical renderings and performances intersect with, comment upon, and add to the larger discourse of history, the things we already know and the debates we already have had about the past.

Oh yes, one more thing: it's time that we historians also learn to leave space for the bird to fly.

2 History-writing as critique[1]

Joan W. Scott

The genuine historian must have the strength to recast the well known into something never heard before.

F. Nietzsche

La critique, ce sera l'art de l'inservitude volontaire, celui de l'indocilité réfléchie.

M. Foucault

It is fashionable these days to talk about poststructuralist theory in the past tense, as a disruptive moment that once threatened to undermine the discipline of history, substituting fancy French distractions for serious empirical investigations. Orthodox disciplinarians, along with journalists, politicians and public intellectuals, have declared this theory to be dead. And not only dead, but thankfully so, since it is held responsible for all manner of ethical lapses, ranging from the decline of academic standards (plagiarism, lack of attention to factual accuracy, radical scepticism about truth and the possibility of objectivity) to the vagaries of multiculturalism (disunity, loss of coherence and shared focus), the erosion of society's moral centre, the defeat of working-class political movements, tolerance for violations of universal human rights in the name of cultural relativism, and even to the 11 September terrorist attacks in New York City and Washington, D.C.[2]

Those who celebrate the passing of poststructuralism (and there is a convergence here of right and left) have in common a yearning for certainty, security and stability. 'Balance' and 'neutrality' are currently the watchwords of political conservatives in the United States who, in the name of students' rights, are against any expression of opinion or point of view by classroom teachers.[3] This is particularly evident in Middle Eastern studies programmes that are under surveillance by right-wing supporters of the current regime in Israel, but also in many courses which take up questions of inequality or social justice. In various humanities and social science disciplines there has been a recourse to scientific models of investigation to eliminate subjective assessments and replace them with solid facts. There has been, too, a closing of borders in what were once disruptive interventions on the left: the formal-ising of some theories that used to encourage innovation, the imposition of orthodoxy in formerly troublesome fields such as women's studies.

Among historians, the search for security takes various forms: a renewed emphasis on empiricism and quantitative analysis, the rehabilitation of the autonomous willing subject as the agent of history, the essentialising of political categories of identity by the evidence of 'experience', the turn to evolutionary psychology for explanations of human behaviour, the endorse-ment of the timelessness of universal values, and the trivialisation and denunciation of the 'linguistic turn' – an attempt to deny it a serious place in the recent life of the discipline.[4] Often the return to traditional disciplinarity is depicted as innovation (once it was the '*new* cultural history', now it's the '*new* empiricism') but this should not mislead us; despite any number of quarrels about the causes of the Civil War or the French Revolution, it's the old rules about the transparency of language (words mean what they say, analytic categories are objective) and the equally transparent relationship between social organisation and individual self-perception (there is no place for alienation, interpellation, subjectivation or the unconscious) that are being asserted as the only acceptable rules of the game.[5] Throughout the 1980s and 1990s – the supposed heyday of poststructuralist theory in the United States – there were, to be sure, resistances in the name of the right way of doing history; but these have now become triumphalist proclamations that no longer engage debate; they simply declare victory. Poststructuralism's harshest critics now regularly congratulate themselves on their prescience. So it surely won't be long before the authors of *Telling the Truth about History* offer their 1994 conclusion as an obituary notice. 'In the final analysis, then, there can be no postmodern history. We turn now to the task of elaborating models for the future of history, models for understanding the search for historical truths within the framework of a revitalised and transformed practice of objectivity.'[6]

I want to argue that such an obituary would be not only premature but foolish, for at least two reasons. The first is that, like it or not, we are in a post-modern age, and poststructuralism – not to be confused, as it is in that 1994 text I just cited, with postmodernism – is a critical practice for the post-modern age. As Elizabeth Deeds Ermarth has maintained, 'To be "against" postmodernity is about as informed a position as it was to be against Galileo and Luther: the perfect gesture for a postmodern Mr Podsnap, Dickens's character who sweeps away with grandiloquent gestures what he will not or cannot understand.'[7] Ermarth's is a historical point: postmodernism is an epistemic moment (of heterogeneity, discontinuity, fragmentation) with its own representational and critical demands (we are, in other words, no longer living in the nineteenth century), and I am arguing that post-structuralism meets some of those demands. This leads to the second reason: poststructuralism is one of the critical theories that inspired the practice of history as critique in its late twentieth-century form, a practice that needs to be protected and reinforced in the face of a conservative revolution that, in the academy as in politics, seeks to discredit critique as disruptive, discordant, even disloyal. Those on the left who welcome the end of poststructuralism in the name of the 'truth' about the experiences of women, workers, post-colonial subjects and minorities unwittingly join their colleagues on the right who associate anti-relativism with morality. They are not only relin-quishing an important critical weapon; they are becoming part of the consensus they say they want to challenge. My argument, to put it briefly, is that a poststructuralist history is not only possible, but necessary. Now more than ever.

History's resistance to theory

The attack on poststructuralism by US historians (even by those who should know better) calls upon, probably reflexively, a long-standing discourse which positions history in opposition to philosophy. (This discourse is not an exclusively American phenomenon; it is characteristic of the nineteenth-century origins of scientific history.) My generation imbibed it in graduate school where we were told that, in addition to taking careful notes and iden-tifying source and page number on every notecard, an eclectic handbag of tools was all we needed to make sense of the past. Something more systematic, more rigorous, would distort the truth, unacceptably distancing us from the people whose experience we must understand. Even when we were inspired by Eric Hobsbawm and E. P. Thompson, it was as often because they were innovative archival hunters as because they were Marxists – this in the 1960s, the heyday of left-wing student/social movements. In the USA social history was about illuminating the lives of the 'common man' – and later woman. And it often combined quantitative methods (based on the premise of objectivity) and revolutionary or at least reformist aspirations. There was indeed a political end for some of us and I don't want to deny its continuing importance: to bring the stories of these lives into consideration, making them visible, as a way of correcting the record of privilege and power that typically excluded them, a way of establishing agency in the present through identification with examples from the past.[8] But the emphasis was on our similarity with the past, not on our difference from it; on continuity; and on the universality of categories such as class, race and gender. In the field of history, second-wave feminism was critical of the exclusion of women, but reticent about theorising it. What theorising there was most often invoked universal structures of patriarchy, and male domination. Even 'gender' quickly became synonymous, if not with 'women', then with an already-known unequal relationship between the sexes. It was a handy label whose application reassured rather than disturbed us, turning questions into answers before they had even been asked.[9]

The great preoccupation, though, has been with 'objectivity'. Of course, it is acknowledged that true objectivity is impossible, but the point is to get as close to it as possible. Or to have the appearance of being close, an appearance created precisely by abjuring any hint of philosophical predisposition, any avowed theory of human behaviour (even when there is one buried beneath the lines); an appearance achieved by insisting that human subjects act in full command of their intentions, that words literally mean what they say, and that 'nature' or 'experience' are transparent categories outside the reach of politics, philosophy or 'theory'. Read the presidential addresses to the American Historical Association since its founding in 1884; with few exceptions they are about substantive matters, maybe about practice or method, but not theory. One of the exceptions is Carl Becker, who was condemned by many of his colleagues for his strong philosophical preoccupations; indeed, his critics thought he ought not to be considered a historian at all. Go back to Lawrence Stone's ill-informed attack on Michel Foucault in the pages of the *New York Review of Books*. Stone dismisses Foucault as a historian *pretendu*.[10] Although he disputes some of Foucault's facts in order to do this, it is the epistemological challenge that, for Stone, puts Foucault outside the company of historians. Read, in historical journals, the negative or ambivalent reviews of books and articles endorsing a 'linguistic turn'; they search for 'objective' occurrences that can be taken to elude the mediation of language – natural disasters, horrific death, illness, sexual difference.[11] Listen to Lynn Hunt and Joyce Appleby, apostles even at the end of the twentieth century of that 'noble dream' – the special objectivity sought by historians.[12] Still in 2004, a thematic issue of the journal *History and Theory* finds historians anxiously discussing the place of ethics in the writing of history. Although most argue against what must by now be a straw man – the idea that 'moral evaluations lie outside any responsibilities that historians ought to be asked to meet' – they do so without interrogating the meaning of the morality they take to be a shared, self-evident set of beliefs.[13] Indeed, 'ethics' for most of these writers refers to a closed system of evaluation, one in which fixed categories of 'the good' and 'the just' are applied to events and actions in the past. The kind of self-reflective examination of the historian's own moral categories (called for by poststructuralists) is largely absent in this attempt to reconcile ethics and historical objectivity.

There is another less confrontational way in which history's insistence on the objective empirical resists theory. This resistance takes the form of superficial acceptance of the vocabulary of theory in the service of its domestication. Think of all those books and articles that begin with grand gestures to theory and then present utterly predictable historical narratives telling us that 'race' or 'class' or 'gender' (or any other identity category) is the predictable effect of capitalism or patriarchy or Western imperialism or its postcolonial aftermath. The questioning of these categories that is called for by the 'theory' being gestured to is absent. It is as if the requirements of the discipline cancel out the potentially disruptive effects of the theory, blinding the historian to the critical tasks theory enjoins. Nowhere is this as clear as in the misappropriation of some of the terminology of post-structuralism, draining critical conceptual instruments of their force. Take the word 'deconstruction', repeatedly misused as a synonym for 'examine' (maybe for 'analyse'), but with no sense of how to perform the critical interrogation of metaphysics that was the aim of Derrida's work.

It is perhaps to be expected that the anti-Marxist animus of most mainstream historians in the United States takes the form of a resistance to theory and an endorsement of 'objectivity' as a standard for practice because, among other things, objectivity is taken to be an antidote to (leftist) politics. But it is disconcerting to find Marxists, too, condemning poststructuralism as a sell-out of truth, echoing Hobsbawm's comments in his recent manifesto, which bitterly blames 'postmodernists' (and the identity groups it spawned: 'nationalists, feminists, gays, Blacks and others') for the failure of the working-class movement he so fervently supported.[14] Before others settled it into orthodoxy, Marx's writing was precisely an endorsement of critique – of political economy's naturalised categories and of the official story of politics offered by bourgeois liberal regimes, but also of its own analytic categories. That its adherents today fail to see their kinship with post-structuralism is dismaying; it says something about the way they have lost touch with the tradition of critique, an important aspect of which was self-critique – so vital for the richest work of Marx and many of his followers.

Critique

Critique is often mistakenly thought to be synonymous with criticism, but it has a more precise and systematic meaning. I take my definition from the literary critic Barbara Johnson, who writes:

> A critique of any theoretical system is not an examination of its flaws and imperfections. It is not a set of criticisms designed to make the system better. It is an analysis that focuses on the grounds of the system's possibility. The critique reads backwards from what seems natural, obvious, self-evident, or universal in order to show that these things have their history, their reasons for being the way they are, their effects on what follows from them and that the starting point is not a (natural) given but a (cultural) construct, usually blind to itself.[15]

The point of critique is to make visible those blind spots in order to open a system to change. Not to replace what is with a fully formulated, ideal plan, but to open the possibility for thinking (and so acting) differently. In the characterisation of critique offered by Theodor Adorno, 'Open thinking points beyond itself'.[16]

Critique has long been associated with philosophers: Plato, Kant, Hegel, Marx, the Frankfurt school, Nietzsche, to name only some. But at least since the nineteenth century, its concern has also been with *history*, with specifying and analysing the mutable social and political contexts within which foundational concepts are deployed. Hegel's critique of Kant and Marx's of Hegel involved attention to the social bases for a morality Kant (and the Enlightenment) took to be universal. In different ways, Hegel and Marx historicised the norms Kant refused to challenge. Nietzsche, too, called for a critique of 'all moral values' through an examination of their genealogy: 'We need to know the conditions from which they have sprung, how they have developed and changed.'[17] Morality, he argued, was a symptom whose precipitating conditions must be elucidated, as well as its consequences and effects – both the symptom and its effects were pre-eminently matters of history. But Nietzsche also warned against the paralytic influence of traditional histories which offered 'the happiness of knowing oneself not to be wholly arbitrary and accidental, but rather growing out of the past as its heir, flower and fruit'.[18] When 'the dead bury the living', he wrote, then creative futures become impossible.[19] 'It almost seems as though the task were to guard history so that nothing could come of it but stories, but by no means history-making events!'[20]

The relationship between history and history-making events was clear to Marx: 'The immediate task of philosophy, which is in the service of history,' he wrote in his *Critique of Hegel's Philosophy of Right* (1843), 'is to unmask human self-alienation in its secular form now that it has been unmasked in its sacred form.'[21] The way to do this was not abstractly with *a priori* philosophical concepts, but concretely, through the analysis of existing historical situations. This would expose the dialectical processes immanent in reality and so challenge the idea that the world consisted of fixed essences and eternal truths. For Marx, the writing of history was one form critique could take.

As for Marx, so for Adorno, history defined the concepts philosophers might employ: 'Whatever takes place within the interior of the concept always reflects something of the movement of reality.'[22] What Adorno called 'critical history' (a part of the critical theory he and his Frankfurt school colleagues elaborated) aimed at unmasking the unexamined presuppositions (including those of critical historians themselves) that served to legitimise social inequality.[23] It called into question assumptions about necessary links between past and present (these might simply be a projection of contemporary conceptions on to the past, an illusion of continuity), stressing discontinuity instead. David Hoy writes of Adorno,

> The effect of critical history is temporal: it focuses our attention on the present. Critical history, however, does this with neither the rationalist intent of making the present seem the culmination of all that has gone before, nor the neo-conservative intent of preserving the status quo. Instead . . . the intent is to make certain the present is still open to the future despite its problematic connection to the past.[24]

The idea of staying open to the future is at the very heart of critique and defines it as an ethical project, though a very different one from that associated with objectivity. The ethics of objectivity, held up by the right or the left, advances a closed agenda; it is politically and methodologically conservative whether it offers a romanticised view of women's or working men's struggles or elegises the individual heroism of national leaders. The ethics of critique, in contrast, lies in its endorsement of an *undetermined history*. Its critics often dismiss this aspect of critique as a kind of negativism (post-structuralists are regularly denounced as nihilists) because it offers no clear map, no plan for what comes next. Critique's proponents reply that that is precisely its value. Kant defended the 'purely negative' utility of critique, as a way of clarifying reason and keeping it free from error. Its purpose, he wrote, 'is not to extend knowledge, but only to correct it and to supply a touchstone of the value, or lack of value, of all *a priori* knowledge'.[25] Although the critics of Kant rejected the idea of a finite body of knowledge, they endorsed the negative utility of critique. Marx, calling for 'A Ruthless Criticism of Everything Existing', (1844) applauded the idea that reformers ought not to have a clear idea of what the future should be.

> That, however, is just the advantage of the new trend: that we do not attempt dogmatically to prefigure the future, but want to find the new world only through criticism of the old . . .
> We shall confront the world not as doctrinaires . . . We develop new principles to the world out of its own principles . . . We only show the world what it is fighting for, and consciousness is something that the world must acquire, like it or not.[26]

With 'consciousness' would come the shedding of illusion and the ability to change the circumstances that produced alienation; what might follow would be inevitably emancipatory, but its form could not be prescribed. Marx associated prescription with dogmatism and so did Adorno: 'A philosophy that would set itself up as total, as a system, would become a delusional system.'[27] Adorno saw the call for 'constructive critique' as a contradiction that would undermine its force: 'it is by no means always possible to add to critique the immediate practical recommendation of something better'.[28] Indeed, 'the repressive intolerance to the thought that is not immediately accompanied by instructions for action is founded on anxiety'.[29] The importance of critique, after all, lay precisely in 'the power to resist established opinions and to resist existing institutions' and at the same time to reflect upon itself.[30] 'An adequate philosophical thinking is not only critical of the status quo and its reified replica in consciousness but is equally critical of itself'.[31] This relentless resistance to common practices and their justifications was, for Adorno, 'essential to democracy'.

> Not only does democracy require the freedom to criticize and need critical impulses. Democracy is nothing less than defined by critique. This

can be recalled simply in the historical fact that the conception of the separation of powers, upon which every democracy is based, from Locke and Montesquieu and the American constitution up to today, has its lifeblood in critique.[32]

It is not a far leap from Adorno's linkage of open-ended critique with democracy to a similar connection made by Jacques Derrida. (Although I should add here that Adorno would have had many criticisms of Derrida, as Derrida did of Adorno – it is not the similarity of their philosophies that I want to insist on, but the shared commitment to the idea of philosophy as critique.)[33] Writing in the early 1980s 'in defense of philosophy', by which he meant the kind of thinking defined as critique, Derrida wrote: "Thinking" . . . must even, in the name of a democracy still *to come* as the possibility of this "thinking", unremittingly interrogate the de facto democracy, critique its current determinations, analyze its philosophical genealogy, in short, deconstruct it.'[34] By 'deconstruct' Derrida meant locate its blindspots, discover its limits, think critically about its operations, not in order to dismantle democracy, but to improve it in as yet unarticulated ways.

Despite the many important differences among them, these philosophers understand themselves as part of a philosophical tradition in which critique is the medium. Adorno puts it succinctly: 'Critique alone, as the unity of the problem and its arguments, not the adoption of received theses, has laid the foundation for what may be considered the productive unity of the history of philosophy.'[35] And Derrida offers the metaphor of the lever, which, according to Alexander Dickow, 'pushes or propels readers towards a new interpretive effort'.[36] Although these same philosophers' insistence on history as contradiction and discontinuity seems to argue against the notion of tradition, the commitment to critique understood instrumentally – as a negative yet productive incentive to action – offers a way of grasping their meaning. For historians, there is a double challenge here: to write the kind of history that will serve as a lever, unearthing the foundational premises upon which our social and political verities rest, in order (and this is the second part of the challenge) to clear space for the operations of a history whose direction cannot be determined and whose end will never come. My argument is that poststructuralism provides such a lever; that it offers a way of revitalising historical enquiry in a postmodern, postcolonial world.

The genealogy of Michel Foucault

One of the great accomplishments of Michel Foucault was to theorise the idea of critical history and to operationalise it, to demonstrate in specific studies how it might be done. (I focus on Foucault because his interest in history as critique was so explicit not because I want to limit our possibilities only to his approach. My intent is exemplification not prescription.)

Genealogy was Foucault's name for his critical history. 'Criticism is no longer going to be practiced in the search for formal structures with universal value but, rather, as a historical investigation into the events that have led us to constitute ourselves and to recognize ourselves as subjects of what we are doing, thinking, saying.'[37] In contrast to Kant's explorations of the limits of reason, Foucault had a different goal, one he shared with Nietzsche; it was to write history that 'serves to show how that-which-is has not always been', and so to show 'why and how that-which-is might no longer be that-which-is'.[38] The reigning concepts of modernity, beginning with reason, were to be historicised, treated not as transcendent categories whose essential meaning awaited the probes of philosophers, but as attempts by historically situated humans to define and redefine who they were. Let others theorise about reason; Foucault undertook to write its history not by echoing the words of its prophets, but by looking at the containment of madness – an attempt both intellectual and institutional, he argued, to fortify reason as the self-definition of man. This attention to the role of difference in the construction of meaning is one of the hallmarks of poststructuralist history.

After reason, Foucault wrote about discipline and sexuality and the emergence of the human sciences in the enunciation of the modern subject. History itself did not elude his attention; indeed, he argued that historical ways of thinking were themselves time-bound. By the nineteenth century, 'History . . . is not to be understood as the compilation of factual successions or sequences as they may have occurred; it is the fundamental mode of being of empiricities . . . Since it is the mode of being of all that is given us in experience, History has become the unavoidable element in our thought.'[39] Foucault's interest was in the way different epochs posed problems and found solutions to them; the way in which some solutions came to seem inevitable and necessary while others were overlooked or rejected. In what he called 'the profusion of lost events', Foucault called into question the self-proclaimed inevitability of any moral or social system.[40] David Hoy calls this 'the history of problematization'.[41] The point, of course, was to treat our current understandings of ourselves as the effects of processes of problem-solving, processes which articulated relations of power as they identified objects of knowledge. Another way of putting this is to say that what counted as history was a series of discontinuous interpretive shifts:

> If interpretation were the slow exposure of the meaning hidden in an origin, then only metaphysics could interpret the development of humanity. But if interpretation is the violent or surreptitious appropriation of a system of rules, which in itself has no essential meaning, in order to impose a direction, to bend it to a new will, to force its participation in a different game, and to subject it to secondary rules, then the development of humanity is a series of interpretations. The role of genealogy is to record its history: the history of morals, ideals, and metaphysical concepts, the history of the concept of liberty or of the

ascetic life; as they stand for the emergence of different interpretations, they must be made to appear as events on the stage of historical process.[42]

Since interpretations were an ongoing, unlimited process – the product of an unstoppable human desire for knowledge – genealogy could provoke this desire rather than satisfy it. When any taken-for-granted idea or established fact is understood to be an interpretation of reality rather than reality itself, its history can be written by specifying its operations and resurrecting its forgotten alternatives. It is not, then, an inevitable consequence of the march of time, but a set of options that prevailed by ruling out others. The result of this kind of enquiry is an opening to reinterpretation.

> History becomes 'effective' to the degree that it introduces discontinuity into our very being . . . 'Effective' history deprives the self of the reassuring stability of life and nature, and it will not permit itself to be transported by a voiceless obstinacy toward a millennial ending. It will uproot its traditional foundations and relentlessly disrupt its pretended continuity. This is because knowledge is not made for understanding; it is made for cutting.[43]

Foucault's history-as-critique provides leverage ('uprooting', 'cutting') for an unspecified future.

Many historians, missing the critical epistemological thrust of Foucault's work, have either quarrelled with his choice of topic, periodisation, or facts (in an effort to discredit him), or (in an effort to emulate him) read his work thematically as a call to study more asylums, prisons or sexual norms, now in comparative perspective. Among the emulators are those who use terms such as 'desire' or 'the subject' as labels rather than levers for excavating meaning. Or those who invoke 'power' as if it were a definable entity rather than a constituted relationship, confirming the objections of others who insist that Foucault's attention to the relational constitution of power in many realms distracts us from its 'real' institutional locations, especially the state. This, I think, is to miss the point; to misread his attempt to theorise critique as an operation of history-writing. That operation, he tells us, must begin with a question: 'In what is given to us as universal, necessary, obligatory, what place is occupied by whatever is singular, contingent, and the product of arbitrary constraints?'[44] The pursuit of answers to this question might take the form of more questions. What counts as universal? (Here the universal human truths of the Enlightenment are treated as mutable products of history.) How has nature (or some other inviolable essence – culture or historical continuity, for example) been invoked to establish the necessity of certain exclusions; of obligatory social behaviours? How do objects of knowledge become political or legal or economic or social subjects? These questions are not meant to have general answers; instead, they direct us to concrete historical investigations, investigations that may offer different explanations than his, different ways of understanding the psychological dimensions of subject formation, for example. The critical point, however, is that the end of these investigations is not to establish timeless patterns of human conduct, but precisely to historicise our belief in such patterns and the categories upon which they rest. 'We want historians to confirm our belief that the present rests upon profound intentions and immutable necessities. But the true historical sense confirms our existence among countless lost events, without a landmark or a point of reference.'[45] Achieving this 'true historical sense' meant refusing the frameworks and analyses of other historians. 'Even if I refer to and use many historical studies, I always do my own historical analyses in the areas which interest me.'[46]

Foucault's interest in the constitution of the human subject has sometimes been taken for a denial of agency when, in fact, his aim is to explain how agency is established, how concepts structure our understanding of ourselves and others, how the traits and characteristics attributed to different kinds of people come into being, affect behaviour, and change. In place of the autonomous willing individual of liberal individualism whose agency is inherent in his humanity, we are given an individual whose very self is articulated – conceptualised – socially, through language, the result of historical processes that need to be explored. The emphasis on discourse was one of the ways Foucault distinguished himself from the Frankfurt school philosophers who, he felt, gave short shrift to the importance of concepts and ideas. For Foucault, 'taking account of that which goes through the head of someone, or of a series of individuals, or in the discourse they hold, is effectively part of history: to say something is an event [*dire quelque chose est un événement*]'.[47]

Foucault talked of the subject, not the self, as a way of insisting on the process which subjected individuals to certain constraints even as it defined them as free-willing agents. Here, too, he rejected the Frankfurt school's humanist definition of the subject, because it endorsed the idea that there was an essence of the human. 'I don't think that the Frankfurt School could admit that what we have to do is not recover our lost identity, or liberate our imprisoned nature, or find the fundamental truth of ourselves; but go in an entirely different direction . . . We have to produce something that doesn't yet exist and of which we can have no idea what it will be.'[48] For Foucault the point was, in the words of one of his Italian interviewers, 'to think about the origins of man in a historical-genealogical sense rather than in metaphysical terms'.[49] The homosexual is a case in point. Foucault insisted that though same-sex behaviour had existed for centuries, the notion that that behaviour was enacted by a person whose very being was defined by his sexuality – who bore the identity of 'invert' or 'homosexual' – was a late nineteenth-century conception.[50] The attribution of identity made homosexuals objects of science and subjects of law, and so provided the grounds for collective identification and, eventually, political action. We can take other examples, some not expressly mentioned by Foucault. Feminists for one, whose agency (and consequent 'illegal' actions), I argue elsewhere, were established precisely by their exclusion as citizens in the age of democratic revolutions.[51] Or women workers who, although they had existed in the ranks of paid labour for centuries, became a problem (and so subjects of the law and also potential 'heroes of their own lives') only in the mid-nineteenth-century context of urban, industrial growth, of ideologies of domesticity, and of new concerns about the form the sexual division of labour should take.[52] By asking *how* homosexuals or women workers (to take only some of many examples we could cite) became a problem, rather than assuming that they had always been one, we can historicise these categories of identity and so the matter of agency, and in the process establish critical distance not only from the nineteenth century, but from our own time.

It is the expansiveness of Foucault's theorising of history as critique that is so appealing, the unlimited nature of its possibility. Not only are any prevailing concepts fair game (the home, the individual, the self, the moral accountability of parents, incest, even bodily experiences such as fever), but so is the idea of their transhistorical meaning. 'Nothing in man – not even his body – is sufficiently stable to serve as the basis for self-recognition or for understanding other men.'[53] If all claims to universality are put into question, then we have a way of thinking beyond Whig history's assumptions not only of progress, but of the inevitable path modernity must take (to secularism, 'civilisation' and an increasing homogeneity of values and cultures). Foucault has been accused of ethnocentrism because he did not extend his histories beyond the West (indeed, often not beyond France), but this is not entirely accurate. His work on ancient Greece is hardly about 'the West', and his writing on Iran at the time of the revolution against the Shah sought to make sense of the new role of religion in politics there in 1978.[54] Although his *History of Sexuality* has been faulted for neglecting both gender and race in the construction of sexual discourses and sexual subjects, in fact there is attention to both. 'Beginning in the second half of the nineteenth century', he writes, 'the thematics of blood was sometimes called on to lend its entire historical weight toward revitalizing the type of political power that was exercised through devices of sexuality. Racism took shape at this point (racism in its modern, "biologizing" statist form).'[55] But even without these examples, my main point is that objections on thematic grounds ought not to prevent our use of his critical conceptual tools. Whether or not *he* addressed it as fully as might be wished, Foucault has enabled *us* to think about the current crisis of Western universalism and the ways its definition of the 'problem' of Islam (for example) rests not on essences but on strategic deployments of essentialised concepts in particular historical circumstances.

The presuppositions upon which Foucauldian critical history rests seem to make some historians uncomfortable, perhaps because they are so clearly articulated or perhaps because they confound any notion that objectivity – pure or qualified – is possible. What are we then to make of truth? How can we argue if we can't 'prove' the validity of our points with what is now being increasingly referred to (in science and history) as 'evidence-based' information? For Foucault, I would argue, there is evidence; it is the evidence of language, of concepts, taken not to reflect reality but to structure it, to make it visible, effective, active in institutions and social organisation. And there are facts and even 'truth', though truth is defined as a system of shared standards rather than a transcendent entity; it is defined differentially, in relation to things that are taken to be untrue. In this way, Foucault restructures the concept of objectivity, opening it to critical interrogation.

> [T]he very question of truth, the right it appropriates to refute error and oppose itself to appearance, the manner in which it developed (initially made available to the wise, then withdrawn by men of piety to an unattainable world where it was given the double role of consolation and imperative, finally rejected as a useless notion, superfluous, and contradicted on all sides) – does this not form history, the history of an error we call truth?[56]

The idea that meaning is established differentially is not Foucault's invention, but, as Ermarth and others have argued, is fully consistent with early twentieth-century theories of measurement (Einstein) and linguistics (Saussure), theories that ushered in the era referred to as postmodernity.[57] Foucault's work is based on the premise that the relationship between words and things is interactive, not reflective; it is differentially established – 'In what ways?' is the question – and mutable. So – and this is the invitation to think critically – the historian needs to probe that relationship rather than assume its transparency. Or, to return to Derrida's metaphor of the lever, s/he has to unearth the disturbing questions about what seems sure or established in order to make new interpretive efforts – and so new futures – possible.

The passion for critique

There is no question that critique is uncomfortable – and not only for historians. To subject the taken-for-granted to new scrutiny is disturbing and destabilising. Adorno, in a passage I cited earlier, attributed the intolerance for critical thought's lack of a new plan for the future to 'anxiety'. An anxiety we might say, following Jacques Lacan, that serves as the obstacle to, the protection against, desire. Indeed, I want to argue, with Wendy Brown and Janet Halley, who have written a compelling introduction to a volume of essays called *Left Legalism/Left Critique*, that desire animates critique, and so yields pleasure. This is not pleasure as comfort or reassurance, or in Elizabeth Weed's terms, 'consolation'; it is instead the 'shock of the new', the disorienting effect of a different perspective, the thrill of thinking beyond established frontiers.[58] 'The work of critique', write Brown and Halley, 'is potentially without boundary or end.'[59] As such it 'hazards the opening of new modalities of thought and political possibility, and potentially affords as well the possibility of enormous pleasure – political, intellectual, and ethical'.[60] Their characterisation of critique uses the language of desire: it is a 'kindling spirit', it produces 'euphoria'; the pursuit of this 'pleasure itself [is] a crucial source of political motivation'.[61]

Brown and Halley are not the first to liken critique to desire; indeed, it echoes through the writings of the philosophers I have been considering here. Some of them see critique as an effect of desire, others equate the two. Whichever it is, the complicated association drawn between desire and critique explains the impossibility of disinterested objectivity on the one hand, and the association of critique with danger and disruption on the other. Passion, of course, has a complicated genealogy, one Albert Hirschman detailed in his classic *The Passions and the Interests*.[62] The 'passion' that modernity worries about can neither be predicted nor contained. When Derrida refers us back to Aristotle's *Metaphysics* – 'All men, by nature, have the desire to know' – he does so to establish an insight of his own: 'The pleasure of useless sensations explains the desire to know for its own sake.'[63] Kant believed there was an innate human disposition to push thought beyond its established boundaries: 'Man', he wrote, 'has an inward need to ponder questions that cannot be answered by any empirical employment of reason, or by principles thence derived'.[64] Nietzsche, who might well have quarrelled with Kant's essentialising of the desire to know (as would have Foucault or Derrida), associated critique with thought's ability to 'tear itself loose and attain freedom'.[65] Adorno considered this kind of thinking 'insatiable', 'its aversion to being quickly and easily satisfied refuses the foolish wisdom of resignation'.[66] He equated the insatiable drive that animated critique with the ultimate form of happiness, the deep satisfaction that comes from learning to see differently: 'The happiness that dawns in the eye of the thinking person is the happiness of humanity . . . Thought is happiness, even where it defines unhappiness: by enunciating it.'[67] Freud linked the pleasure associated with the desire for knowledge explicitly to sex. He posited 'an instinct for knowledge or research', evident in children between the ages of three and five, that stemmed from their curiosity about sex: 'Knowledge in children is attracted unexpectedly early and intensively to sexual problems and is in fact possibly first aroused by them.'[68] It is not surprising to find Freud making knowledge and desire synonymous, though it was Marx who said it more eloquently and succinctly: 'criticism is not a passion of the head, but the head of passion'.[69]

This is the passion Foucault describes in the Preface to *The Order of Things*. It is startling – at once delightful and disconcerting:

> This book first arose out of a passage in Borges, out of the laughter that shattered as I read the passage, all the familiar landmarks of my thought – *our* thought, the thought that bears the stamp of our age and our geography – breaking up all the ordered surfaces and all the planes with

which we are accustomed to tame the wild profusion of existing things, and continuing long afterwards to disturb and threaten with collapse our age-old distinction between the Same and the Other . . . That passage from Borges kept me laughing a long time, though not without a certain uneasiness that I found hard to shake off.[70]

The uneasiness, Foucault tells us, has several sources and not just the questioning of the belief that the fundamental codes of our culture reflect an incontestable empirical reality. Uneasiness is a symptom of insecurity, of a loss of familiar markers in a moment of surprise. As with any passion, the known limits are hard to discern.

It is tempting to shake off this kind of uneasiness by sticking with the already known, by doggedly continuing to explore familiar terrain and, through that exploration, confirming its boundaries, fortifying its existing frontiers against unwelcome incursions. Foucault did not opt for this kind of security, choosing instead to follow desire where it led even if, or perhaps because, it meant trespassing on the field of established history. For some of us, following his lead has led to exciting challenges. We have resisted what Robyn Wiegman called 'the impulse to reproduce only what [we] think we already know', instead interrogating the grounds of our knowledge, both the historical accounts and the analytic categories that established their inevitability.[71] For feminist historians such as myself it has meant not simply restoring the visibility of women, but – following Denise Riley's incitement – treating the very category of women as an object for historical study.[72] These efforts have not always been welcome; indeed, they have sometimes earned the scorn of those who righteously uphold an unquestioned belief in the real and eternal existence of women and their agency as touchstones of a one true feminism. If we understand this scorn as an expression of unease or anxiety, we can understand it too as a retreat from or resistance to critique. This retreat is a great pity, since feminism has historically derived its strength and influence from its own desire to interrogate the 'fundamental categories, methodology, and self-understanding of Western science and theory'.[73] That some feminists seem now to have retreated from this position, or solidified it into an orthodoxy which refuses the kind of ongoing self-examination required by critique, is, I submit, a sign of the times.

The ethics of critique

Although critique has been discounted as negative and impractical, it is in fact driven by a desire for change – and one that is not always 'progressive' or 'left'; there are critiques from the right too, although my focus here has been on those from the left. The aim of critique is to make things better. In our world, this is often defined in terms of fulfilling the ideals of democratic society – liberty, equality, justice – although with no pre-drawn plan in mind.

The notion is that any legitimating authority – even one founded on these ideals – will become so invested in its own power that it will resist innovation and attempt to put a stop to history; the opening to a different (and by definition better) future is protected (though by no means guaranteed) if critique can continue to operate. The emancipatory goals of Marx and Adorno were clear (to raise the consciousness and so change the fate of those oppressed by bourgeois capitalism), but so were those of Foucault when he retold liberal Whig stories as the emergence of new regimes of power. The point was to bring down established boundaries in the interests of 'liberty'.[74] 'Bodies and pleasures', the enigmatic ending of the first volume of the *History of Sexuality*, points in the direction of greater freedom of sexual expression even if it takes as a given that there will always be some form of regulatory norm in operation that itself will have to be subjected to critique. 'The most ruthless critique', Derrida wrote at the time of the founding of the Collège de Philosophie – an attempt to institutionalise philosophy as critique within and against the grain of established academic philosophy –

> the implacable analysis of a power of legitimation is always produced in the name of a system of legitimation . . . We already know that the interest in research not currently legitimated will only find its way if, following trajectories ignored by or unknown to any established institutional power, this new research is *already underway and promises a new legitimacy* until one day, once again . . . and so on.[75]

Critique is never satisfied with the regimes that claim to fulfil its desire; futurity is guaranteed only by the persistent dissatisfaction of critique.

This is where history-writing comes in. And with it, a different kind of ethics from the one the historians writing in that special issue of *History and Theory* were worrying about. It is not a question of judging whether the actions of men and women in the past were good or bad from some contemporary ethical perspective (whether or not, for example, Sartre was a willing dupe of communists, or Fanon an unacceptably violent man, or slavery an oppressive institution). Of course, historians are free to make such judgements and base their work upon them and that work often has undeniably important political resonance, making previously ignored people visible or revising prevailing interpretations. I'm not calling for an end to studies of that kind; we surely need them. But I don't think they usually constitute critique. Instead, they comfortably confirm our own sense of moral superiority, our own sense of who we are.

Critique ought to make us uncomfortable by asking what the sources of those values are, how they have come into being, what relationships they have constituted, what power they have secured. This is not the kind of negativity that leads to denying the Holocaust or justifying slavery or the oppression of women. It is not at that level that the interrogation takes place. Rather, the attempt is to make visible the premises upon which the organising categories of our identities (personal, social, national) are based and to give them a history, so placing them in time and subject to review. This kind of history-writing takes up topics not usually considered 'historical' because they are either objects taken to be self-evident in their meaning (women, workers, fever, incest) or categories of analysis outside of time (gender, race, class, even postcolonial). The object of critical history-writing is the present, though its materials come from the archives of the past; its aim is neither to justify nor to discredit, but to illuminate those blind-spots Barbara Johnson referred to (in the quote I cited at the beginning of this manifesto) that keep social systems intact and make seeing how to change them so difficult. This kind of critical history-writing serves the interests of history in two senses: it opens doors to futures we might not otherwise have been able to imagine and, in so doing, gives us ever more material for the writing of history.

Notes

1 An earlier version of this paper, titled 'Against Eclecticism', was published in *differences* 16:3 (Fall 2005): 114–37. This paper was strongly influenced by the work I did with graduate students in a seminar on 'Critique' at Rutgers University in the fall of 2005. I am grateful for their hard work and their insights, individual and collective. I would also like to thank Andrew Aisenberg, Caroline Arni, Wendy Brown, Brian Connolly, Geoffroy de Lagasnerie, Didier Eribon, Carol Gluck, Denise Riley, Sylvia Schafer, Donald M. Scott and Elizabeth Weed for their critical comments on this paper.

2 For example, see Emily Eakin, 'The Theory of Everything, R.I.P.', *New York Times*, 17 October 2004; Jonathan Kandell, 'Jacques Derrida, Abstruse Theorist, Dies in Paris at 74', *New York Times*, 10 October 2004; Edward Rothstein, 'An Appraisal: The Man who Showed us How to Take the World apart', *New York Times*, 11 October 2004.

3 There is even now (2006) a bill pending in the Arizona state legislature that would give students the right to have alternative readings more suited to their tastes than those required on course syllabi.

4 For a critical response to one such effort, see Carla Hesse, 'The New Empiricism', *Cultural and Social History* (2004): 201–7. See also Dominick LaCapra, 'Tropisms of Intellectual History', *Rethinking History* 8:4 (December 2004): 499–529, especially 522.

5 The return of the sociobiology of the 1970s as the all-new evolutionary psychology is a similar phenomenon. So also is the use of neuroscience by some scholars who would entirely replace the theorised subject with a hard-wired mind.

6 Joyce Appleby, Lynn Hunt and Margaret Jacob, *Telling the Truth about History* (New York: Norton, 1994): 237.

7 Elizabeth Deeds Ermarth, 'Ethics and Method', *History and Theory* 43:4 (December 2004): 61–83, 68.

8 For a powerful critique of this see Jacques Rancière, *La Nuit des prolétaires: Archives du rêve ouvrier* (Paris: Fayard, 1981). See also, Joan W. Scott, 'The Class We Have Lost', *International Labor and Working Class History* 57 (Spring 2000): 69–75.

9 Joan W. Scott, 'Preface' to the second edition of *Gender and the Politics of History* (New York: Columbia Press, 1999).

10 Lawrence Stone, 'Madness', *New York Review of Books*, 16 December 1982; Michel Foucault, 'An Exchange with Michel Foucault', *New York Review of*

Books, 31 March 1983. In the exchange with Stone, Foucault replies, furiously, that his footnotes prove his credentials as a historian.

11 See, for example, John E. Toews, 'Intellectual History after the Linguistic Turn: The Autonomy of Meaning and the Irreducibility of Experience', *American Historical Review* 92 (October 1987); and William H. Sewell, Jr, 'Gender, History and Deconstruction: Joan Wallach Scott's *Gender and the Politics of History*', CSST Working Paper 34, University of Michigan, Ann Arbor, August 1989. See also, Joan W. Scott, 'The Evidence of Experience', *Critical Inquiry* 17:4 (Summer 1991): 773–97.

12 Appleby, *et al.*, *Telling the Truth about History*. 'That noble dream' refers to Peter Novick's book, *'That Noble Dream': The Objectivity Question and the American Historical Profession* (New York: Cambridge University Press, 1988).

13 'Historians and Ethics', special themed issue of *History and Theory* 43:4 (December 2004): 9.

14 Eric Hobsbawn, 'Le Pari de la raison: manifeste pour l'histoire', *Le Monde diplomatique*, (December 2004): 1, 20 and 21.

15 Barbara Johnson, translator's introduction to Jacques Derrida, *Dissemination* (Chicago: University of Chicago Press, 1981): xv. See also Barbara Johnson, *The Wake of Deconstruction* (Cambridge, Mass.: Blackwell, 1994).

16 Theodor Adorno, *Critical Models: Interventions and Catchwords* (New York: Columbia University Press, 1998): 293.

17 Friedrich Nietzsche, *The Birth of Tragedy and the Genealogy of Morals*, trans. F. Golffing, (New York: Doubleday, 1956): 155.

18 Friedrich Nietzsche, *On the Advantage and Disadvantage of History for Life* (Indianapolis: Hackett Publishers, 1980): 20.

19 Ibid., p. 18.

20 Ibid., p. 29.

21 Robert C. Tucker (ed.), *The Marx–Engels Reader* (New York: Norton, 1978): 54.

22 Adorno, *Critical Models*, p. 10.

23 The emancipatory thrust of critical theory was clear. For another example, see Max Horkheimer, 'Traditional and Critical Theory', in his *Critical Theory: Selected Essays*, trans. M. J. O'Connell (New York: Herder and Herder, 1972): 188–243.

24 David C. Hoy and Thomas McCarthy, *Critical Theory* (Cambridge, Mass.: Blackwell, 1994): 139.

25 Immanuel Kant, *Critique of Pure Reason*, trans. N. K. Smith, (New York: St Martin's Press, 1965): 59.

26 Tucker (ed.), *The Marx–Engels Reader*, pp. 13, 14–15.

27 Adorno, *Critical Models*, p. 7.

28 Ibid., p. 287.

29 Ibid., p. 290.

30 Ibid., p. 281.

31 Ibid., p. 133.

32 Ibid., p. 281.

33 Jacques Derrida, *Fichus: Discours de Francfort* (Paris: Galilée, 2002).

34 Jacques Derrida, *Right to Philosophy*, Vol. I: *Who's Afraid of Philosophy?*, trans. Jan Plug (Stanford: Stanford University Press, 2002): 42.

35 Adorno, *Critical Models*, p. 8.

36 Alexander Dickow provides an illuminating discussion, 'Derrida's Summons: Responsibility in "Mochlos", or, the Conflict of the Faculties', unpublished, Vol. II: *Eyes of the University* (Stanford: Stanford University Press, 2004), paper, Rutgers University, December 2005, p. 14. See also Jacques Derrida, *Right to Philosophy* pp. 110–11: 'Now, when one asks how to orient oneself in history,

morality, or politics, the most serious discords and decisions have to do less often with ends, it seems to me, than with levers.'
37 Michel Foucault, 'What is Enlightenment?', trans. C. Porter, in Paul Rabinow (ed.), *The Essential Works of Michel Foucault, 1954–1984*, Vol. 1 (New York: New Press, 1997): 315. See also, Foucault, 'What is Critique?', trans. L. Hochroth, in David Ingram (ed.), *The Political* (Malden, Mass.: Blackwell, 2002).
38 Cited in Hoy and McCarthy, *Critical Theory*, p. 48.
39 Michel Foucault, *The Order of Things: An Archaeology of the Human Sciences* (New York: Vintage Books, 1994): 219.
40 Michel Foucault, 'Nietzsche, Genealogy, History', in Donald F. Bouchard (ed.) and trans., *Language, Counter-Memory, Practice: Selected Essays and Interviews by Michel Foucault* (Ithaca: Cornell University Press, 1977): 146.
41 Hoy and McCarthy, *Critical Theory*, p. 163.
42 Foucault, 'Nietzsche, Genealogy, History', pp. 151–2.
43 Ibid., p. 154.
44 Foucault, 'What is Enlightenment?', p. 315.
45 Foucault, 'Nietzsche, Genealogy, History', p. 155.
46 Michel Foucault, 'Entretien avec Michel Foucault', in his *Dits et Ecrits II, 1976–1988* (Paris: Gallimard, 2001): 895.
47 Ibid.
48 Ibid., p. 893.
49 Ibid., p. 894.
50 There have been debates about this timing. Among them, see Didier Eribon, *Hérésies: essais sur la théorie de la sexualité* (Paris: Fayard, 2003).
51 Joan Wallach Scott, *Only Paradoxes to Offer: French Feminists and the Rights of Man* (Cambridge, Mass.: Harvard University Press, 1996).
52 Joan W. Scott, 'The Woman Worker', in Georges Duby and Michelle Perrot (eds), *A History of Women*, Vol. IV (Cambridge, Mass.: Harvard University Press, 1993): 399–426.
53 Foucault, 'Nietzsche, Genealogy, History', p. 153.
54 See Janet Afary and Kevin B. Anderson, *Foucault and the Iranian Revolution: Gender and the Seductions of Islam* (Chicago: University of Chicago Press, 2005); see also, Pankaj Mishra, 'The Misunderstood Muslims', *New York Review of Books* 52:18 (17 November 2005): 15–18.
55 Foucault, *The History of Sexuality*, Vol. I: *Introduction*, trans. Peter Hurley (New York: Vintage, 1980): 149.
56 Foucault, 'Nietzsche, Genealogy, History', p. 144.
57 Ermarth, 'Ethics and Method', pp. 68–75.
58 Elizabeth Weed, 'Luce Irigaray and the Waning of Critique', paper given at the University of Buffalo Humanities Institute Inaugural Conference, 28–9 October 2005. To be published in a volume of essays from the conference.
59 Wendy Brown and Janet Halley (eds), *Left Legalism/Left Critique* (Durham, NC: Duke University Press, 2002): 26. See also Wendy Brown, 'Untimeliness and Punctuality: Critical Theory in Dark Times', in her *Edgework: Critical Essays on Knowledge and Politics* (Princeton: Princeton University Press, 2005): 1–16.
60 Ibid., p. 29.
61 Ibid., p. 32.
62 Albert O. Hirschman, *The Passions and the Interests: Political Arguments for Capitalism before its Triumph* (Princeton: Princeton University Press, 1977).
63 Derrida, *Right to Philosophy*, Vol. II, pp. 130–1.
64 Kant, 'Introduction', *Critique of Pure Reason*, p. 56.
65 Nietzsche, *On the Advantage and Disadvantage*, p. 4.
66 Adorno, *Critical Models*, p. 292.
67 Ibid., p. 293.

68 Sigmund Freud, *Three Essays on the Theory of Sexuality*, trans. J. Strachey (New York: Basic Books, 1975): 60.

69 Tucker (ed.), *The Marx–Engels Reader*, p. 55.

70 Foucault, *The Order of Things*, pp. xv and xvii.

71 Robyn Wiegman, 'What Ails Feminist Criticism? A Second Opinion', *Critical Inquiry* 25:2 (Winter 1999): 362–79.

72 Denise Riley, *'Am I That Name?' Feminism and the Category of 'Women' in History* (London: Macmillan, 1988); see also her 'A Short History of Some Preoccupations', in Judith Butler and Joan W. Scott (eds), *Feminists Theorize the Political*, (New York: Routledge, 1992): 121–8.

73 Seyla Benhabib and Drucilla Cornell (eds), *Feminism as Critique: Essays on the Politics of Gender in Late-Capitalist Societies* (London: Polity Press, 1987): 1.

74 On the connection of Foucault's critique to contemporary political movements, see Didier Eribon, 'Introduction: *L'Art de l'inservitude*', in Eribon (ed.), *L'Infréquentable Michel Foucault: Renouveaux de la pensée critique* (Paris: EPEL, 2001): 9–18.

75 Derrida, *Right to Philosophy*, Vol. II, pp. 126–7.

3 Manifesto for a history of the media

Mark Poster

> He had been taught . . . that history, along with geography, was dead. That history in the older sense was an historical concept. History in the older sense was narrative, stories we told ourselves about where we'd come from and what it had been like, and those narratives were revised by each new generation, and indeed always had been. History was plastic, was a matter of interpretation. The digital had not so much changed that as made it too obvious to ignore. History was stored data, subject to manipulation and interpretation.
>
> William Gibson, *All Tomorrow's Parties*

Marx theorised a changed relation between men and machines. Machines had changed: they had been hooked up to natural energy sources, first steam, then petroleum, then electricity. So men could change too: their work relations and skills could be reorganised. In the Industrial Revolution, labourers acted upon natural materials but only through the mediation of increasingly complex machinic apparatuses, so complex and expensive that, unlike their artisan forebears, industrial workers could not own their own tools. The consequences of these alterations in the daily work life of men and women were played out in the politics and society of the past two centuries and were increasingly the main focus of historical investigations. History took into account a new relation of humans to machines.

Now machines are changing again. They are processing information, not raw materials, and they are globally networked. Today all elements of culture (texts, images and sounds) are coded into digital logic and uploaded into a global network that incorporates all human groupings, however unequally. Texts, images and sounds are exchanged between humans increasingly only through the mediation of networked computers. The work of human beings changes accordingly. No longer Chaplinesque cogs in assembly lines; workers are increasingly monitors of work processes and manipulators of symbols in close conjunction with computers. The historian's task is thus to theorise the implications of this transformation, to create research projects that explore its many aspects, and to write its histories with an eye to the political possibilities it opens up.

The discipline of history is haunted by the spectre of the virtual. Historians have bathed in the real for too long, writing about events and structures, people and institutions, attitudes and behaviour, consciousness and action, as if access to these phenomena through archival documents afforded them dips into the sea of the past as it actually was. In the 1970s and 1980s, historians took umbrage at Hayden White and the whole intellectual current of critical theory for even suggesting that writing history was a form of narrative with a variety of tropes introducing meaning into the historian's text that could not have emerged directly from the archive. Historians also objected to the arguments of poststructuralists that history was infused with assumptions deriving from Western cultural habits which were then the objects of investigation, forming a vicious circle of cultural closure and paro-chialism. Historians were so seduced by the past, so engrossed in the tragedies and victories over oppression that filled its moments, so impressed with the importance and weightiness of it all, that they forgot they were writing texts, reading texts, creating texts, processes which have logics in themselves, requiring attention to their internal complexities. Historians desperately needed theory and, for the most part, they adamantly refused it. So by the mid-1990s, when the media began to achieve a density and extensiveness that could no longer be ignored, when the virtual encroached undeniably upon the real, historians by and large were not prepared. The 'real' and the 'virtual' became inextricable and cultural (textual, visual, aural) at the same time. It is time historians took this change to heart, rethinking the 'real' and their methods of representing it.

Historians were certainly not alone in facing the future shock of mediated culture. Teachers in universities were astonished when students in large numbers began to download paper assignments from the internet, when they brought laptop computers to class to take notes, when they did email in class, when they wanted to hand in work on floppy disks or CD ROMs, when they answered mobile phones in class and communicated text messages on them, when they asked that instructors' notes be posted on university websites, and finally when they turned automatically to the internet as research tool, not the library, every time they were given an assignment. The media, digital media in particular, had arrived in the hallowed halls of ivy. And it affected all of the disciplines, not just history. A technology of networked computing that was born largely within the university community was now coming back to disrupt the habits of the classroom and carefully elaborated protocols of advanced research. Each of the disciplines needed to come to grips with the new technology of information machines.

In this manifesto I propose a framework for histories of media that rests outside the well-trod humanist approaches of looking for agents and victims, ideas and actions, influences and innovations. While this framework continues to inspire research into media history, that history must also be understood, I contend, as the construction of combinations of humans and information machines. In such assemblages the logic of the information machine is as significant as the logic of human beings. Until now historians of the media have worried about the question of technological determinism versus human freedom. Either machines shaped human practice or humans deployed machines as tools for instrumental purposes. But this dilemma becomes salient only if the humanist frame is already at play in the historian's vision. If we focus instead on the interplay of humans and information machines, the question of technological determinism is nullified. The field of investigation no longer consists of subjects (humans) and objects (information machines) but as complexes of the two elements in which neither plays the role of subject or object. The *first* principle in the field of media history then will be the couple humans/machines in their complex interactions and mutual effects.

Historians need to approach media history with the couple humans/machines in the forefront because information machines affect not natural objects, as mechanical machines do, but cultural objects. Information machines – the apparatuses of media – operate upon texts, images and sounds. In conjunction with humans they produce, reproduce, store and disseminate these cultural objects. When machines work on cultural objects they alter the basic conditions of culture. They disrupt and reconfigure time and space, body and mind, object and subject, the living and the non-living, the organic and the inorganic, the ideal and the material. They introduce into language, visuality and aurality a new level of materiality, one that is outside human perception and the Newtonian physical world, but is fully material at the micro-level of electrons, chemical switches and light pulses. In this way, culture, the processes through which meanings appear and are disseminated in society, is altered by information machines that code, crunch and work upon the bearers of meaning – texts, images and sounds.

These changes in the structure of media were not visible during the half millennium of history that began with printing machines. Until recently information machines operated upon cultural objects in the perceptible realm of the analogue. Inked paper 'looks like' handwriting; photographs trace light patterns upon chemically coated film; grooves in phonograph records force needles to generate movements that can be transduced into radio frequencies that mimic sounds; telephones (until the recent introduction of digital technology) change spoken words first into electro-magnetic waves only to return them into sounds after they are transmitted to a receiver. In each case the information machine produces at a different physical level an analogue of the text, image and sound initiated by the human. Such changes to the physics of the cultural object enable drastic innovations in their reproduction, storage and dissemination. Printing presses outperform teams of scribes in reproducing texts; telephones transmit sounds far beyond the capacity of the human voice; photographs store images much better than memory cells in the brain, and so forth. But analogue information machines have severe limitations, operating as they do within the Newtonian domain of human perception. These limitations become visible to the historian or observer only after the advent of the digital. The analogue only becomes analogue once it is defined as such by the difference of the digital. Perhaps that helps explain why historians of media tended, until recently, to overlook the message of the medium.

With the advent of networked digital information machines, the restrictions of the analogue are transcended and, as a result, the impact of media upon culture vastly increases and changes in quality. Culture is now mediated by a different physical region, one governed by laws of time and space, for instance, which are drastically different from those of previous information machines. This translation is carried out through several operations. Digital machines do not mimic traces of human sounds and sights. They translate these cultural objects into a machine language of zeros and ones, a binary logic of on and off, yes or no, a code that operates outside human perception in a microscopic realm that pulses light, switches tiny chemical charges, moves invisible electrons. Once transcoded into the binary logic of the digital machine, culture may be infused with the properties of a new physical domain. What makes sense in the analogue world of mediated human perception no longer necessarily applies. A copy of a cultural object, for instance, does not require new resources, energy, space or time, invalidating the principle of scarcity that is the basis of modern culture. The individuality and intentionality of a user does not affect the truth value of an entry into a digital database so that anyone can be anyone else in the network. The digital domain of media imposes new ethics, new conditions of trust.

But digital information machines are not independent of humans. The machines and the humans interact continually with one another through interfaces that are able to connect with both domains, to converse with each, to transact across the divide of the analogue and the digital. Information machines and humans continually and relentlessly *change each other*. With analogue media, the cultural object is independent of the human user. The cultural object – book, film, radio broadcast – is in direct contact with the user. In the case of the computer, a series of interfaces stand between the user and the information machine. Monitor, printer, keyboard, mouse and other devices function to translate back and forth between the user code and the machine code, between the 'culture' of each. Texts, images and sounds that are comprehensible to the user are impenetrable to the computer's central processing unit. By the same token, the CPU's digital code is meaningless to the user. Without interfaces that translate from the user to CPU (keyboard) and from the CPU to the user (monitor), digital information machines could not function. One might say that other electronic media – telephones, radio and television – also require interfaces such as tuners that transform radio frequencies into sounds waves and images. The continuities and breaks between earlier electronic media and current ones must be researched in detail by historians. It will then be recognised, I believe, that digital code requires a much more complex set of interfaces than earlier media in order to function as information media for the user.

At all of these levels, computers introduce a change in the relation of humans to machines. Historians of media must account for this discontinuity or break by rethinking the figure of the human and the figure of the machine as agents of history. If the human persists in historical texts as agent or subject and the machine continues to be represented as object, the specific configuration of the assemblage of human and machine in computing is lost. The culture in general has certainly recognised the problem (even if historians have not). Without going back to Mary Shelley's *Frankenstein* (1818), the increasing spate of films that portray humans and machines in life and death struggle (the Wachowski brothers' *Matrix* trilogy of 1999–2003 may stand in for dozens of them) registers a deep anxiety over the relation. The doggedness of historians' usage of the human–subject/machine–object binary serves to misrecognise the new configuration and to stabilise the older cultural norm. It functions as a profoundly conservative ideological limit to obscure newer forms of antagonism and possibility in the relation of humans and machines. We must then write the history of the human/machine assemblage without the instrumentalist ideology of machines as tools that characterises much of previous historical work.

Computers are no longer stand-alone devices but linked to a worldwide network. This feature of digital information machines also introduces profound changes in human culture, changes that require attention by historians. First, the network is global and politics is national. This contradiction results in conflicts, for example, over copyright law. United States law provides for copyright for ninety-five years after the author's death; Australian law limits copyright to fifty years from death. So works fall into the public domain forty-five years sooner down under. The text of *Gone with the Wind* is available now in Australia but not in the United States. Yet anyone connected to the network may easily obtain it from Australia's Project Gutenberg (Shannon, 2004). National sovereignty is thus defeated in this and many other cases. Many cultures do not even have copyright law. Yet they too must adapt to the strictures of global processes as these are being generated by the World Intellectual Property Organisation. Cultures become thereby transnational, inducing a set of new issues that require much negotiation, translation and mutual understanding. While long-distance telephone use achieved similar conditions, the global network normalises translational communications.

The registers of time and space – basic conditions of cultural coherence – are also reconfigured by networked computing. One's sense of locality changes when communications are rapid across thousands of miles, as they are on the internet. Massively multiple online games, for instance, connect players across the globe in synchronous activity and thus inject a second order of temporality into players, one out of joint with their physical location. Challenged by innovations in transport systems in earlier centuries, geographic specificity is today complicated by speed dimensions that nullify spatial distance. In many contemporary communications systems spatial location recedes in importance. One no longer waits by the phone but takes it along. As for the internet, user location means little in most network functions. To receive an email from someone you know tells you nothing about that person's location on the globe. Numerous technologies fold into the internet in this regard: satellite communications, global positioning systems, multi-band digital telephones with visual displays, webcams hooked into GPS, and so forth. Theorists such as Paul Virilio and new media artists such as Stelarc in turn bemoan and explore the vast transformations affecting the body in the new spatial and temporal modalities.

With its divisions into nations and continents, the discipline of history is ill-suited to account for these novelties. The recent trend towards world history will help in this respect but much of it still operates in geographic frameworks of earlier cultural domains. And academic posts in history departments are defined as continent or nation. Undergraduate history curricula are filled with courses titled by time and place, not by problem or theme. Ph.D. candidates are classified by national field or fields. Temporal and spatial categories in the discipline are increasingly out of sync with historical tendencies and inherently conservative in their inability to call into question such phenomena as the nation state or to trace the history of phenomena that do not fall within national boundaries that are deeply transnational. The temporality introduced by networked computing adds on to other temporalities – those of natural cycles, of work and of other media such as the 'flow' of television – producing a multiple, heterogeneous complex of culturally inscribed time, destabilising the dominant temporality of Western clock time and rendering anachronistic the foundational habits of mind of most historians. The time of the nation, 'local time', is no longer hegemonic but part of a complex of temporalities that must take each other into account. The nation state may not be disappearing but it is certainly becoming relative to other spatial formations, from regional groupings like the European Union to sub-national ethnicities and global NGOs, corporations and cultural movements. History departments need to open positions for scholars to study these phenomena.

The digital culture emerging from networked computing furthermore initiates a massive shift in the nature of cultural objects. Modernity relies upon fixed cultural objects: printed materials, photos, CDs, celluloid films, broadcasts, and so forth. These relatively stable objects constitute the foundation of Western culture. They may be altered to some extent by users, but they are reproduced as uniform things by printing presses, CD factories and broadcast companies, regardless of changes made in individual copies by consumers. Films, television shows and books may be commented upon by audiences and reviewers, lauded or criticised in the minds of readers and viewers. Still, these modern cultural objects persist unchanged by their circulation in society. They are reliable, solid analogue blocks of matter. As such they militate for a clear line of separation between those who made them and those who purchased them. Modern cultural objects, in other words, construct and continuously reproduce the producer and the consumer as two distinct subject positions. The celebrity/author and the consumer of cultural objects are decidedly modern subject positions. Histories of their emergence ought to include analyses of the role of fixed cultural objects in this process.

Things were certainly not the same before modern society and the printing press, the camera and the mechanisms of broadcasting. Throughout the millennia before 1500 most cultural objects were made and remade continuously by their users. Their creation was integral to their recreation. Songs and stories were performed by the audience and were altered with each enactment. Before the existence of media of reproduction, cultural objects were variable to some extent and by and large did not introduce a sharply etched division between producer and consumer. When human memory was the only basis for storing and archiving cultural objects, exact reproduction was impossible. Without the stability of the record, written or otherwise, creators of cultural objects could not be elevated to the status of author.

Networked computing combines elements of modern and pre-modern types of cultural objects. Like modern society, digital cultural objects are stored and distributed in material forms that may be reproduced as exact copies. A digital text file, image or sound on one's hard disk may be copied and disseminated without change. Unlike modern culture, digital culture accomplishes this task at very little cost and extends this capability to anyone with an online computer. Each user is thus at the same time a producer, like Disney or Scribner's. Such democratisation is in itself potentially of great import. Digitisation also transforms texts, images and sounds into the same material form: the computer file. By doing so, digitisation erases the analogue differences between cultural objects and renders the same individual capable of producing, reproducing, storing and distributing any cultural object. A single online computer user functions as a printing press, a broadcaster, a film-maker and a music company. But the networked computing of digital cultural objects goes considerably beyond the amplification of modern forms. It also captures some elements of the pre-modern condition of cultural objects: as easily as a computer user may copy and distribute texts, images and sounds, so may they alter them and distribute them in their altered state. As a result, digital cultural objects depart from analogue, fixed objects of modernity in yet another significant way: they are variable. The human/computer assemblage may change a text, image or sound almost as easily as reading, viewing or listening to it. Digital cultural objects have no more fixity than liquid. The content of culture becomes, in the regime of the digital, evanescent and permanent at the same time. Data or information on the internet is changeable, temporary, or what I call 'underdetermined'. Like a folksong or oral narrative, each instance of the digital cultural object may be different from all others. And yet one cannot be sure. The variability of cultural objects creates special problems for the historian, to be sure.

Some aspects of digital cultural objects avail themselves of the changeability of the file more than others. Text files saved in the .pdf format of

Adobe are more difficult to alter than those in the .txt, .rtf or .doc formats. Stumbling blocks to text manipulation are introduced in some computer files as a form of resistance against their inherent malleability. At the other extreme producers of computer games have yielded to the hacking of users who often made changes in the game ('Doom' is a good example) and redistributed the resulting files on the internet. Commercial game producers consequently sometimes include a feature that allows users to make changes in the game and redistribute it. Like the free software and open source movements in the realm of computer programs, a culture of open content has emerged in networked computing that takes advantage of the variable character of digital cultural objects.

But modern institutions resist the variability of cultural objects. The culture industry attempts to restrict the user's ability not only to change the object but even to 'consume'. Regional restrictions are imposed on DVDs. The music industry has attempted to prevent playing CDs on computers. So-called 'Digital Rights Management' techniques attempt to restrict how many times a song or a movie can be played, on what type of machine, and how, if at all, it might be copied. Similar restrictions are imposed on cable, satellite and broadcast high-definition television. Digital audio-tape machines, from the start, could not record at the same bit rate as commercial CDs. Commercial software programs have also been fitted with copy protection, authorisation systems and the like. It is the ease of copying and changing digital objects that leads to a fundamental incompatibility with modern cultural practices, such as the passive figure of the consumer and copyright law. This highly controversial area will no doubt lead to much conflict and the resolutions of the conflict will deeply affect the shape of culture in the coming decades.

For historians, the change from variable to fixed and back again to variable cultural objects must be a central dimension of media history. Not only is this phenomenon in itself a salient aspect of culture; these changes have ripple effects on other important aspects of culture, most notably the configuration of the individual, or, to use the term often cited by historians, the 'agent'. Historians depict individuals in modern society as autonomous agents, most often rational and conscious beings who struggle against domination or suffer as victims of its injustices. Like Michel Foucault, I contend that the chief problem of cultural history in the modern era is not to describe how these agents act and think in structures and events but rather to account for the construction of such a figure of agency or individuality in the first place. Just as historians blind themselves to the nation as a geographic unit by fixing it as the premise of their research and teaching, as the category that divides up the field of history, so they blind themselves to the great question of the historical construction of the modern ideology of individualism by repro- ducing in their texts and lectures the very figure of such an individual, as if it were a natural being or a given fact of life. Agents populate ubiquitously the pages of modern social history as the fauna of the West.

The most recent term for this cultural inscription of individuality is 'identity'. All individuals, historians write, have identities in the same way as elephants have tusks. In book after book written by American historians since the 1970s the reader is presented with narratives in which individuals and groups seek or assert their identities. One finds the question of identity popping up in the most unlikely places, in sixteenth-century France or the Italian Middle Ages, places where the term itself was never used and would not easily be comprehended. Yet how individuals are understood to have identities is a most interesting historical question and is closely tied to the history of media. Of critical importance to the emergence of identity as a characteristic of the self were media of recording, media that were not invented or disseminated throughout societies until the modern period. Fingerprinting, brain measurement, the discourse of taxonomy, photography, printing, the practice of counting populations, identity and credit cards with numbers unique to each person, passports, and the discursive practice of the case file – all of these, as well as more recent media of databases, biometrics and gene analysis, have been conditions for the possibility of individuals having identities. Identity has been constructed as a social and cultural fact outside the consciousness of the self and in the media or recording and storage. The vaunted agency of the individual could not exist before such media practices were in place.

And now that digital media have spread across the globe, however unequally, 'identity' and 'agency' are increasingly giving way to new forms of the cultural construction of the self. In online chat rooms and games, 'identity' becomes not a given figure of the self but a practice of self-fashioning, not a natural attribute but a manufactured result, not a permanent centre of individuality but a temporary and changing aspect of personal development. A new kind of agency or identity is in the process of emerging, in and through media practices. This subject position does not appear to have the characteristics so valued by the modern individual: autonomy, privacy, a stable centre, privileged rationality, self-reliance, consistency of character. Instead, the subject position of digital culture appears as a node in network, a relay point, changeable in time and space, amorphously defined, internally inconsistent. One might contrast these subject positions as fixed and variable, mirroring the cultural objects that surround them in their respective social landscapes.

There is no question here of preferring one type over the other, of celebrating the new or weeping nostalgically for the disappearance of the old. *The project for historians is to grasp the process of cultural transformation and to trace its trajectories.* This requires, as I have argued, a clear understanding of the role of media in the process and a post-humanist willingness to look for changes in relations of humans to machines. We will not comprehend the emergence of new subject positions and new forms of agency if we treat, for example, the history of computing as a problem of assigning credit to inventors, as in earlier forms of the history of technology. The problem is not that such information is irrelevant – far from it – but that if historians look for agents of the modern type in the history of the media they will be unable to discern the history of new types of agency in new configurations of humans and machines.

Perhaps a convincing way to illustrate the change in agency connected with changes in media is to examine the methods of historians and ask about their agency in archival work. As archives become digitised, they fall into the domain of variable cultural objects. I will set aside this aspect of the question, one that raises many highly challenging issues, and look instead at the way digitised archives have new relations to information machines. Digital archives require for access the mediation of computers, perhaps networked or online computers. There are serious questions about formatting and compatibility between the data and the computer, but again we may at present leave aside this question. What cannot be ignored, however, is that this historian, in the case of digitised archives, becomes dependent upon a complex information machine: the computer and its software programs. This dependence is new. Before digitisation, nothing but language proficiency and bureaucracy stood between the historian and the data in the archive. True enough, the historian had to travel to the archive, often with great difficulty and cost, a disadvantage of analogue records that does not necessarily apply to digitised archives which may be online and accessible from any online machine. The dependence of the historian on the information machine also appears in the search functions of the database software: the historian may find his or her data only with the help of the information machine. The machine, in this way, becomes an aspect of the agency of the historian, an integral part of the research project. With the vast quantity of data becoming available and the digital quality of that data, historians become only as good as their search engines in retrieving significant materials.

In sum, changes in the media since the mid-twentieth century pose a sharp challenge to historians. Differences in the physical domain of new media introduce ruptures into culture that must become central questions for historians in the decades to come, especially for historians of media. The interface of humans with networked, digital information machines constitutes a new phenomenon in human history, one that promises to change for ever the habitation of the planet. These machines are harbingers of unprecedented forms of cultural practice that are already emerging in online domains and spill over into the 'real' world of politics, economics and social life. Historians of the future will be writing a history of the virtual, a task that is as daunting as it is exhilarating, but in either case requires a fundamental rethinking of the basic constituents of historical texts, historical research procedures, theoretical frameworks for establishing research questions and agendas. This huge task of reinventing the discipline will be the preoccupation of coming generations of historians.

Reference

V. Shannon, 'New Economy: One Internet, Many Copyright Law', *New York Times*, 11 August 2004.

4   The closed space of choice
A manifesto on the future of history

Elizabeth Deeds Ermarth

The most obvious sign of the failure of the American-led global anti-terror war is the pervasive, frequently expressed, and growing sense of vulnerability that defines much of the West, especially the United States and Britain. The certainty that something equivalent to or bigger than 9/11 is going to happen is matched by the almost total inability of the US and UK political leaderships to comprehend the real nature, causes and aims of the terror groups that target them, like Al Qaeda. Consequently, the US and UK counterterrorism strategies are failing across the board. Fear and ignorance together are a deadly combination.

Rami Khouri

We are difference.

Michel Foucault

Information has nothing to do with imagination or culture.
Henri Cartier-Bresson

The 'growing sense of vulnerability' that Rami Khouri (2005) notes in the West, and that so many feel today, arises primarily not from malign external threats but from internal incapacity. This is an incapacity persistently shored up and maintained by habits of thought that have become increasingly outdated for at least a century but still maintain their hold in Anglo-American culture, especially in the United States, where we and our gurus apparently lack the strength to confront our own cultural challenges and instead prefer to listen to the siren songs about economic indicators that keep us cycling in denial.

The epigraphs above mark three ideas I will set out in this manifesto: first, and most important, the idea that conventional historical explanation plays a significant role in the general sense of cultural failure; second, that changing definitions of knowledge offer new definitions of individuality and process and therefore new opportunities for historical writing that are not being pursued; and third, that in seeking remedy for our incapacity we must look to method, not information or data or 'facts' which, taken alone, can be worse than meaningless.

A manifesto has what Spinoza called a 'prophetic function' in that it gives expression to the desire of a multitude. That is a daunting standard; but whether or not I manage to meet it, I hope at the very least to connect with those readers who find conventional historical explanation unsatisfactory and are interested to experiment in new directions. What would I like to see historians do that they are not presently doing? I would like to see historical writing that finally comes to terms with language; not language as ornament or secondary reflection, but language as Saussure and his many heirs have defined it for us. I want to see historians write in ways that are adequate to the fullest and most generous contemporary understanding of how meaning and knowledge are generated and preserved. In other words, I want to see historical writing that acknowledges what I call the Discursive Condition (Ermarth, 2000), not just in its footnotes and arguments – though that would certainly be a welcome change – but in its entire format and methodology. This manifesto will be about what is involved in making that very considerable change in how history is done.

Seeking ways around conventional history is no small enterprise, given the deeply rooted commitment to empiricism that grounds historical writing in Anglo-American culture. Success would mean finding alternatives to the key instruments of conventional history – for example, the gathering and collation of information or 'facts', the reference to actions of 'individuals', and reliance on productive causality as an explanatory mechanism. Historians (including most popular novelists) who write comfortably – and, let's admit it, comfortingly – using such tools of thought continue to get away with it because they ignore, and they persuade us to ignore, their format, their method. The tools are not in question. But unfortunately, and as every true artist knows, the form *is* the content, the How *is* the What; and in the Discursive Condition everyone including the historian carries the responsibility for creative intervention in the forms and mediums of their culture.

The first section deals with the tools of conventional historical practice and how they might be contributing to a sense of cultural failure; the second section deals with the alternative conditions and tools provided by Saussure and his heirs in practice. My usage of the term 'historians' includes not only the teachers and students who might be called 'professional' historians but anybody who uses historical conventions to explain things to themselves, which means just about everybody in Anglo-American culture. We are all historians, whether we seek our explanations in political argument, in planning our life projects, in therapy or in narrative. Historical conventions function for us as basic tools of thought; it is difficult even to think about personal or collective projects without them. First this happened, and then that, therefore something. It seems as 'natural' as breathing, despite the fact that historical explanation is the ultimate artifice and is anything but natural (Ermarth, 1998a: chs. 1–2). In considering the way forward, historians of both kinds, professional and pedestrian, badly need to pay attention to the *function* of conventional historical method and to shake the still-prevalent assumption that, at base, historical writing is about the neutral discovery, collation and interpretation of evidence, information or facts. That idea – the child of centuries of empiricism – commits us to the practice of treating concretes as fodder for the higher levels of generalisation that eventually bring us to the scientific law or causal explanation at a level abstracted from concretes. Such abstract forms, and the causalities that supposedly produce them, have functioned at the heart of Western thought for two thousand years; they are what Alfred North Whitehead meant when he characterised Western philosophy as a series of footnotes to Plato. But as I explain in the second section below, these causalities do not work well in the Discursive Condition.

For reasons explained in the first section, I adopt phrases such as 'conventional history' and 'standard historical conventions' as shorthand for the fairly recent (two-hundred-year-old) idea of history that we take for granted as 'natural' (this shorthand is not just my invention; see Munslow, 2003). I hope professional historians will accept this shorthand in good humour for the sake of brevity. The term 'conventional' is not a term of opprobrium; it indicates only that history has generally operated according to certain rules and assumptions – that is, conventions – and that those rules and conventions are limited to a period of roughly six centuries, between the Quattrocento and 1900, and to a mainly Eurocentric culture.

Another unavoidable shorthand here has to do with identifying the arguments I have made elsewhere that sustain the present argument. Those arguments cannot be summarised here but at appropriate points I note in passing five of the most important so that interested readers can pursue the fuller case.

Conventional history

History as conventionally understood and practised involves relatively little attention to the question of what, exactly, its function is in our cultural life. Take, for example, the key instruments of conventional history that I have just mentioned – facts, individuals and emergent causalities. The implicit claim made by the unreflexive use of such instruments is that they are the harmless means of producing an accurate picture or representation of 'reality', the more neutral the better: as accurate a picture as possible of Roman politics, Michelangelo's personal life, the year 1776, Mary Wollstonecraft's influence, civil war in the United States or Bosnia, revolution in China, Shell in Niger. By virtue of its methodology conventional history implicitly claims that its proper work is a culturally neutral task: one of providing accurate portraiture, or the production of resemblances in which we are to recognise ourselves, especially our 'reality' composed of 'individuals' who motivate and are motivated by emergent causalities. Such resemblances are the long-familiar quarry of modernity, the era that put the world of forms on the horizontal and that for the first time ever introduced projective, even productive, motion into everything from making maps to planning revolutions.

But what is the cultural function of such claims to be mapping resemblances? One of its functions certainly is to keep reconfirming the essentially Platonic idea that there is such a thing as a knowable 'reality' well past the point where that claim can be defended even by science. One of the epistemological scandals for empiricists, including conventional historians, is the claim associated with relativity theory that what we can measure includes our measurement and thus a foundational difference inimical to the objectification of the universe fundamental to modernity. Even granting that a stable, 'real' physical reality may exist among rocks and stones and trees – though even there our knowledge is infected by now outdated explanatory habits – still, in human and cultural terms such a 'real' either remains a desert or it is unknowable (Zizek, 2002; Belsey, 2005). The fictional side of 'reality' soon shows up when attempts to objectify cultural 'reality' encounter the many differences within and across cultures that make empiricist generalisations about them difficult or impossible.

Where method silently inscribes ideas that themselves are never spoken or weighed, method wields immense power, and such is the case with conventional history. In fact, speaking and weighing that method amount to scandal; decades after Hayden White's *Metahistory* it still is taboo to suggest that historical writing is not basically objective: that its methods are fundamentally literary, or that historical conventions belong to a historically limited phase of Eurocentric culture, or that historical writing functions to produce a 'reality effect', or that narrative of 'the' past is 'just us back there throwing our voices' (White, 1973; Ermarth, 1998a; Ankersmit, 1989; Jenkins, 2003). Conventional historical practices are protected by taboo, and they have the appropriately mythopoetic functions associated with taboos. In this case the mythopoetic function has to do with securing for the human world a common-denominator universe: the one that guarantees we can achieve objectivity, albeit by a never-acknowledged sleight-of-hand. That objectification in turn guarantees all the things we still regard as 'natural', such as representation (pursuit of resemblance) across the range of practice: in art and politics, in empirical science and philosophy, and in historical explanation. This mythopoetic function is rarely acknowledged. Why should we want alternatives to information, individuals and emergent causalities?

Some might say that in resorting to method that I define history too broadly, and that history is simply all and only the sum total of written records – a kind of archive of humanity. Right away we can argue about what a 'record' might be. Could the historical record include writing about recently discovered archaeological remains of a people remote in time and space? If so, in what sense is that document a 'record', and of what is it a record? A remote people? Or our desire to rationalise the differences that occupy the cultural distances between us? The official, self-serving Serbian 'record' of the 1990s war in the former Yugoslavia is nothing more than, as one witness put it, 'a lie, a deceit' (Drakulič, 2004). Even the smallest, most immediate 'record' can be wholly unreliable. For example, the written 'record' of my brief testimony at a local municipal hearing consisted of words wholly invented by the secretary and differing completely from what was on the tape; had I not accidentally discovered that fact and complained, the written 'record' would have been entirely a 'lie' by my standard and probably by most standards of historical truth. Fortunately there was a tape. But how often is that the case when something important is at stake, and if there is, how frail (e.g., erasable) is such a 'record'?

The written record exists in the first place because it objectifies events that 'we' want to remember in the way we want to remember them. In the USA the selective 'record' excludes more than it includes, in some cases even 'events' such as private conversations that result in financial catastrophes affecting millions. It includes such markers as the Civil War, Joseph McCarthy's attack on civil rights, the taking and release of hostages in Iran, and the refusal of Rosa Parks to play the game of humiliation provided for her by a racist culture. The 'written' record in these latter cases often consists of police records, staged photos and videotaped interviews which have immense value and powerful functions. But as 'records' of events they are full of holes, like most 'reality'. The true function of those partial records is a cultural function and has much more to do with constituting collective memory than with accuracy. They satisfy an assumption about how things work and how people define themselves. In other words, they have a mythopoetic function similar to the legends that permitted certain people on the shores of the Indian Ocean to recognise a tsunami-in-progress even though they had never previously seen one. Mythopoetic functions obviously have their practical side. Whether we are talking about written records or a more general set of descriptive rules, in the case of Western historical explanation the question remains, what actual function do such records or descriptions have for us?

To approach such functions we must begin with a wider canvas and with the commonsense idea of history – one that is everywhere assumed and nowhere acknowledged in professional historical writing. That commonsense idea is this: that history is a condition, a medium, something almost indistinguishable from time itself. This is quite a different idea of history from that of a written record. 'History' in this expanded sense stands for everything that has ever happened and will ever happen, whether we know it or not, whether we record it or not. In this long view, history is not limited even to humanity, the definition of which has changed more than once over the centuries. No, the idea of history as a universal medium is larger than any manifestation and contains them all. When we speak – as we often do – of 'making' history or 'changing' history, we speak of influencing something that far exceeds any documentary frame.

Historical explanation thus creates and maintains this ultimate and still largely unacknowledged fiction: that time is a neutral, unproblematic, universal medium 'in' which everything happens. Such time functions as a neutral, common-denominator medium that guarantees mutual relevance among things widely separated in time or space. The sheer fact that absolutely everything can be accommodated in a single system of measurement sustains history's crucial guarantee of objectivity (Ermarth, 1998a). This neutrality, furthermore, is infinite, extending beyond all perceivable horizons. Can we have a history of the cosmos? A history of the earth? A history of species? It seems we can. The function of conventional history is to confirm and reconfirm this all-important unifying neutral condition 'in' which it becomes possible to make mutually informative measurements between, say, the Hebrew and Greek manuscripts of the Bible, the (corrupted) medieval versions and the King James translation. History in this sense is nothing less than a gigantic perspective system that includes, or at least implicitly claims to include absolutely everything in a single system of measurement operable from the origin to the end of time. *That time, neutral time, is the most important effect or product of historical explanations.* That neutral time is what conventional history inscribes and re-inscribes; it is the common denominator that links conventional history with empiricism in science and philosophy, with cartography and exploration, with visual realism and representational politics; in short, with every cultural institution that depends on such highly abstract common denominators in order to objectify the entire universe and unify its field.

That neutral time was unknown to Homer or Augustine, to Molère or even Gibbon. Shakespeare toyed with it only in his history plays; the eighteenth century in continental Europe, Britain and the United States had other fish to fry. Around 1800, however, and relatively suddenly by conventional historical standards of incremental development, historical time as we understand it became disseminated everywhere in the English-speaking world, in personal and social narrative, in biology, in geology, and by 1900 in most humanistic fields of education. Within fifty years (by 1850) in Britain this definition of time included everything from geological and evolutionary time to the social and personal time of everyday people. That last step – so long in coming, that inclusion of common life – was key to the establishment of history as an explanatory mechanism for the social order. It is a step that belongs to the great British and European social experiments of the nineteenth century and their sometimes violent political outcomes. Society came into its own then as an entity capable of study like any other object, rather than just one of the 'humane' platforms of a cosmic hierarchy. (The United States conducted its experiment in political not social terms and did not experiment nearly as broadly with historical explanation; it continues to have no social idea or a very weak social idea compared to its British and European cultural sources.)

This history – a supposedly universal, neutral medium 'in' which we reside, and 'in' which causalities have unfolded since the dawn of time – is a relatively recent, relatively local European invention. The nineteenth century normalised it for us, especially for Anglo-American culture, in the work of Charles Lyell, Charles Darwin, and Walter Scott and his many heirs. Popular narrative before Scott had a very different form, although some eighteenth-century women novelists in England had begun to experiment with new formats in yet another case of artists working on the breaking edge of cultural change. Scott's novels were the first histories disseminated right across Euro-centric culture, including North America. In his day he was an international superstar and bestseller for one powerful reason: because he provided his culture with the new kind of narrative it was looking for, one based in four centuries of cultural development, and one that established a universal common denominator (the neutral time of history), and thus a basis for comparing things that had previously inhabited different worlds: for example, rich and poor, native and foreign, black and white. Although Scott's achievement was profound, it was only a late manifestation of a cultural function that had been first disseminated four centuries earlier in different terms. The painters and architects of the Quattrocento used the same kind of perspective apparatus to rationalise sight and neutralise space that Scott used four centuries later to rationalise consciousness and neutralise time.

There is more at stake here than 'accuracy' of description or 'life-likeness' in art. At stake are the powers of choice and creativity. Conventional historical explanation gives us mental tools that require the increasingly burdensome effort of functioning in an infinite horizon and of making those comparisons between widely separated cases which define empiricism and representation. By convention, the neutral time of history goes on for ever. Over the near horizon there is another horizon, and another to infinity; beyond the immediate future is another, farther future, and another beyond that to infinity. In such conditions individual choice has a daunting potential for future influence and yet seems, looking forward from the present, to have relatively minuscule power. It is daunting and confusing, a bit like the relationship in Protestantism between works and salvation: the one so small and ultimately ineffectual, the other so profoundly consequential. On the one hand, everything is at stake; on the other hand, my individual power over the outcome shrinks to nearly nothing in a horizon of infinite possibility. It is enough to make me procrastinate; there will always be time to make that choice tomorrow. Always time. This is one of the siren songs of conventional history.

In such conditions choice is easily diminished, postponed, even trivialised, and this is one of the foreclosures enforced by conventional historical knowledge. Historical knowledge *by definition* involves perspective, not action. On the vast plain of history causalities remained veiled, abstract and accessible only in retrospect. Choice is little more than a gamble: potentially hugely consequential and yet in the present moment relatively trivial and almost accidental. No wonder we are all at home 'counting our Porsches', as one commentator put it. The difficulty of pursuing political agendas on the infinite field of history is too great; action always happens at times and in places that are 'always somewhere else' (Boyle, 1987: 8). Besides, it is always possible that your Porsche may be a sign of grace.

This may be the condition of 'freedom', but I doubt it; it seems more the condition of *anomie*. I fully appreciate the importance of information and 'facts'; flying blind is not desirable and is not the only available alternative. But the case for studying conventional history is precisely that, by giving us the facts, it can guide choice. Perhaps someone will give me examples of where this has happened? How has 'never again' worked to prevent genocide in Darfur? How well did neutrality work in Srebrenica? Hindsight would suggest a course of action that seems clear enough intellectually, but it produces no action. The inability to recognise this fact currently plagues liberalism in the USA, both in education and in politics. Historical knowledge does not appear in itself to sponsor creative action, and that is no accident. The temporal infinities of history, and the invisible causalities and identities they sponsor, dematerialise the present, turning it from a point of concrete and even qualitative value into a point of transit where abstract causalities produce their emergent forms. The values in such transactions are quantitative (how much, how far, how long, how big) not qualitative (how complex, how effective, how new, how organised).

Facing such insoluble dilemmas, it is easier to go shopping; at least there choice and its consequences seem perceivable, if somewhat trivial. I do not exaggerate. Consumer 'choice' in the United States – or at least the appearance of choice – is practically an American metaphysic. When George W. Bush told people to respond to 9/11 by going shopping he was not tripping over his tongue, though it may have sounded that way to Europeans who, while they have fewer items to choose among, nevertheless are accustomed to having far more actual choice than Americans have. Shopping, and the advertising that goes with it, keeps a future open and makes choice possible, albeit at the cost of trivialising both choice and the future.

The problem of choice brings me to the 2005 film that inspired the title of this manifesto, 'The Closed Space of Choice'. The film is *Good Night, and Good Luck*, and it makes my point about history and choice with special brilliance, through artistic creativity more than argument. Artists usually are ahead of the curve. The film is about the influential journalist Edward R. Murrow, his troubled times, and especially the political and cultural problems in the United States of the 1950s, resurgent in the United States *circa* 2002–6. It is hard to imagine a wider historical horizon for the protagonist of this film, Murrow, or for the implications of his campaign against the fascistic persecutions conducted by Senator Joseph McCarthy. The actions in the film, many of which are drawn from video archives, have their *éclat* precisely because they qualify as historically profound. They are actions that could qualify as 'world historical', enacted by men who qualify as cultural heroes and world historical agents, larger-than-life examples of conscience and courage. The stakes are nothing less than the survival of democratic principles in the United States.

If John Ford or George Lucas had made this film, they might have provided viewers with the wide horizons and infinities so customary in American cinema in which such issues play out over time. But not the director of this film. It has none of that big sky and long trail of consequences found in every-thing from *Stagecoach* to *Star Wars*. Instead, *Good Night, and Good Luck* takes place almost entirely in very tightly enclosed interior spaces: the offices of CBS broadcast news, a booth in a restaurant, or tiny parts of a couple's domestic space. While hindsight assures us in retrospect that these are world historical heroes – Murrow, Fred Friendly and, almost as fully, the head of CBS, William S. Paley – the film insists through its format that the space of choice is not infinite but closed, very limited, and very personal. At the moment of choice there are no outcomes to consult in order to work back-ward to find the 'right' choice; no one then knew what the future outcome would be and no one had the luxury of much reflection. Any preparation – in terms of building character and courage – had to have been done already. The space of choice here has nothing to do with the infinite horizons and possible futures of history. Of course, an important dimension of this film is the fact that most of its audience knows which futures were realised and which were not, so its success is a case precisely of reasoning backward from the outcomes to the 'right' choices that made them possible, and putting those choices on display. But the most important part of the film's effect is its format, its medium, the How that is also the What. What viewers experi-ence there is the closed space of choice. The infinite neutralities of history have to take care of themselves. In that closed space, *and only there*, is the opportunity for creative intervention in complex, consequential political, economic and social systems.

The Discursive Condition

In contrast to the common-denominator universe of historical time (Ermarth, 1998a), the Discursive Condition (Ermarth, 2000) is characterised by the limitations and opportunities provided by the ways in which Saussure and his heirs have taught us to understand language. Where neutrality and its objectivity once were, code now is. Conventional history in this environ-ment takes its place as one system of meaning and value among many, one code enabling some options and foreclosing on others, just as any code does. The fundamental ideas about language come from early twentieth-century lectures by Ferdinand de Saussure at Geneva, later collected from student notes after his early death into a small volume, *Cours de linguistique générale* (1915), which was translated into English in 1959. Saussure was not the only one to compromise the neutralities foundational to six centuries of modernity – Picasso and Joyce compromise the neutral time and space of modernity; phenomenology attempts to erase the gap between object and subject; Einstein makes measurement part of what is measured; existentialism and existentialist theology define identity differentially – but Saussure's influence has been huge in academic disciplines such as anthropology, linguistics, philosophy, literature, art and cultural studies of all kinds.

The kind of cultural study that would unfold the paradigmatic nature of these shifts has hardly been attempted in the United States, and when the subject of what comes after modernity has been raised the discussion has too often been narrow and trivialising rather than generous. In the public domain the idea that there is something called 'modernity' and something that comes after it (postmodernity) has about as much traction as is necessary to justify using the term 'postmodern' in clothing adverts or in uncomprehending comments on National Public Radio (where you could learn, as I did recently, that 'postmodernism is a literary device'). A few thoughtful artists, especially some film-makers, have grasped the nettle and recognised that a paradigmatic shift is under way that justifies changes in method, not just content; and that change in method can even be fun. Their work is wildly, unexpectedly popular, but they are too few.

Although Saussure is more broadly familiar to academic readers than to others, the implications of his work still seem inadequately understood, especially as they bear on historical conventions. So let me summarise, very briefly, the key ideas. Saussure claims that language, far from being the unproblematically neutral instrument of modernity, is arbitrary and operates differentially. It is arbitrary in the sense that it has no necessary link with nature (if it did, we would all speak the same language; as it is, 'dog' or '*chien*' can be understood only within the context of English or French). Language operates differentially in that linguistic meanings only arise negatively within the system of differential relationships that constitute a language. To understand anything means to understand its function in a differential system of meaning and value; in other words, in terms of a code. Within that code the more we know about what something is *not*, the more we can understand how it functions and thus what it 'means'. For example, we understand 'dog' in English not by reference to an object but by knowing it is 'not-dot' and 'not-log'; in other words, 'dog' is most precise when we know most about what it is not. In short, linguistic value arises from a complex, largely subliminal system of differentiations: difference is constitutive, resemblance is not.

This is all bad enough for conventional history because it confines all identity, all process, indeed all consciousness, to what Saussure called 'semiological' systems. And things only get worse with the third and final step Saussure takes, that of making language the model for *all* systems of meaning and value, so that any code, whether verbal or not, operates like language; in other words, through differential function where all definition is negative. Saussure says almost in passing that language is the most complex of 'semiological' systems, and thus a model for all of them. This means that for 'language' we can consider usage in all kinds of systems of meaning and value: political systems, domestic systems, traffic systems, fashion systems. All are semiological systems. Because the term 'language' tends to imply verbal language, it is fruitful to shift to the term 'discourse' which has a little more cultural upholstery and can indicate all differential systems of meaning and value.

The Discursive Condition, then, is the condition in which such semiological (differential) systems of meaning and value lie at the basis of knowledge and consciousness. This means that we use and understand all sign systems in the same way we use and understand verbal languages: differentially. The *langue* (whether verbal or non-verbal) consists of the implicitly understood (and rarely, if ever, articulated) rules governing possibility, and the particular enunciation or usage (*parole*) specifies in some particular way that potential, those possibilities. The beauty of Saussure's theory lies in the split nature of linguistic usage: *langue*, the system of rules that is never spoken and never exhausted; and the enunciation (*parole*) that is always partial specification of the general systemic potential. The system itself – the sets of rules by which it operates – is largely or completely implicit and exists only in a wholly disseminated state. 'English' is all – and only what – native speakers say it is, not something extracted in textbook rules. Usage in any system depends on the tacit knowledge by its users about what is and is not allowed by these rules. This is true for 'English'; it is also true of usage in politics, domestic life, traffic, fashion and so on. We exercise our code-knowledge this way all the time as we choose our enunciations, and we implicitly understand when the rules are broken even if we never articulate them. Few native speakers of English articulate its rules, but even so, every native speaker can spot a mistake. The same is true for all the codes or semiotic systems in which we function. Like native speakers of verbal languages, we know when a code is being misused: at the office, in traffic behaviour, at the White House. The trick for historians may be to learn how to articulate those rules. System-knowledge amounts to a kind of collective intelligence that operates well before any logic of ideas; getting to grips with that knowledge, a fundamentally linguistic (differentially grounded) knowledge, remains the challenge of our time.

What is more, we operate simultaneously in multiple codes, not in one at a time. Although the emphasis may differ from one to another, no one functions sequentially first as citizen, next as parent, next as professional, consumer, fashion slave, and so on. In this multiplex Discursive Condition, the moment of creativity and choice is thus ever-present and richly prepared and necessarily constrained by the rule sets necessary to any enunciation at all. The moment of enunciation is the constrained moment of choice when we can either replicate conventional usage or depart from it. Students have always easily grasped the simplicity and elegance of Saussure's ideas about language; they recognise in them models more adequate to their actual experience than the tools of thought inherited from empiricism and codified in conventional history. Historical conventions, in the name of productive postponement, foreclose almost entirely on this powerful and creative power of enunciation.

Once we accept both that language lies at the basis of our knowledge and that no universal common denominator exists to enforce neutrality in our 'codings', several things follow that make conventional historical explanation seem increasingly parochial. First, the definition of 'individuality' changes and with it the definition of agency (Ermarth, 2000, 2001). There is no such thing in the Discursive Condition as that free-floating monad known as 'the' individual, or Foucault's 'founding subject' of history, or the miserable treasure of autonomous selfhood, or the Cartesian *cogito*. To be sure, enunciation is always an individual usage, however conventional that usage might be; but usage implies systemic values that pre-exist any individual and that limit and enable what he or she can do within the system. Thus, one can say that language speaks us, in the sense that we are born into multiple semiotic systems and can do only what they allow us to do; an English-speaker has complex temporal inflections that are not available or even necessary in languages with other forms of inflection. But the fact that language speaks us does not mean that there is no room for individuality, choice and creativity; on the contrary, the moment of enunciation is an ever-present opportunity for choice and even creativity and an expression of individuality more complex than anything allowed to the 'founding subject' of history and its growing *anomie*.

Our job in the Discursive Condition is not to find results independent of usage but to find ways to make our usages independent and not slavish. We already 'are difference', just as Foucault says (1972: 131); in the systems we inhabit our place is unique and our opportunities to act are immediate and ongoing. The question is thus no longer the old modern question, how do we 'make a difference'? The only question is the postmodern one: do we, by the choices we constantly make each time we 'enunciate' this rather than that, make the differences we intend and want to make? In the Discursive Condition individuality is a process not a result – an idea already familiar to J. S. Mill in the mid-nineteenth century. In the uniquely limited discursive situation, and only there, lies the immediate power to change usage within the available systems.

The second change brought by the Discursive Condition has to do with the historicist and empiricist idea of accuracy in the sense of 'evidence' consisting of 'facts' and even statistics. The Discursive Condition reveals the invented nature of such 'facts'; the truth to the saying of Benjamin Disraeli that there are lies, damned lies and statistics. The idea that 'evidence speaks when victims can't' – contained in the subtitle to the popular, retrograde TV series *CSI* (*Crime Scene Investigators*) – simply denies the presence and power of language; in other words, the collectively established semiotic conditions of meaning and value. This denial is precisely what *CSI* accomplishes in a visual system (putatively 'science') consisting largely of eyedroppers subjecting liquids to mechanised tests. Human readers are scarcely necessary in this world of self-evidence; all they do is work the mechanism. Sounds a bit like The Market, really – another mechanism that we can supposedly trust to work its results with marginal human input. In fact, The Market is a recognisable example of the way conventional history fosters thinking in terms of resemblances instead of differences: positing structures and essences that mask their fictionality and their function. (Adam Smith certainly would turn in his grave, twice, to see his ideas used to justify the very syndicalist and corporate evils he railed against.) Relinquishing 'evidence' does not at all mean losing precision; far from it.

For example, certain narrative practices in the Discursive Condition give tremendous value to detail (the 'detail is all'; Nabokov, 1969: 76) precisely because that detail is not required to establish a generalisation and thus to produce an abstraction that supersedes its materiality. Instead of being ephemeral servants of that abstraction, material details in the Discursive Condition become irreducible alphabets of construction. Like the poetic echoes in Shakespearean language, the details of semiotic usages specify the powers of multiple semiotic structures that call attention to the pattern-making, meaning-making rules of construction quite apart from the specific pattern or meaning. Detail does not get lost in the Discursive Condition *because the difference it makes is precisely what grounds the system of meaning and value.* The basis of order is difference, not resemblance. In discursive practice detail always has that kind of irreducible precision. The stories of Borges, Kafka and Nabokov are full of precision precisely because they do not serve empiricist rationalisations. Precision leads nowhere; as Alain Robbe-Grillet says of Kafka, 'there is nothing more fantastic than precision' (1989: 164–5).

Finally, the writing proper to the Discursive Condition is inhospitable to the kind of emergent causalities that underwrite conventional historical explanation and its sponsored ideas of 'growth' and 'progress' in everything from education to economics. In the Discursive Condition what we can know stops at the limits of the discursive system or set of systems within which we operate; even science must take the measuring system into the measurement. In the Discursive Condition history cannot rely on its usual alibi, causality, but it does have new options to pursue: for example, iden-tifying and studying the differential relationships – the systemic values – that constitute the possibilities of particular operating codes, as at Enron, or the Pentagon, or the World Trade Organisation; or studying what kinds of value the operating codes enable or foreclose; or studying the differences between operating codes.

Foucault's work remains the gold standard when it comes to such writing. He establishes his investigative field not in terms of serial causalities but in terms of blocks which provide a basis of comparison. For example, when considering penal practices in *Discipline and Punish* (1977), he calls our attention to the differences between the practice of public execution and the practice of imprisonment. He does not need to posit a historical field unified by neutrality in time because he is not interested in how one changed into the other – something that may have happened fairly suddenly as other cultural balances shifted in the large, imbricated, unrationalisable scene of cultural practice. What interests him is the conjuncture, the comparative opportunity, the point of difference. It is a focus entirely foreign to the founding subjects and unfolding causalities of conventional history. In this kind of historical writing the emphasis rests on comparative systems, on comparative code. Difference, not resemblance.

What, then, about 'the' past? That past in conventional history is constantly turning our present into a graveyard beneath our feet. 'The' past belongs to the common-denominator universe of empiricism and thus functions as a dematerialised launcher in the perpetual disaster of receding time. The Discursive Condition forecloses on that disaster by treating various 'pasts' as a present function in this or that system of meaning and value. Given the obviously multiplied and complex nature of our own present conditions, it makes no sense to assume that 'the' past was any less complex and multiplied, or had a more secure identity than our present. As in Borges's 'Garden of Forking Paths', pasts pullulate in every present, but not all pasts in all presents. Pluralising the past in this way is not at all the same thing as consigning it to 'point of view', that creature of historical conventions. There is only this past or that past, functional in some codes but not others. This just means that anything described as 'the' past, as Einstein said of time itself, is a function of a system, not an envelope containing it. This allowance for alternative codes is not something conventional history can accomplish because, by convention, its code is *the* code; that is what makes its formalities so powerful (Ermarth, 1998b). The Discursive Condition pluralises code and thus pluralises 'the' past which has different functions in different codes.

This is the kind of thing that drives conventional historians nuts, and I feel for them, I do. But the problem with their rationalist agendas is that they have allowed them and their cultural functions to remain unquestioned for too long. Meanwhile, unnoticed, the world has moved on, and in it our mental tools, derived so substantially from conventional history, are increasingly inadequate. As Václav Havel remarked some years ago, there is no point in 'looking for an objective way out of the crisis of objectivism' (Havel, 1992). Our sense of cultural vulnerability involves the large methodological issues raised here, not just small, rectifiable problems of tactics or even policy. We have lost our common denominators in the Discursive Condition. Get over it. The options are not worse, just different. Instead of seeking to objectify 'reality' and thus finally to close off the play of difference that sustains meaning and value, why not consider the advantages of mapping the differential systems of meaning and value that function so powerfully in actual affairs? At the moment, conventional history just ignores them.

The Discursive Condition thus releases the past from the dialectical causalities to which conventional history confines it. In Foucault, and more brilliantly in the various artists who have been revising the narrative formats of Eurocentric culture for more than a century, the play of difference remains open and, with it, multiple possibilities. In this multiplied discursive condition what is past is an iterative, ever-present, ever-renewed capability that can lead in several directions and that is neither lost in the disaster of receding time nor trivialised by a world historical future. Once 'the past is no longer part of a dialectic' it can confess its function in the present (Ermarth, 1992: 133). The focus of attention shifts from the secondary picture or resemblance and moves to the primary arena of enunciation and practice, and to the recognition of differences within and between codes. That recognition is not 'knowledge' in the conventional sense: not the outcomes of causal sequences in which the detail is only interesting as the carrier of a generalisation and something to be kicked away once it yields that product. The Discursive Condition even offers new ways to conceptualise time: for example, as rhythmic iteration (Ermarth, 1992) or as punctuated equilibrium (Gould and Eldridge, 1977).

The Discursive Condition thus offers us new mental tools for writing the history of discursive formations, especially an ability to recognise systemic values and the subtle differentiations that constitute them. In the United States we could use a whole lot more of this in the approach to contemporary political and educational problems which currently border on the Kafkaesque. The need for experiment with method is urgent and the stakes are high. The universe of historical 'fact' and determinable causality is more circumscribed and limiting than any actual materiality or practice. There is no way to turn that complexity into conventional history, or into any other explanatory result, except by suppression and exclusion. The Discursive Condition requires acknowledgement of that limit and, in so doing, opens a new and productive gap between discursive system and enunciation: not a gap between 'past and present' to be filled with emergent causalities and the data that confirm them; but a gap between potential and enunciation that invites creativity and remains always open. Creative opportunity appears in that gap which is literally the space of choice: closed, limited and personal, yet respectful of the collective intelligence, the social memory, contained in the semiological systems available to individuals every moment of every day. Which choices we make from the occupation of our unique discursive circumstances are up to us; they can be original and new, or conventional and repetitive. But this is a moment of opportunity for the discursive historian who describes material practices in order to find and focus the systems of meaning and value that inform and sustain those practices. *A list of new methodological rules might include the following*: emphasise difference rather than resemblance, especially the differences that define this or that discursive system of meaning and value; be sure your narrative line sponsors digression-and-return more than progress and production; forswear any pretence of 'naturalness' in the enterprise of writing history; seek the contrasts between cultural systems, not causalities that produce them; develop key elements into figures or patterns, not structures, causalities or resemblances; value any past as a function of present systemic iteration; never say 'individual' or 'fact'; always write in a personal voice; never stick to one disciplinary ambit.

The moment of enunciation need not be, and usually is not, particularly creative; but it is the immediate and ever-present moment of choice where creativity becomes possible for those willing to act anew. Not everyone can alter conventional usage in whatever medium; in other words, not everyone can be an artist. But the choice is always present and immediate. In this way the Discursive Condition rescues creativity and art from the cultural marginality forced on them by the Enlightenment and returns them to the heart of social renewal.

In long-gone eras, when historical writing was the front guard of a new political and religious order (Tudor England, for example) or a new social order (the nineteenth century, for example) it may have taken courage to write history because it was a new and potentially blasphemous thing to confront vested authority with an alternative system. Today it takes no courage to collate sources to the point of coma and hide behind them like a legionnaire behind the forward phalanx. What takes courage today is to make the cultural syntax, the discursive system, appear (just as the surrealists proposed), and then to interpret the discursive systems that operate in everything from domestic life to the global economy. And to do so in one's own voice and with the humility borne from knowing that interpreting is like breathing – it goes on every moment in every mind. A history adequate to the Discursive Condition will redefine individuality in terms of its true complexity and discursive function; it will find new latitude in the description and comparison of codes; and it will rematerialise the present moment as the restricted but infinitely rich site of choice, creativity and renewal.

References

Frank Ankersmit, *The Reality Effect in the Writing of History: The Dynamics of Historiographical Tropology* (Amsterdam: Noord Hollandsche, 1989).

Catherine Belsey, *Culture and the Real: Theorizing Cultural Criticism* (London and New York: Routledge, 2005).

James Boyle, 'My Turn', *Newsweek*, May 1987.

Elizabeth Deeds Ermarth, *Sequel to History* (Princeton: Princeton University Press, 1992).

—— *Realism and Consensus*, 2nd edn, Part One. (Edinburgh: Edinburgh University Press, 1998a).

—— 'Time and Neutrality: The Media of Modernity in a Postmodern World', *Cultural Values*, special issue on 'Time and Value', 2 (1998b): 2–3, 355–67.

—— 'Beyond "The Subject": Individuality in the Discursive Condition', *New Literary History* 31: 3 (2000): 405–19.

—— 'Agency in the Discursive Condition', *History and Theory* 40 (December 2001): 34–58.

Slavenka Drakulič, 'The War on People – and on the Truth – in Croatia', *Chronicle of Higher Education*, 11 June 2004, Sect. B, pp. 6–8.

Michel Foucault, *The Archaeology of Knowledge*, trans. A. M. Sheridan Smith (New York: Pantheon and London: Tavistock, 1972): 131.

Stephen J. Gould and Niles Eldridge 'Puncturated Equilibrium: The Tempo and Mode of Evolution Reconsidered', *Paleobiology* 3 (1977): 115–51.

Václav Havel, 'Address to the World Economic Forum in Davos', *New York Times*, 1 March 1992: A15.

Keith Jenkins, *Refiguring History: New Thoughts on an Old Discipline* (London: Routledge, 2003).

Rami Khouri, 'Europe Learns, America Provokes', 3 October 2005. Available at: www.TomPaine.com. (Khouri is editor of the Beirut-based *Daily Star* newspaper, published throughout the Middle East with the *International Herald Tribune*.)

Alun Munslow, *The New History* (London and Edinburgh: Pearson, Longman, 2003).

Vladimir Nabokov, *Ada, or Ardor: A Family Chronicle* (New York: McGraw-Hill, 1969).

Alain Robbe-Grillet, *For a New Novel: Essays on Fiction*, trans. Richard Howard (Evanston: Northwestern University Press, 1989).

Hayden White, *Metahistory: The Historical Imagination in Nineteenth-Century Europe* (Baltimore: Johns Hopkins University Press, 1973).

Slavoj Zizek, *Welcome to the Desert of the Real* (London: Verso, 2002).

5 'Humani nil alienum'

The quest for 'human nature'

Beverley Southgate

Introduction

The formulation of a manifesto for 'history' for the future involves not only speculation but advocacy – not only a theoretical presentation of one's hopes and fears but some practical ideas of what one might do about them. All too often, and especially of late, it seems to me that the philosophy of history has become detached from its practice – taking off into scholastic-style 'cobwebs of learning' that seem of little relevance to toilers in the field; and at the same time those toilers (empirically orientated historians) themselves have had minimal impact on the way people actually live their lives. I shall start, then, with a diagnosis, and some attempted assessment of where, educationally and culturally, we are and where we seem to be heading; and then, in the light of that, propose my own remedy, or treatment, or manifesto which – at the risk of reducing tension by revealing my plot at the outset – will be based on the Roman poet Terence's idealistic embrace of all things human.[1]

Diagnosis

As he surveyed learning in the early seventeenth century, Francis Bacon criticised the then current emphasis on 'theory' at the expense of 'practice'. Intellectuals, or philosophers (whether metaphysical or moral or natural), were, he raged, imprisoned within an ancient framework of thought, or 'paradigm', which not only predetermined the parameters within which thinking could be done but preordained its purpose. The categories into which ideas had to be integrated were essentially those of Aristotelian metaphysics and – in the context of the long-enduring Thomist synthesis of Aristotelianism with Christianity – the *point* of any knowledge gained thereby was ultimately theological, not so much material as spiritual improvement. After centuries of constraint within that conceptual straitjacket, thought had turned in upon itself – spinning intellectual cobwebs of admirable fineness, but lacking any pretence of material utility or profit. It was, then, as Bacon insisted, time for a revolution – an intellectual and moral upheaval

– and it was, in the event, no less than that which he and his followers over the next century succeeded in effecting.

Central to that revolution was the principle that theory should be linked with practice, with the ultimate goal of human betterment; that knowledge, with all its implications of empowerment, should be applicable to the needs of men and women. I want to ground my own manifesto for twenty-first-century history on that principle. For as heirs of the Baconian legacy and the early-modern cultural revolution, we face problems of our own. Some of those problems, paradoxically, would be recognised by Bacon as being not so different from those that he himself confronted; while others, ironically, he might acknowledge as deriving from his own prescription for their remedy. Taking those in reverse order, one outcome of the Baconian philosophy, institutionalised in the embryonic Royal Society and soon established as an orthodoxy, has been a secular emphasis denying the importance, or 'relevance', of any learning lacking direct applicability to material benefit; hence continuing attacks on the humanities as 'useless'. But as a paradoxical corollary to that, disciplinary developments – and more specifically developments in history – have resulted in a renewed dichotomy between theory and practice, which has implied a denial of the propriety, in principle, of any intrusion of 'utility' (such as might derive from political or ethical commitment) into an essentially 'pure' intellectual endeavour (which is not to say that in practice history has not been put to many uses). Those seemingly contradictory ingredients of 'modernism' themselves now constitute a part of an 'intellectual correctness' whose rules are as hard to transgress as those of its Aristotelian predecessor.

For it is hard, as Bacon knew and as Nietzsche later reminded us, to break free from 'an unconscious canon of *permitted* sagacity' – from those presuppositions that we, by definition, no longer feel a need to question, but which circumscribe the limits of our thought and of what we are allowed to count as wisdom. Warning of the dangers of 'enclosing oneself within a bounded horizon', Nietzsche railed against our 'unthinking subjection to an acquired habit', our confinement within the equivalent of 'a mole-tunnel', which may be 'the right place for a mole', but not for any human being.[2]

Yet it sometimes seems that, another century on, we persist in burrowing blindly, or at best with tunnel-vision, and not least in the field of historical study. For it is, as the American essayist Ralph Waldo Emerson noted, not only 'the state of the world' in general, but its 'history' more specifically that is 'at any one time directly dependent on the intellectual classification then existing in the minds of men'.[3] So much has been conceded by some historians themselves: in the nineteenth century J. T. Merz noted, with more philosophical acumen than is often shown today, that in future centuries 'the objectivity on which some . . . [contemporary historians] pride themselves will be looked upon not as freedom from but as unconsciousness on their part of the preconceived notions which have governed them'.[4] So problematic concepts (such as 'objectivity'), to which historians so often refer unthinkingly, themselves require historicisation – as does the concept of 'history' itself – in order to highlight the contingency of what is regularly taken to be natural, or simply 'given' as a part of nature.[5]

Indeed, it is not hard to spot one of the central paradoxes by which, as indicated above, the discipline of history has long been confronted: that, working within the 'modernist' paradigm, it has on the one hand aspired to attain and then retain respectability through acceptance of the orthodox model of an empirically orientated science; but, with an inherent tendency (if not requirement) to look backwards, it has with its other hand retained some grip on older styles and values, of which sight has been often lost elsewhere. As a consequence, history has confronted, and continues to confront, the dilemma of whether or not to lay claim to 'practicality' or some material advantage – alternately citing the pragmatic need to 'learn from the past' (whether directly or through the medium of supposedly 'transferable skills'), and more idealistically asserting the inestimable value of pure 'knowledge for its own sake'.

That dilemma, and the schizoid nature of historical studies, is emblematic of wider tensions in a society torn between material and spiritual aspirations. In that context, education in the humanities is perennially but increasingly under threat, required constantly to justify itself in terms that are essentially alien – in terms, that is, of practical utility and economic benefit. And there is evidence of a widespread *'trahison des clercs'* – a renunciation of such humanistic values as are needed as a counterbalance to prevailing orthodoxies, and a tendency, noted long ago by Julien Benda, to become subsumed within a consensus and (worse still) construe that as a virtue. When that happens – and Benda believed that, in the 1920s it already had – the 'clerk' has been 'not only conquered . . . [but] assimilated'.[6]

Whether conscious or unconscious of that assimilation, historians have, then, been complicit in the construction and maintenance of a 'modernist' structure, or paradigm, or regime of truth that has proved as admirable, and socially, politically and psychologically convenient as its Aristotelian predecessor; its coherence and stability proving no less effective in resisting challenges and change. Typically progressive historical narratives have played an important therapeutic role in boosting individual and national confidence and self-esteem, providing purpose and meaning, and confirming identities; and it is for such reasons that 'history' has continued to be seen as a vital and central part of education – even (or perhaps especially) in our current supposedly multicultural, diversity-embracing times. So, for example, as British society fractures, we are encouraged to revert to earlier and simpler (and supposedly definitive) accounts of 'our island story', which may serve as a common base for a narrative embracing, and to be shared by, all: 'a knowledge of history is of paramount importance to a civilised society. Best get it right!'[7]

In other countries, similarly carefully constructed histories are designed to provide stable foundations for societies that can be at peace with themselves – and so be less likely to cause or suffer from internal trouble or disruption. In the United States, Ken Burns' simplified narratives are specifically designed to appeal to a diverse audience and achieve 'an emotional consensus', restoring American self-confidence in a shared identity; his huge popularity indicates that he is serving a felt need. Similarly, the newly prescribed textbooks imposed on Iraq, as a part of their democratic revolution, aim to underpin a newly reconstructed national identity, and so omit all reference to its less than democratic, and so supposedly aberrant and readily disposable, immediate past.

It is the presentation of a single storyline as representing – literally re-presenting – the 'truth' about what happened in the past that continues to characterise much, if not most, history today; and there is a corresponding public perception, as evidenced almost daily in the press, that there is an identifiable 'true story' of events which it is the function of reporters (as contemporary historians), cleansed of any 'bias' and imbued with ideal 'balance', to report. Hence the repeated criticisms of the BBC and Hollywood, as well as other media, by politicians who blame them for failing to conform to their own, obviously 'correct', perceptions. My point then is that, despite theoretical protestations, there remains a widespread belief in the unitary nature of 'truth' about the past (however recent), and that there remains considerable pressure on both news reporters and historians themselves to conform to and contribute to the consensual view of a (by definition) largely unquestioned paradigm. In other words, again, it is hard to break out from the bounds of our strictly controlled and patrolled conceptual 'mole-tunnel'.

To be thus confined within limits is, of course, comforting – especially when we feel that our choice of confinement is our own and we are anyway blind to alternatives. But we are reminded from time to time of what life outside those limits can be like – forced to confront the situation of others less well placed; and the problem – the dis-ease I am diagnosing here – is the seeming impotence of history as currently constituted to do anything about it. History, as we are constantly reminded, is about what is (or was), and not about what should be. But that surely provokes the question of what on earth the point can be of simply describing a situation without any intention of doing anything about it. That way lies an *in*-humanity – an attempt to deny the validity of John Donne's more enlightened perception that 'No man is an island', and that the bell that's tolling is doing so for us.

So we are left with the disagreeable conclusion that 'history' as currently constituted (however complicated by ongoing debates about theory and practice and utility) may actually be complicit in maintaining a status quo that is characterised all too often by man's inhumanity to man.

Treatment

If that is so, what is needed is a fundamental reconfiguration. For it is not only diagnosis of dis-ease that we, as manifesto-writers, are concerned with here, but the prescription of some remedy; and we are bound to ask (and try to answer) in what ways history might provide help or treatment for the condition diagnosed.

That condition, so far as history is concerned, boils down to two main points: first, that history is essentially conservative – emphasising *consensus* and supportive of existing (disciplinary and socio-political) structures; and second, that it continues, paradoxically, to claim scientific status for itself, while disclaiming any pretence to the *practicality* by which science itself, since Bacon's time, has been defined. This is in the wider context of a condition all too often characterised by *inhumanity* – an inhumanity that has been recorded in histories from the earliest times and seems unlikely to be changed within the next fifty years, but will, with accelerating globalisation, become ever more intrusive into the consciousness of all.

My proposed treatment, then, is to focus on the last (inhumanity), and apply to that a 'history' that will need to be transformed in relation to the characteristics identified above as consensus and practicality. In brief, by deliberately *opposing consensus*, histories might be *practically used* to challenge existing (intellectual and socio-political) frameworks, with the ultimate goal of human betterment.

At the centre of our reformed study, then, will be a reconsideration of what it means to be 'human': in what does, and in what might, 'humanity' consist? That does not entail a search for *essences* – a historical quest for some essential characteristics originally bestowed on a part of creation by some all-powerful god or nature. It entails rather a historical and moral enquiry into what has been and might be approved and disapproved as characteristically 'human'. 'Human nature' is to be not so much defined as aspired to. For defining inevitably narrows down, imposes closure, denies alternative options – and what is required is, rather, a widening and opening up of potentialities and possibilities. So historical study specifically takes on a singularly important role – of presenting (making clear in our present) models of 'humanity' that otherwise may not occur or seem to be available. For definitions and perceptions of human nature have undoubtedly changed, as our relationship with the external world of nature has been modified through time – not least in the early modern intellectual revolution.

At that point in history, it might be claimed that, with insistence on objectification, and the strict dissociation of human subjects from the objects of their study, something had been lost – that scientific gains had been bought at the price of human loss. Certainly there was an awareness at the time of the experience of some loss, the traces of which have continued to be felt and periodically brought to the fore again within the counter-cultural tradition of Romanticism. Goethe, for example, and William Blake and Keats – all enabled, as poets, to extend their vision beyond the limited perceptions of their times – expressed concern with such unfashionable matters as a loss of spirituality and of an appropriate relationship with nature. Keats' lament for the rainbow, robbed of its wonderment by Newtonian optics, is emblematic; and it is significant that such critics of mechanisation are poets, whose function is, as T. S. Eliot has reminded us, to enable vision beyond the range of what normality, at any time, permits. It is significant, too, that by the early eighteenth century poetry itself was perceived as having degenerated from its previous position as head of the disciplinary hierarchy, to become accounted no more than 'an extravagant and a vain amusement', written out of education as economically profitless.[8]

That collateral loss was embraced as a veritable virtue by such major thinkers in the Western tradition as have seen narrowness of focus a small price to pay for greater acuity of the vision required in pursuit of their own objectives. John Locke, for instance, not only repudiated poetry, but famously advocated 'common sense' as an antidote to wasting time on such matters as lie beyond the reach of human ken – thereby implicitly redefining the objectives and aspirations appropriate, not only for philosophers, but for all human beings. There was, he indicated, little point in frustrating ourselves by setting targets beyond our range; better to live contentedly (or is it complacently?), accepting with equanimity our inbuilt limitations. Hume too, having personally suffered the angst induced by sceptical doubt and questioning, proposed as remedy a simple acceptance of the world as it is: one may, as a philosopher, be tortured by persistent doubts and uncertainties, but one does better, as a normal human being, to get on with life. Dining and conversing with friends takes our minds off those metaphysical questions, which were later to be confidently and finally consigned to the realm of the 'meaningless'; and advocacy of a 'contented' acceptance of the world as it is currently experienced, the deliberate exclusion from consciousness of all that lies beyond a deliberately narrowed range of human experience, persisted (under the aegis of fashionable Western philosophies) well into the twentieth century. That, of course, constituted an equally deliberate narrowing of the concept of 'humanity' – a transition and a redefinition so widely accepted now as to require historical analysis to remind us of alternative possibilities.

For alternatives, as we have seen, do exist, or have in the past existed. The mechanisation of nature and, more recently and increasingly, of people, has not been achieved without a fight; and there are even now growing signs of a more popular reversion to 'pre-scientific' attitudes. In this 'greener' movement historical study can play its part, not least by laying bare the traces of earlier emphases as an alternative to current values; and by presenting an alternative model of humans' relationship with a 'nature' that itself requires re-visioning, history can help to redefine – or rather open up – what is meant (or what we want to be meant) by 'human being'.

That fundamental investigation, though, will require input from elsewhere – from religion, for example – which is another facet of human experience that has for many been lost in the process of secularisation in modernity. Fundamentalist dogma is not the point at issue, but rather an acceptance of religious awe, or wonder, in the face of what cannot be readily explained in scientific terms. The optimism of Enlightenment thinkers, who aspired to total explanation through resort to their then new science, has persisted to the present time – and not without reason, as the application of that science has resulted, at least locally, in hugely enhanced material standards of living. But in the face of imminent ecocide, the self-confidence of humans, who believe in their ability ultimately (or at least in principle) to achieve total mastery of their environment, will need to be further historicised and shown to be but one, somewhat circumscribed, vision of ourselves and of our relationship with the universe.

For insistence on the virtually unlimited power that derives from a certain sort of knowledge is another aspect of the Baconian inheritance, and another example of how Baconian definitions – in this case of both 'power' and 'knowledge' – have been unthinkingly adopted and incorporated in a progressive historical narrative. Further analysis of such terms within a more theologically orientated context would reveal their limitations – their arbitrary imposition on a field of human experience which is potentially much wider; where, that is to say, 'power' and 'knowledge' may be defined in ways that lie beyond the purview of Baconian-style analysis and vision.

At which point we are confronted by issues not only, in a general sense, 'religious', but psychological; and this must indicate a further major area of historical enquiry. For we need to know how humans seemingly become entrapped, sometimes for centuries, within a particular horizon of understanding or regime of truth, within a Nietzschean 'canon of *permitted* sagacity'; and we need to know how breakouts from such intellectual prisons are finally achieved. What, for instance, accounted for the long dictatorship of Aristotle? And how was his dominion finally supplanted by that of a new 'world-view'? To answer such questions, as they relate not only to the past but to the present (and thence future), we need above all a historical and psychological enquiry into those nonconformists who contrived to break out from their mole-tunnel – those revolutionaries who fought against and overcame 'the power of the actual'. For by so doing we may come to some understanding of the contingency, as well as the power, of such systems of thought as we are still constrained by: this is how we might contrive 'to educate ourselves *against* our age'[9]; for to be against might actually be to be (in another sense) *for*.

That is true not only in broadly intellectual but more specifically in socio-political terms, where no less it has always been hard, and sometimes dangerous, to see beyond the boundaries of immediate constructions. It would, in classical Greece, have been a brave, and uncharacteristically imaginative, Spartan to advocate democracy; it would have taken a suicidal Roman in imperial times to propose a return to republicanism; and it takes a contrary nature now to try to think beyond the categories inherent in a capitalism widely seen (in the Western world) as constituting the very end of history. In both psychological and socio-political contexts, then, a future historical study will be needed to expose the contingency of what is, at any time, simply accepted as 'natural'.

And for evidence of alternatives, historians will need to look more widely than current disciplinary constraints sometimes allow: in the context of the Terentian dictum that, in defining humanity, nothing human is to be accounted alien, the historical traces left in cultural or artistic artefacts may need more emphasis; and that, so far as my educationally orientated manifesto for the future is concerned, would have the additional advantage of helping to fill what might be identified as a growing 'cultural deficit' and alienation from such creative aspects of the past as hint at possibilities that lie beyond conventional horizons.

By that I mean that enquiry into any period of the past will need to widen its embrace of a *cultural* history focused on what human beings not only thought but *felt*. For the expression of emotion is best found in works broadly defined as lying within the purview of the arts – imaginative literature, poetry, painting and music: it is here that we detect imaginative responses to the varied experiences through which men and women live, and here also that we are most likely to find indications of alternative (even utopian) possibilities that might transform our expectations and our lives. So it is here that we need to focus attention in our attempts to understand the nature and potentialities of humanity at any given time.

There is, of course, nothing new in that proposal. Well over a hundred years ago, Leslie Stephen, in his *History of English Thought in the Eighteenth Century*, aimed not only to indicate the application of philosophical and theological principles to 'moral and political questions' but 'their reflection in the *imaginative literature* of the time'. For, as he clarified, 'The imaginative literature of an age must express the genuine *feelings* of the age'; so that we can often best learn from such poets and 'literary' figures as Pope and Swift and Addison, 'what were the deepest convictions of their age'.[10]

Two decades later, J. T. Merz similarly noted how a history of thought 'demands its completion by a study of that large body of thought which is buried in the poetical, artistic, and religious literature of the whole period'. For him, it was Goethe whose 'work embodies for us probably the deepest thought of modern times', with *Faust* constituting 'a comprehensive embodiment . . . the classical expression of nineteenth-century doubts and aspirations'. Any history, therefore, clearly needed 'to include the spontaneous literature and the artistic creations of the period, the inventions of the poetical and the manifestations of the religious thought of the age'.[11]

Such a widely embracing study will require skills generally associated, since the time of Merz and Stephen, with a variety of disciplines – literary, visual and aural; and it will additionally require a mind impatient of such distinctions as are regularly made between cultures 'high' and 'low'. One of the last bastions of an outdated class structure has been precariously erected and defended on the chasm claimed to lie between Beethoven and the Beatles; but although listeners may not respond equally to both, it is not clear why the sensibilities required to listen to (if not appreciate) both should not be fostered as a part of education in the humanities, with each providing the historian with evidence of imaginative human responses to human situations – and so potentially contributing to a fuller understanding of what can, even now and for the future, constitute 'humanity'.

Conclusion

History in modern times has fulfilled the role of meaning-giver – a secular replacement for those who have accepted the death of a god previously perceived in terms of Providence, or of a 'destiny' made conveniently manifest to some. Histories, that is to say, have been written to underpin a 'now' that needs justification – that needs to be seen as a meaningful, purposeful outcome of what has gone before; histories, both personal and public, have contrived to make some sense of human life, importantly endowing it with a sense of direction of its own – and so relieving us of any responsibility for choice; they have, as Nietzsche wrote, spun a 'web over the past' and so contrived to subdue it[12] – or to subdue the anxieties that might derive from seeing that past (and so our present) as an open-ended jumble of alternative possibilities.

That role of meaning-giver must, it seems to me, persist indefinitely – and certainly in our futures. So the question is: who or what will determine what meaning is to be given? Contemporary reversions to extreme, or fundamentalist, religions might seem to indicate a potential return to theological control of histories; and present attempts, in the face of globalisation and multiculturalism, to resuscitate past ideals of patriotism and national identities are likely to result increasingly in political demands for reactionary histories based on the virtues of the nation-state. Such theologically or politically based histories would imply the reintroduction of seemingly necessary paths to an end preordained by a superior authority, possibly superhuman at its source but anyway conveniently conveyed to earth through human representatives and powers.[13]

In the face of such possibilities (which, as I write in 2005, appear to be imminent), my preference would be for histories driven by a necessarily unending quest for what it means to be *human*. Historians would then present their works as contributions to an ever-ongoing conversation; and refusing to accept disciplinary distinctions, they would (however idealistically) embrace all things that might potentially be included within the boundlessness of human experience, putting some emphasis on such aspects of that experience as might be becoming, at any time, forgotten and lost. Histories would thus be far from excluding the 'superhuman' or transcendental, for it is that which might continue to give hints, or (as Augustine claimed) leave traces, of something ever beyond, just out of reach, to which humans might continue to aspire. And, so far from excluding the political and ethical, they would embrace them at their core in their very practical quest for human improvement, and serve, in Nietzsche's words, 'to expand the concept "man" and make it more beautiful'.[14] History would, in short, by focusing on the nature of an ever-evasive 'humanity', constitute an endless quest in which nothing – and here we return to our starting point with Terence – would be accounted out of bounds or alien or none of our concern.

Notes

1 'Homo sum; humani nil a me alienum puto', which might be rendered: 'As a man, I consider nothing human outside my concern' (*Heauton Timorumenos*, I.i.25). Significantly, perhaps, Terence (*c*. 190–159 BC) was brought to Rome from North Africa as a slave.

2 Friedrich Nietzsche, *Untimely Meditations*, ed. Daniel Breazeale (Cambridge: Cambridge University Press, 1997): 120, 170–2.

3 Ralph Waldo Emerson, 'Circles', in *The Complete Prose Works* (London: Ward, Lock, 1890): 78.

4 J. T. Merz, *A History of European Thought in the Nineteenth Century*, 4 vols (Edinburgh and London: William Blackwood & Sons, 1896–1914): vol. 1, 7.

5 In the case of objectivity itself, Peter Novick has shown the way in *That Noble Dream: The 'Objectivity Question' and the American Historical Profession* (Cambridge: Cambridge University Press, 1988).

6 Julien Benda, *The Great Betrayal* (*La Trahison des Clercs*), trans. Richard Aldington (London: Routledge, 1928): 145. For a recent and timely lament along similar lines, see Alun Munslow, 'Getting on with History', *Rethinking History: The Journal of Theory and Practice* 9 (2005): 497–501.

7 So John Rimington, director of Bernard Sunley Charitable Foundation, which has contributed £2,000 for the republishing in 2005 of H. E. Marshall's *Our Island Story* (1905), quoted in the *Daily Telegraph*, 22 June 2005, p. 18.

8 John Keats, 'Lamia' (1820), Part II, lines 229f.; T. S. Eliot, *Selected Prose*, ed. John Hayward (Harmondsworth: Penguin, 1953): 95–6; John Dennis, *The Grounds of Criticism in Poetry* (London: Geo. Strahan & Bernard Lintott, 1704): 01; John Locke, *Some Thoughts Concerning Education* [1690] (London: Sherwood, Neely, and Jones, 1809): 207–8.

9 Nietzsche, *Untimely Meditations*, pp. 170, 146.

10 Leslie Stephen, *History of English Thought in the Eighteenth Century*, 2 vols. (London: Smith, Elder, 1876): vol. 1, vi; vol. 2, 348 (my emphases).

11 Merz, *A History of European Thought*, vol. 1, p. 61; cf. p. 76; vol. 4, pp. 786, 788–9.

12 Nietzsche, *Untimely Meditations*, p. 91.

13 Since writing this, I have come to realise that I fail to do justice to the potentialities of theology. See in particular Mark I. Wallace's persuasive advocacy of 'a *postmodern theology with an emancipatory intent* that critically retrieves language and imagery from previous . . . sources in order to enable personal and social transformation in a world at risk' ('God is Underfoot: Pneumatology after Derrida', in John D. Caputo (ed.), *The Religious* (Oxford: Blackwell, 2002): 203; emphasis in original).

14 Nietzsche, *Untimely Meditations*, p. 68. See also *The Gay Science*, ed. Bernard Williams (Cambridge: Cambridge University Press, 2001): 128, where Nietzsche writes of 'the power to create for ourselves our own new eyes and ever again new eyes that are ever more our own – so that for humans alone among the animals there are no eternal horizons and perspectives'.

6 History and the politics of recognition

Dipesh Chakrabarty

In thinking about the pressures that the cultural politics of recognition in democracies have brought to bear on the academic discipline of history over the last twenty or thirty years, thus determining, to some degree, the debates that will shape the discipline and its futures, I have found it helpful to think of a particular mix of history and memory that I have come to call the 'historical wound'. My use of this expression grows out of Charles Taylor's discussion of 'the politics of recognition' in multicultural societies. Within the perspective of this politics, wrote Taylor, 'misrecognition shows not just a lack of due respect. It can inflict a grievous wound, saddling its victims with a crippling self-hatred'.[1] I work with the same idea of 'wound' but I assume that, for a person or group so 'wounded', to speak of the wound or to speak in its name is already to be on the path to recovery.

To be able to speak thus, however – that is, to speak self-consciously from within a history of having been wounded – is itself a historical phenomenon. The rhetoric and spirit of decolonisation of the 1950s and 1960s contributed to its formation. The spread of anti-colonial rhetoric back into the ex-colonial countries gave rise to a broad consensus in particular democratic polities that some marginal and oppressed social groups owed their present disadvantages in the main to discrimination and oppression suffered in the past.[2] I take this consensus to be the basis for the formation of what I am calling 'historical wounds'. The indigenous peoples in Australia, New Zealand and Canada, and the formerly 'untouchable' groups in India – now called the *dalits* (the oppressed) – are examples of such groups. Sometimes, other disadvantaged minorities who have also long suffered oppressive pasts – African-Americans in the United States, for example – have aspired to and struggled for the same kind of politics of recognition but with varying degrees of success in forming the necessary social consensus.

Let me spell out what I see as the salient features of 'historical wounds'. *Historical wounds are not the same as historical truths but the latter constitute a condition of possibility for the former.* Historical truths are broad, synthetic generalisations based on researched collections of individual historical facts. They could be wrong but they are always amenable to verification by methods of historical research. Historical wounds, on the other hand, are a mix of history and memory and hence their truth is not verifiable by historians. Historical wounds cannot come into being, however, without the prior existence of historical truths. For instance, the act of calling (in the 1990s) the generations of Aboriginal children who were forcibly removed from parental custody by the colonial government in Australia or missionary agencies the 'stolen generations' was a matter of speaking to a sense of historical wound. That there had been such removal of Aboriginal children was a piece of historical truth, a generalisation open to empirical verification. But the epithet 'stolen' packed into the expression an emotional intensity that could not be measured by the historian's scale. Its instant popularity in the nineties, however, was due to a broadly emergent social consensus about the historical plight of the Aboriginal people.

Historical wounds are thus dialogically formed, dependent as they are on acknowledgement from groups seen as givers of the wound in the first place. The Aboriginal sense of historical wound that I speak of found conditions favourable to its formation in the twenty or so years after the demise of the White Australia policy – that is, from the late 1960s to the early 1970s – when Australian non-indigenous, mainly white, historians (such as Henry Reynolds) began to write histories that were definitely pro-Aboriginal in sympathy. This historiographical move, supported by both Liberal (i.e., conservative) and Labor governments in the 1980s and 1990s, resulted in the creation of a new academic subject in Australian universities: Aboriginal history, with journals and other disciplinary paraphernalia devoted to it. It was in this period that the 'stolen generation' narrative gained ground.

Historical wounds, however, are not permanent formations. The social consensus on which they are based is always open to new challenges and thus, in principle, can be undone. Now that a neo-conservative, right-wing government is in power in Australia, there is a concerted attempt to dislodge the consensus around certain historical truths on which the Aboriginal sense of historical injury is founded. A maverick and reactionary historian, Keith Windschuttle, has recently gained much publicity for seeking to destroy the professional reputation of pro-Aboriginal white historians by showing up alleged deficiencies in their archival research. The debate continues but it does show that, as cultural formations, historical wounds live precarious lives, for the mainstream social consensus that sustains a sense of historical wound may come under attack from quarters that want to dissolve it.

Historical wounds are unevenly formed across different democracies. I have found the Australian context very helpful in thinking about the idea of historical wound. But the necessary social consensus is not always easily achieved and even when it is, it does not bear the same relationship every-where to the academy. The *dalits* in India are usually recognised as people who have been disadvantaged by their histories. Nationalist leaders such as Gandhi and Ambedkar helped achieve this consensus among the hegemonic social groups in India. But, unlike in Australia, where academics played a critical role as public intellectuals in helping to mould social opinions in favour of the Aboriginals, the transformation in India has been brought about by *dalit* political activism from the colonial times, aided later in no small measure by the compulsions of India's electoral democracy. Upper-caste Indians did not so much respect the historical injuries of the caste system as accept the fact that the *dalits* and other 'lower castes' together constituted a majority of the voters. Their political power in public life simply could not be ignored. So there is a question of 'historical wounds' in the case of the *dalits* but it forms more an ingredient of political life in India than something actively attended to in mainstream academic work.

The situation is far more contested when it comes to the disadvantaged minorities in the United States: the African-Americans, the Native Americans, the Hispanic-Americans and others. There are, of course, sub-disciplines within history departments or programmes devoted to studying the pasts of these groups but the fierce battle over intellectual consequences of 'identity politics' shows that these sub-disciplines have never achieved the commanding heights gained by, say, Aboriginal history in the Australian academy since the 1980s. Yet this is not to say that politics of historical wounds do not exist in the American context: they do in public life and, often seen negatively as 'identity politics', have played a role in fomenting important methodological debates among professional historians. Here, again, the story varies between rich, private institutions and publicly funded universities.

Finally, the politics of historical wounds often pose a challenge to the discipline of history by seemingly privileging 'experiential' access to the past. I can best illustrate this proposition with the help of two or three anecdotes. The first comes from the time – the mid-1980s – when I was teaching in the history department at the University of Melbourne and when Aboriginal history was first introduced as an academic subject at the undergraduate level. The first teachers of the subject, necessarily all non-indigenous, ran into an important pedagogical problem quite early on in the course. They wanted to introduce their students, some of them of Aboriginal descent, to evidence bearing on cases of early twentieth-century massacre of Aboriginal groups by European settler communities. Aboriginal students refused to engage with the evidence, saying that it hurt them too much to read it. The very basic principle of historical distance became a first, major issue in the debates in that class.

My second anecdote also relates to a young Aboriginal intellectual, Anthony Birch, who is a poet and whom I knew as a Ph.D. student in the history department in Melbourne. When Tony, as he was known among friends, finished his Ph.D., he was offered two lecturing positions, one in the history department and one in the English department. I was disappointed as a historian when he opted for the position in the literature department. Asked why, he said, 'Because I can write my history better as poetry.' I recently had an opportunity to confirm that this was indeed what he had said. His email reply reiterated the point:

> Sounds like me, doesn't it? . . . Academic history is a very limited discipline, particularly in its ability to represent the past. 'Professional' history poses as truth and fact through the authority given to empiricism . . . The past is sometimes represented equally, or at times, more accurately through a range of textual forms, including story-telling and poetry.[3]

It is clear that in saying that a poetic rendition of the past could be more 'accurate' than a historical one, Birch was not using the historian's idea of empirical veracity. Accuracy was more a matter of being 'true' to his personal experience of the past.

We in India have encountered a similar resistance to disciplinary history in the course of producing *Subaltern Studies*. Starting the series in the 1980s, we soon faced criticism in India that our editorial board and our contributors contained not a single person of *dalit* or low-caste origin. We therefore invited a respected *dalit-bahujan* (referring to the idea of a political bloc of *dalits* and other low-caste groups, *bahujan* meaning 'majority') activist and intellectual, Kancha Ilaih, to contribute an essay to *Subaltern Studies*. In the essay he wrote for us, Ilaih, a university-trained political scientist, deliberately set aside all academic procedures in order to claim for the *dalit-bahujan* peoples a past that would not necessarily be vindicated by the methodological protocols of the historian or the textual analyst.[4] Ilaih's radical claim was that the existing archives and ways of reading them – the discipline of history, to be precise – had to be rejected if *dalit-bahujans* were to find pasts that helped them in their present struggles.[5] He would much rather write out of his direct personal *experience* of oppression. In his words:

> The methodology and epistemology that I use in this essay being what they are, the discussion might appear 'unbelievable', 'unacceptable', or 'untruthful' to those 'scholars and thinkers' who are born and brought up in Hindu families. Further, I deliberately do not want to take precautions, qualify my statements, footnote my material, nuance my claims, for the simple reason that my statements are not meant to be nuanced in the first place. They are meant to raise Dalitbahujan consciousness.[6]

I still remember the debate among the editorial members of *Subaltern Studies* that preceded our decision to publish this essay that deliberately – and as a political gesture – used personal experience as a way of understanding history. But how could one have an interest in subaltern politics and not engage with the gesture of rejection of academic discipline that was an inherent part of Ilaih's vision of the political?[7]

II

The appeal to one's present 'experience' as a guide to one's past – an appeal built into the politics of historical wounds – has proven unacceptable to most historians who are, on the whole, sceptical about the 'evidence of experience'. The capacity to assume a certain distance from the past has been central to the idea of 'historical objectivity'. Experience collapses this distance. Historians do not deny that their questions arise from the present and that they are not free of bias, but the discipline has rested on an assumed and trained ability to separate the past from the present. All this is commonplace, but what is significant about the last fifteen or twenty years is the fact that some very important historians of our time have felt the need to reiterate and defend in print these very basic principles of the discipline. Consider books like Carlo Ginzburg's *Wooden Eyes: Nine Reflections on Distance*, his *History, Rhetoric, Proof* or his essay 'Only One Witness' in Saul Friedlander's edited book on the Holocaust, *The Limits of Representation*; Jaques Le Goff's *History and Memory*; Peter Novick's *A Noble Dream: The 'Objectivity' Question in American History*; Eric Hobsbawm's collection of essays in *On History*; Natalie Davis's *Slaves on Screen*; Richard Evans's *The Defence of History*; or Joyce Appleby, Lynn Hunt and Margaret Jacob's jointly authored *Telling the Truth about History*. They are all, in one way or another, sophisticated defences of the idea of 'historical objectivity'. The 1990s were in fact bookended by two important essays – Joan Scott's 'The Evidence of Experience' and Lee Kerwin Klein's 'On the Emergence of Memory in Historical Discourse' – both of which expressed radical scepticism about the usefulness and political value of 'experience' or 'memory' as a reliable guide to history.[8]

The gap, in this respect, between academic histories and those told in institutions of public life such as museums is therefore telling. While the cloistered speech of professional historians has remained critical of the rhetoric of 'experience', museums have increasingly turned to foregrounding 'experience' not just in terms of what target spectators get out of their visits – 'a museum experience' that gives to 'experience' a commodity form – but as a way of accessing the past. A look at the various issues of the journal *Museum Management and Curatorship* (previously called the *International Journal of Museum Management and Curatorship*) shows how concerned, since the mid-1980s, museums have become with managing the experience of the people who visit them.[9] As Richard Prentice, a museologist, said in 1996, 'Museums, like many other heritage attractions, are essentially experiential products, quite literally constructions to facilitate experience.'[10] Eilean Hooper-Greenhill, a teacher of Museum Studies at the University of Leicester, said in her 1994 book *Museums and Their Visitors*: 'For too long, museums have defended the values of scholarship, research, and collection *at the expense of* the needs of visitors. The challenge today is to preserve these traditional museum concerns, but to *combine them* with the educational values that focus on how the objects cared for in the museums can add to the quality of life for all.'[11] This is recognised also in the following remarks made in 1997 by Zahava Doering, then the director of the Office of Institutional Studies at the Smithsonian: '[The] most satisfying exhibition[s] for visitors are *those that resonate with their experience* and provide information in ways that confirm and enrich their [own] view of the world.'[12]

This shift from the Habermasian public sphere (to which the historian with his or her dependence on the written word belongs) has also meant that museums have become embroiled in some of the pressing questions of identity and representation that mark contemporary liberal-capitalist democracies. Underlining the shift, Stephen Weil writes:

> In a dozen different contexts, identity and interest groups of every kind insist that the mainstream museum is neither empowered nor qualified to speak on their behalf. Increasingly, such groups are creating their own museums from which to speak their own voices and address what they consider to be their own issues. In recent years, Native Americans, Asian Americans and African Americans have been partially active in the establishment of specialised museums.[13]

An eminent historian of our times reports a certain feeling of unease with the way film-makers market 'experience' as a way of getting at the past. I refer here to Natalie Davis's discussion of two films, Stephen Spielberg's *Amistad* and Oprah Winfrey's *Beloved*, both depicting slavery on screen. Winfrey thus explained her own objectives in creating this filmic rendition of Toni Morrison's novel: 'I wanted people to be able to feel deeply on a very personal level what it meant to be a slave, what slavery did to people, and also be liberated by that knowledge.' She is reported to have said to her scriptwriter and fellow-producer, 'This is my *Schindler's List*.'[14] Spielberg similarly used 'considerable dramatic license', reports Davis, in *Amistad* so as to make it 'symbolic of a struggle that continues to this day' in the form of 'immigrants brought in illegally to work in sweatshops'.[15] Davis, as a historian, is clearly unhappy about this collapsing of the distance between the past and the present. But she does not go as far as Louis Gottschalk of the University of Chicago did when, in 1935, he wrote the following to the president of Metro-Goldwyn-Mayer:

> If the cinema art is going to draw its subjects so generously from history, it owes it to its patrons and its own higher ideals to achieve greater accuracy. No picture of a historical nature ought to be offered to the public until a reputable historian has had a chance to criticize and revise it.[16]

Clearly, it has been a losing battle in the last seventy-odd years for those on Professor Gottschalk's side. Davis presents a weaker version of the

Gottschalk argument but, clearly, for her, filmic presentism is an issue. She writes: 'The play of imagination in picturing resistance to slavery can follow the rules of evidence when possible, and the spirit of evidence when details are lacking.'[17] At the very least, film-makers should follow the principle of separating the past from the present and not collapse that distinction into one single experience. 'Strangeness in history', she writes, should be sustained 'along with familiar'. Or, as she puts it later, historical films should 'let the past be the past'.[18]

III

Let me then say what in my view was problematic in the clash between the discipline of history and the cultural politics of recognition in the eighties and the nineties of the last century. The important historians – Carlo Ginzburg, Natalie Davis, Lynn Hunt, Lawrence Stone and Eric Hobsbawm among them – who felt called upon to restate and defend the idea of historical objectivity repeated an older epistemological debate internal to the discipline as to whether or not the presentism built into the rhetoric of 'experience' destroyed objectivity. It was as if the idea of 'objectivity' and concomitant techniques for producing a sense of distance from the past had come under challenge. On a theoretical register, the fight was with postmodernism, poststructuralism (or even Hayden White's structuralism), deconstruction and certain varieties of postcolonial writing – all of which were seen as purveyors of versions of 'absolute moral relativism'. But it is not difficult to discern more directly political concerns behind the theoretical niceties. Challenges to historical objectivity, it was feared, would feed identity politics (in the United States and elsewhere) if not fascist or reactionary tendencies. The rhetoric of 'experience' was feared because, by collapsing the past and the present, 'experience' could produce only an irresponsible, if not inflammatory, mix of history and memory. What was missed and what went unremarked in the whole debate was the fact that a particular history of 'experience' was at issue – 'experience' seized by the commodity-form, 'experience' itself as a marketable commodity in contemporary public life. This was 'experience' moulded by globalisation and late capitalism.

I do not deny the many philosophical and logical problems that dog the category 'experience' are critical to the politics of historical wounds. It is also true that the mix of memory and history can take both benign and malignant forms – the recent deliberate attempts by the Hindu right in India to create anti-Muslim and anti-minority memories have impelled many respectable Indian historians such as Romila Thapar to defend the discipline's idea of objectivity. But also undeniable is the fact that questions of historical wounds and mediatised 'experience' have been central to the recent political uses of the past in diverse contexts of democracy – the Truth and Reconciliation Commission in South Africa, the Waitangi Tribunal in New Zealand, the demand for reconciliation with – or at least an apology to – the Aboriginals in Australia, discussion of the issue of sovereignty for the indigenous people of Canada, the Indian *dalit* response to the recent UN conference on racism held in Durban all come to mind, not to speak of the enormous amount of writing on memory and history around the Holocaust. None of these political instances would be imaginable without the active presence of the media.

Globalisation is no doubt a process with multiple and often contradictory trajectories. To the degree that globalisation succeeds in injecting into our lives a logic of placelessness – as understood, say, by Messrs Negri and Hardt – there may come into a play an attendant logic of pastlessness, and history may indeed come to be written, strategically, without reference to anyone's experience of the past.[19] Attempts by some *dalit* and *adivasi* ('tribal') activists in India to seek the label 'indigenous' for themselves in UN forums and the creation of websites that deliberately invent new global histories for themselves would be cases in point.[20] In such instances it may be said that globalisation is leading to construction and use of identities that are mainly strategic. Globalisation, similarly, may also create new historical wounds claiming global recognition. The increasing traffic of refugees and migrants may result in greater racialisation of governance and society and create new social injuries in the long term. The reported anger of young Muslims all over the world after 9/11 may be seen as an attempt at a politics of global recognition in relation to a perceived 'historical wound' – an incomplete process for the putative 'oppressor' has not recognised the justice of the claim. At the same time, there will be contexts where struggles for recognition will find co-ordinates within and not outside the nation. I doubt that the claim to land rights by Australian Aboriginals will ever refer to a de-territorialised and virtual country.

But even within these multiple possibilities, mediatisation and commodi-fication of experience will remain a constant for some time to come. Two developments in particular will (and should) continue to challenge the idea of historical objectivity. Whatever our philosophical problems with the category, 'experience' in a commodity-form will continue to mediate people's relationships to their pasts. I think here not only of museums but of television, videos and films. The film-studies critic Tom Gunning has emphasised how films make the past available by making it vivid, thereby converting it directly into an object of embodied 'experience'. This is very different from the ideal of re-enacting the past in the historian's mind. In Gunning's words:

> [F]ilm provides indelible images of some of the twentieth century's great events. Our horrified consciousness of the Holocaust relies partly on the filmed images from the liberation of the camps, and our knowledge of the devastation of the Atomic bomb comes partly from motion pictures of Hiroshima or of A-bomb test explosions. Conversely, twentieth-century disasters or traumas that went unrecorded by motion pictures – such as the genocide of the Armenians or mass starvation in Asia – are less present in public consciousness because of the lack of vivid images

... Fictional films serve as historical evidence in the same way that other representational art forms do – by making events vivid . . . [A]s a form of mass visual entertainment, films reflect social attitudes in a specific and vivid manner.[21]

Future historians working on our own times will thus have to turn to films, museums and the electronic media that archive human lives in an age of globalisation. This will itself lead to reconsideration of the meaning of historical objectivity.

Second, as the struggles of indigenous and other subaltern groups multiply the various chartings out of political paths and strategies that democratise the world in unforeseen ways, it will become increasingly obvious that historical objectivity is not always to be found on the side of justice and that the traditional archives of the historians themselves belong to certain relations of privilege. The Australian anthropologist Diane Bell has remarked how, in the politics of Aboriginal Australia, the view that traditions are 'invented' – an expression coined and popularised in the 1980s by two progressive historians, Eric Hobsbawm and Terence Ranger, who assumed that their coinage would serve as a weapon of the oppressed – can actually lead to the 'denial of rights' and to the 'destruction of [sacred] sites' as 'bureaucrats and experts' with 'access to archives' end up devaluing oral history by making it 'less authoritative'. What Diane Bell instead prefers as a means of research-ing Aboriginal claims about the history of their relationship to land is indeed 'experience' – 'being there'. She writes: 'There are stories that capture the spirit of a place and its peoples more faithfully than do others. These are subtle truths . . . They require context, getting to know a range of histories and politics. They require being there.'[22] Bell thinks of 'being there' in unproblematic terms. 'Being there', for her, is a question of travelling to experi-ence first hand the event, let us say, of the dispossession of the Aborigines. But the media – all the films and television serials and newspaper and magazine essays to do with the historical wounds of the Aboriginal people – ensure that there is no 'first-hand' experience to be had. Yet this does not mean that there is no 'experience'. There is, but a mediatised one. Today's presentism in the politics of historical wounds cannot be understood with-out reference to the media and to what I have called the 'commodity-form of experience'. Historians defending the discipline in the eighties and the nineties of the last century did so by repeating the arguments one might rehearse against a Dilthey or a Gadamer. Yet 'experience' cannot any longer be critiqued without some engagement with the question of how it became a marketable commodity while recognising, at the same time, that the mediation through the commodity-form does not, *eo ipso*, falsify experience.

I want to end by pointing to the very different horizons of what one might call 'the time of democracy' built into the two positions: first, that of historical objectivity; and second, one that recognises the fact of the mediatisation of experience and memory. Those insisting on historical objectivity argue, in effect, against the idea of instantaneous persuasion. For them, the time-consuming process of marshalling evidence and 'proof' is part of the logic of persuasion. In the realm of the media, however, as the emphasis on vividness in the quote from Gunning above suggests, persuasion is instantaneous, working as it does through an appeal to the senses and thus to the embodied person. The first position, however well intentioned, temporises on the question of democracy; it looks towards the temporal horizon of the 'not yet'. Mediatised memory and experience, however, speak to the temporal horizon of the 'now'; it thus speaks more eloquently to the postcolonial mood. Democracy now involves the deployment of both of these horizons. As historians sensitise themselves to popular uses of the past in a global and media-dominated world, they may very well see the need to renew the charter of the historians' guild that has been wedded so long to nineteenth-century ideas of citizenship.

Notes

1 Charles Taylor, 'The Politics of Recognition', in Amy Gutman (ed.), *Multiculturalism: Examining the Politics of Recognition* (Princeton, NJ: Princeton University Press, 1994): 26.
2 Taylor's text suggests this colonial connection: see p. 31.
3 Tony Birch, email to the author, Melbourne, 6 September 2005.
4 See Kancha Ilaih, 'Productive Labour, Consciousness and History: The Dalitbahujan Alternative', in Shahid Amin and Dipesh Chakrabarty (eds), *Subaltern Studies: Writings on South Asian History and Society* (Delhi: Oxford University Press, 1996): 165–200. Ilaih began by saying: 'Mainstream historiography has done nothing to incorporate the Dalitbahujan perspective in the writing of Indian history: *Subaltern Studies* is no exception to this'.
5 Ibid., p. 167.
6 Ibid., p. 168.
7 Here also we must note that Ilaih's rejection of academic disciplines cannot ever be total, living as he does in structures dominated by visions of governmentality. Thus, he must employ, minimally, some sociological or anthropological reasoning to find and identify his 'Dalitbahujan' constituency on the ground.
8 Joan Scott, 'The Evidence of Experience', *Critical Inquiry* 17:4 (1991): 773–97; Lee Kerwin Klein, 'On the Emergence of Memory in Historical Discourse', *Representations* 69 (2000): 127–50.
9 See Roger Miles, 'Museum Audiences', in *Museum Management and Curatorship* (*MMC*) 5 (1986): 73–80.
10 Richard Prentice, 'Managing Implosion: The Facilitation of Insight through the Provision of Context', *MMC*, 15:2 (1996): 169.
11 Cited in Sue Millar, 'Education: Museums and their Visitors', *MMC* 15:2 (1996): 212.
12 Cited in Stephen Weil, 'Museums and their Publics', *MMC* 16:3 (1997): 265.
13 Ibid., p. 262.
14 Winfrey cited in Natalie Zemon Davis, *Slaves on the Screen: Film and Historical Vision* (Cambridge, Mass.: Harvard University Press, 2000): 99.
15 Davis, *Slaves*, p. 131.
16 Gottschalk cited in Robert A. Rosenstone, 'The Historical Film: Looking at the Past in a Postliterate Age', in Marcia Landy (ed.), *The Historical Film: History*

and Memory in the Media (Rutgers, NJ: Rutgers University Press, 2001): 50. The quote originally occurs in Peter Novick's *A Noble Dream*.

17 Davis, *Slavery*, p. 136.

18 Ibid., pp. 131, 136.

19 Michael Hardt and Tony Negri, *Empire* (Cambridge, Mass.: Harvard University Press, 2000).

20 See my 'Politics Unlimited: The Global *Adivasi* and Debates about the Political', an afterword to Bengt A. Karlsson and Tanka B. Subba (eds), *The Politics of Indigeneity in India* (London: Routledge, 2006): 235–46.

21 Tom Gunning, *Making Sense of Films*. Available at: <http://historymatters.gmu.edu/mse/film/>.

22 Diane Bell, *Ngarrindjeri Wurruwarrin: The World That Is, Was, and Will Be* (Melbourne: Spinifex, 1998): 421–2. See also Eric Hobsbawm and T. R. Ranger (eds), *The Invention of Tradition* (Cambridge and New York: Cambridge University Press, 1983).

7   The gift of the past
Towards a critical history

Patrick Joyce

The present does not seem auspicious for the writing of manifestos. The term appears out of kilter with the time, something more in line with what were the passions of the nineteenth and twentieth centuries than what is the general air of post-ideological disengagement of the new century, at least in Britain. Besides, historians, especially academic ones, are not used to writing 'public declarations of policy', which is one *Oxford Dictionary* definition of the meaning of 'manifesto', a meaning decidedly reminiscent of the last century. However, they *are* more at home with another meaning of the term, namely making manifest, 'showing plainly to the eye or mind', in the sense of revealing or making explicit something that was hidden or implicit. It is with this sense that I would like to begin my 'manifesto', for it seems to suggest that between the 'critical history' of my title and this business of revealing and making manifest there may be an important connection.

For what else does a historian do than practise a critical method, directed towards his or her own work and existing historical accounts, and validated with reference to the established and collective protocols of that entity known as 'the discipline'? So in advocating a critical history as the object of my manifesto, am I not just doing what historians, and for that matter other academics, are doing anyway? To some extent yes, and to some extent no, is the not unexpected answer of an academic. 'Yes' in the sense that the potential is there, and 'no' in the sense that it is not always realised. Doing what academics do anyway can be said therefore to have the capacity for something like a manifesto, for saying something that, if not exactly 'policy', is something that can and should be made public. The audience which forms my public should not, our editors have directed, be an audience of peers but one of students and any others who may be interested. So, in taking the view that the critical spirit, if that is not too grand a term, is central to the practice of history, I commence the very unfamiliar task of writing a manifesto.

A critical history, like the discipline of history itself, is about the creation of knowledge. In being about knowledge it is always related to power. The equation between knowledge and power has become such a commonplace in recent times that we need to be reminded of the full force and significance of the connection. In being about the creation of meaning and action, in situations always of competing meanings and actions, knowledge depends upon the mobilisation of the resources of human society. If knowledge is about the dispositions of power in this way, so then is the creation, one might even say the production, of history. But is not this matter of how power is disposed an ethical matter, and indeed in the end a political matter? For how we dispose of power over ourselves and others is ethical, and how power is organised at a collective level is political.

We can think further about this by conceiving of the historian, and the archive or the institution in which he or she encounters the 'sources' or 'traces' from which histories are written, as different 'sites' of memory, thinking of memory of course more widely than as individual memory, but as collective memory, *public* memory. Historians and their archives are therefore a means by which societies organise their pasts. Public memory is shaped by many forces, but in the era of professional history in academic institutions which are always in some sense *public*, historians are among the most important custodians of that memory. In short, the creation of history is a *political* matter.

It is also an *ethical* one, for if the sites of memory that the writing of history occupies are involved in power, where then does the truth of history lie? Is truth possible when all truth has a history that is inseparable from power and the politics of knowledge? One way of pursuing this ethical aspect further is to ask how history creates its own 'credibility', how it makes its particular claims on truth. These seem in fact to be closely related to the archive. I am thinking about the archive here at a conceptual level, rather than simply a literal one, and I quote the social theorist Thomas Osborne as follows: 'Just as for the anthropologist the notion of fieldwork represents both a form of truth and knowledge and a certain ethical authority, a certain right to speak, so the archive confers similar rights on those – whoever they are – who seek to generate credibility on its basis.' Talking about history in this way involves talking about ethics: responsibilities are incurred as a consequence of this 'right to speak' that is gained in the practice of history.

This authorisation that the archive gives can be understood as a gift as well as a responsibility, a gift from the past to the future which entails an obligation in the form of the reciprocity of the historian, something tradition-ally understood in terms of a very close, scrupulous and critical attention to the traces of the past. In moral terms, the reciprocity entailed by the gift can be understood as involving a sort of duty to doubt. Doubt about the innocence of the archive is therefore axiomatic to historical method as a form of *criticism*. It is because historians doubt that they must criticise. Therefore, history can be said to be generically a critical discipline. The great French philosopher Paul Ricoeur has drawn attention to this critical aspect of history as a *vocation*, an ethical matter of obligation to real people in the past.

A critical history would therefore involve enlarging the scope of collective memory as a means of paying its debt to the past. In dealing with the collective, something in our sort of society typically taking the form of the public, we again encounter the political, and it is apparent how the ethical and the political are inseparable. Understanding the nature of history in this way, attempting to realise its potential in this manner, involves practising history as a criticism of power, the power contained in archives, in historical narratives, in institutions at all pedagogic and political levels, and in the selves of the historians (whether writers/academics or readers/students). It being only a short journey from power at these levels to power in society at large, a critical history would always be concerned with the general as well as the specifics of power.

In thinking about the shape of a critical history it seems to me to be a good idea to begin in one's own backyard, as it were, with academic history's own politics of knowledge and the history of this politics. The shape of this backyard, from about the early part of the nineteenth century, has traditionally taken the form of a 'discipline' itself. It is the discipline that regulates the practice of history, and still defines the identity of the historian. A discipline is a way of practising upon the self, in the sense of a mental discipline, which I have already said has the potential as a critical activity for looking squarely at this academic self, in fact for a sort of critique of criticism itself. However, a discipline is also a collective entity, something social and public. In both senses, the individual and the social (although I shall concentrate on the latter), there is the inherent connection to power, and the full meaning of 'discipline' needs to be kept in mind, as a way of controlling and shaping the behaviour of oneself and others and not merely a purely intellectual entity. Of course, there are existing histories of the history discipline, as of the phenomenon of the discipline itself, but not I think done quite in the way I have in mind.

In thinking about the discipline, the 'department' has for long been the essential institution linking the individual to the broader institutional world. So, let us have the development of a 'historical consciousness' that starts by inspecting this favourite corner of the backyard, conceiving of the department as a sort of technology, or as a sort of machine, for producing the credibility of history by producing in turn histories, historical 'periods', historical 'schools' and approaches, and indeed for producing the discipline as a unitary entity, however much 'interdisciplinarity' is currently mooted. Like all technologies, this one is made up of human and non-human entities, so that one would need to know to a serious depth the entire material infrastructure of institutions. Historians have in large measure until fairly recently ignored the world of things, the material world, a world that simply does not stand to attention when we call.

The fabrication and use of the pedagogic 'interior' in all its glory (the lecture room and its table, the seminar room and its chairs), and the means of pedagogic communication (the voice, deportment, email), all these and many other things not only do not merely stand to our attention, but as it were shape that attention itself. They are tools of knowledge, and like all tools they leave their mark upon that which they fashion. So, informed by this understanding, and starting most definitely from where we have got to today, it might be a good idea (and more fun than most existing courses) for a first-year student introductory course to involve consideration of the history of the academic 'career', particularly in view of current transformations in the nature of research in Britain. Candidates for inclusion in our history here would include the politics of research funding, of course, but also the political economy and social anthropology of 'the paper', as well as the journal, the conference and the lecture (the latter following the lead of the inimitable Irving Goffman).

However, behind this infrastructure one would have to consider another sort of infrastructure, namely the dense personal and highly political networks that underpin academic patronage, and therefore the career and the salience of particular kinds of history. This is not to mention the dispensation of academic 'honours', for instance the hermetic, intellectual freemasonry of the British Academy. All of this sits very awkwardly beside the avowedly transparent and meritocratic agenda of academic institutions and the contemporary state. Of course, situations vary across states and other forms of political organisation and my comments relate to my own immediate turf, the British one. But all turfs have their histories, so that comparative turf history as an element in a student course would be indispensable.

The increasingly specialised, and increasingly scrutinised and regulated, academic environment of today would need to be situated in terms of the long ascendancy and then rapid decline, between the late nineteenth century and the late twentieth century, of the whole system of the professional governance of institutions, disciplines and disciplinary identity. Like all contemporary disciplines in higher education, history in Britain is being made assessable and accountable in the new dispensation, literally accountable, in that academic history has become just one more item within what has been called contemporary 'audit society'. This is particularly the case on the British turf, and within the Anglophone academic world the USA is still significantly different, as are other examples, although so-called globalisation sets up common experiences as well.

Central to these experiences is the problem of translation, of how different disciplinary traditions might speak to each other in the clearest possible way, so that here the history of the backyard seems to be simply another way of talking about the history of the world. For example, within Central and Eastern Europe since 1989 there have been many appropriations of Western European historical traditions and approaches, but these have been grafted on to an older legacy, often going back long before communism but also including it (this reflects the – often unsuccessful – grafting of political institutions). While the long history of intellectual transmissions across borders has always and inevitably rested upon misreadings of what is transmitted, deliberate and otherwise, in the multiple readings and rereadings of academic institutions and practices now apparent in the world, there would seem a place for comparative turf history as a means of creating some sort of common lexicon in the interests of translation.

In the British case, but of course much more widely in 'Western' intellectual traditions, the 'liberal education' that underpins the study of history also needs to be understood historically as it has gone, and is going, through what have been a series of profound transformations. The often highly illiberal characteristics of this education have to be historically remembered, namely its post-Renaissance authoritarian roots and the social distinctions upon which these rest, and the legacy of the late nineteenth-century emergence of the current institutions of liberal education. This legacy is evident, for instance, in the modern idea of the tutor–pastor and the 'tutorial', upon which the development of the 'profession' of the historian has been, in part, grounded. The modern forms of research can themselves be understood as uneasy amalgams of older forms of pastoral power and modern forms of state power. It is to this chequered legacy that present attempts to negotiate state power must look, seeking for both the strengths and weaknesses of a liberal education, not forgetting that this history *is* chequered, and traditionally deeply implicated in the constitution of governance of the self and of the selves of others, but above all of the self so that it might govern others.

Beside the history of a liberal education there is the history of the liberal educator, in which the discipline of history from the early twentieth century went some way to succeed classics as the principal medium of instructing the educator. Marx called the bureaucrat the 'high priest' of the state. Perhaps we should call the academic the high priest of civil society. The sense of there being a sort of secular vocation to both professions is strong, and we have seen how, for example, Paul Ricoeur has referred to the 'vocation' of the historian as being central to his or her purpose. In employing this term we call attention to the common emergence of the bureaucrat and the academic as key figures in the emergence of contemporary 'Western' society. The fashioning of the *personae* of both of these archetypal figures and the material and human fashioning of the institutions they have shaped and been shaped by, particularly the role of classics and history in this process, are central to the development of the modern state, particularly the modern liberal state. In many other respects too the connection between the emergence and consolidation of professional, academic history and of the modern state has been close. In intellectual terms, until relatively recently, the nation-state supplied the primary narrative focus of a very great amount of historical writing, and it still continues to be of importance in the intellectual organisation of the discipline.

The inherently political nature of the sort of critical history I am considering will be apparent, but something more needs to be said about the place of the political in the self-understanding and self-critique of disciplines. Until the 1960s, at least in Britain, the national narrative had a distinct political character, broadly Tory and Whig/radical, and this continued, to some extent, in the social history that displaced the more narrowly political history which had previously dominated the agenda. The Marxist influence on British social history was considerable, but even that had the stamp of the nation upon it, albeit the English nation in the form of the place of class in the national story, and of a radical English populism.

However, social history itself and the cultural history that has followed in its wake have introduced a set of questions and techniques/methods which have tended to displace the centrality of the national narrative. The prodigious increase in the size of the higher education sector has given rise to a high degree of specialism and this has worked to similar effect. The result is that it has become increasingly difficult to produce synthetic accounts of national history which can incorporate the subtlety and sophistication of some – but by no means all – of the specialist histories. Social and political developments have also contributed to this: for instance, changes in the economic and cultural experience of women have been reflected in women's and gender history, and these have either led away from, or been only partially integrated in, national narratives. With the decreasing salience of class in British politics, and to some extent in British life too, what had served as one major principle of synthetic accounts no longer served. These social changes were themselves related to what in intellectual terms came to be called the end of grand narratives, among them class and nation. This outcome and the transition from social to cultural history were also aspects of the emergence of the cultural turn, and what historians have promiscuously taken to calling postmodernism.

In the 1960s and 1970s being a social historian carried a certain political charge, directed as social history was against the academic and to some extent the political *ancien régime*. This charge was predominantly, but by no means completely, of a left-liberal sort. In the 1990s and after, being a cultural historian carried much less, if any, political sense, with political identity and engagement in the wider political culture themselves having become much more problematic than before. The 'political' itself came in the interim in important measure to be redefined in identity terms, and this included academic identity, so that to some degree a political identity came to be expressed in the academic life. My 'manifesto' for a critical history can, to some extent, be seen in this light – an ethics of the discipline expressing a political identity.

Even if this is the case, and the nature of the political has changed, in the change from social to cultural history there nevertheless seems to be a loss. Cultural history – as, it must be said, to some degree social history before it – has become increasingly hegemonic in the discipline, and increasingly routinised, so that what political energy there is has in considerable measure been swallowed up in the great maw of the academy, which feeds off the new with an insatiable appetite. The result is often an indiscriminate, and sometimes vacuous, borrowing of 'theory' and methods in which a lack of theoretical rigour is very apparent, when indeed there is any real interest in theory at all.

What social history did have, and what has been largely lost to view in subsequent developments, is a much more critical engagement with theory and other disciplines, especially the social sciences, with social history politicising and actively helping to theorise the approaches of those other disciplines. This was evident in Marxism, in the influence of *Annales* history, the latter with its emphasis on 'total history', and in relation to American social science. The view of history was nothing if not ecumenical. The decline of grand narratives has mistakenly been understood as meaning the end of such an understanding. Social history, for all its failings, was challenging and innovative, and carried a political energy, because it attempted to get beyond the old narrowness of historical interpretation and understandings.

Ironically, rather like the social history it originally attempted to move beyond, cultural history has tended to take the concept of culture for granted, understanding it very narrowly, as something involving purely representation and meaning systems. There has been a marked failure to rethink the social in the light not only of the cultural turn but of subsequent social and political developments in the contemporary world. This rethinking has gone on in the social sciences, but has only fitfully been expressed in cultural history. The fixation with representation has also meant that there has been a failure to rethink the nature of materiality. The result is that cultural history has ignored not only the social but the economic. Ironically, for all its innovation, the result has been largely to leave in place an existing and narrowly understood economic history. The same may be said of political history, although to a lesser extent. Because of this, the incapacity of large parts of cultural history to help us rethink the political is apparent. This failure is a loss for critical history, which in this context can be understood as a sort of social history of power and the political. As such, it is well positioned to be of use in this process of rethinking.

However, I advocate a critical history, and offer an account of liberal education and educators, from within the sanctuary of the institution of a liberal education itself. Is not my 'critical history' only a form of a liberal historical consciousness itself? Is my advocacy of doubt, suspicion and a critical spirit simply a reproduction of rather familiar liberal aspirations? While it would be foolish to say that the discourse that comes out of a particular institution is somehow determined by it, there is more than a little point to these questions. However, what do we mean by 'liberal' in this regard? In fact, in the present day, which might in the Anglophone world loosely be called a 'neo-liberal' day, concern with the nature of 'liberalism' is peculiarly intense.

A critical history should contribute to this debate in part by exploring in much more depth than hitherto the true nature of 'liberalism' in the past (so that so-called 'neo-liberalism' might be quite the wrong term to employ). What do we mean by the term 'liberalism' as it is commonly used? Also, how might we think about the term and the series of questions and concerns to which it has given rise in new ways? Central to these concerns has been the nature of freedom, and a critical history would need to be involved in thinking historically about the many pasts of freedom in relation to its various presents and its future possibilities. Any major rethinking of liberalism and freedom, and any potential post-liberal understanding of these, would, for example, need to explore the relationship between their extra-political and political deployment and appropriations.

Of course, there are political limitations to the critical history I espouse: it does not have a clear political message, for example, like Marxist history. However, perhaps the present day is not yet the time for clear political messages, at least in relation to societies of an advanced liberal sort. So much would be implicit in my concern for an understanding of the past as a contribution to what is an ongoing rethinking of the present of liberalism. Therefore, whatever it might be in the future, while I believe a critical history does have political clout, or at least the possibility of clout, this clout accrues its strength more from a politics of academic knowledge than from an openly and clearly enunciated political programme, insofar as this would be possible in the present.

It is with this in mind that my manifesto would advocate what could be understood as a history of the present, recognising that it is the present, and a continuous stream of presents before ours, which have written the past in such a way as it will respond to our needs and our outlook. However, a historian is by definition somebody concerned with the past. It seems to me, therefore, that to be a historian of the present is not enough. The dangers of this position, at least narrowly conceived, are clear enough: if present concerns dictate readings of the past, then there is a very real possibility that preconceived ideas of the present may simply negate the possibility of the past suggesting new routes to and new ways of understanding the present. Perhaps we need a history of the present past, or of the past present, thinking always about the relation between the two terms, starting from the trains of thought occasioned by juxtaposing our historical tenses like this.

It could be said, then, that social scientists (at least the critical ones) approach matters in the first way of looking at these things, and historians (again the critical ones) the second, that is of the past present, in which the distance between the two is recognised more in terms of the 'otherness' of the past, the way in which it is a foreign country, yet one which we always come to from our own. Or perhaps there is a third way between these, just as there is surely a third way between 'theory' and practice in the writing of history? Historians have notoriously been averse to what they like to call theory, yet it seems to me that a critical history is at once inherently 'theoretical' and irreducibly empirical, the former because it is alert to how history is always structured by different sorts of intellectual framework, and the latter because it is concerned with developing theory through practice, and regenerating and refining practice through theory. Indeed, perhaps, what is arrived at is neither theory nor practice. Echoing the terminology of the anthropologist Clifford Geertz, what we would then have would be not so much thick description as tough description.

I wish to end by returning to that sense of the past as a gift. The gift given is a debt and a responsibility incurred. The gift *of* the past involves the gift of the past *to* the present, and to the future. And it is usually a pleasure as well as an obligation to be given a gift, so I am conscious in ending that I have neglected to talk about the endless pleasures of the past, of finding out how the seemingly familiar is in fact strange, but above all how the present is irradiated by the past. The great French historian Marc Bloch spoke of how the past gave off a charge, akin to an electrical charge, and this I think says it well. Once the force of this charge is felt, things are never the same again.

As I hope was apparent in what has been said so far, power is intrinsically part of the conditions of existence of history writing itself, and a critical history would begin, as I suggest, by looking first at its own practice. So, too, is power intrinsically part of our own conditions of existence as humans: it is not simply about discipline and control but about enabling action and realising thought. Therefore, the many powers of history, including political powers, accrue to all those who study, read and write it, making it essential to how we conceive of ourselves as actors in the world. As actors in the world, the question is: how do we reciprocate to the gift of the past? How do we repay the gift?

I have talked exclusively about academic knowledge, but I am deeply conscious of how other workers on the past repay the gift, and in doing so also bear its burden. And they do so often much better than historians. The powers of the twentieth century have been unimaginably awful in their consequences, the awfulness of this legacy making their burden of unimaginable weight. Few have carried that weight so heroically as W. G. Sebald, whose extraordinary works of literature have borne the pain of witness from the twentieth into the twenty-first century. Before him, bearing the pain of witness in a different way, the great Jewish elegist of the Habsburg Empire, Joseph Roth, made the nineteenth century meaningful to the twentieth century in a similar way.

Historians, of course, do a different job to novelists. But like novelists they address a public. I have said that in our sort of society historians, and their institutions, are a means by which societies have organised their pasts, so that historians have become in effect custodians of public memory. In our sort of society that public has increasingly become one that consumes things, and in their consumption defines what these things are. The same is true for history, which has also become a commodity. Academic history directly addresses an academic audience, but indirectly, in fulfilling the purpose of a liberal education, it helps to shape a public that is historically conscious. In doing so, it has to guard against this commodification of history.

This is present in the UK in many forms, among them a debased public culture and public media in which history has become the new gardening, when it is present at all. This is apparent not only at a so-called popular level but at the level of the 'educated classes', where a widespread, and depressingly familiar, anti-intellectualism sells history light, something the antithesis of history critical. History is not a commodity, and therefore a critical history has an uphill task against the power of the mass, capitalist market. However, critical history is not powerless: in bearing the gift of history from the past to the present, and to the future, it helps cut against the grain of the present, offering a critique of present power by its acts of remembrance.

Suggested reading: some works considered in the text

Peter Becker and William Clark (eds), *Little Tools of Knowledge: Historical Essays on Academic and Bureaucratic Practices* (Detroit: University of Michigan Press, 2001).

Pierre Bourdieu, *Homo Academicus* (Cambridge: Polity Press, 1988).

—— *The State Nobility: Elite Schools in the Field of Power* (Cambridge: Polity Press, 1996).

Michel Foucault, *The Essential Works*, Volume 3: *Power* ed. James D. Faubion (London: Penguin Press, 1994).

Irving Goffman, *The Presentation of Self in Everyday Life* (Ann Arbor: Anchor, 1959).

History of the Human Sciences, special issues on the Archive, 11(4): (November 1998) pp. 1–140; 12:2 (May 1999) pp. 1–122, especially Thomas Osborne, 'The Ordinariness of the Archive' and Patrick Joyce, 'The Politics of the Liberal Archive'.

Patrick Joyce, *The Oxford Reader on Class* (Oxford: Oxford University Press, 1995).

—— 'The Return of History: Postmodernism and the Politics of Academic History in Britain', *Past and Present* 158 (February 1998) pp. 207–35.

—— *The Social in Question: New Bearings in History and the Social Sciences* (London: Routledge, 2002).

—— *The Rule of Freedom: Liberalism and the Modern City* (London: Verso, 2003).

Pierre Nora, *Realms of Memory: Rethinking the French Past*, English edn, three vols. (New York: Columbia University Press, 1996–8).

Thomas Osborne, 'The ordinariness of the archive', *History of the Human Sciences*, 12:2 (May 1999) p. 54.

Paul Ricoeur, *Time and Narrative*, three vols (University of Chicago Press, 1984–8).

Nikolas Rose, *Powers of Freedom* (Cambridge: Cambridge University Press, 1999).

Joseph Roth, *The Redetzky March* (London: Penguin, 1995).

—— *What I Saw: Reports from Berlin 1920–33* (London: Granta, 2003).

W. G. Sebald, *The Natural History of Destruction* (London: The Modern Library, 2003).

—— *Austerlitz* (London: Penguin, 2002).

Christopher Stray, *Classics Transformed: Schools, Universities and Society in England, 1830–1960* (Oxford: Oxford University Press, 1998).

8 Performing cross-culturally

Greg Dening

Here I am ending studies that have preoccupied me for fifty years. But in the theatre of history, there is never really an ending. There is only an exit-line that begins another conversation. I am not inclined to make that exit-line a manifesto, though. There is much too much certainty in a manifesto, and not a little aggression. I would much prefer my exit-line to be dialogic. Dialogue is not just an exchange of ideas. It is also an exchange of the gift of self. There is always the self-denial that listening demands in dialogue. Who was it that wrote that the letters of the word 'listen' are also the letters of the word 'silent'? Any manifesto of mine would be in part silent.

Fifty years ago I made a discovery that changed my life. I discovered that I wanted to write the history of 'the other side of the beach', of indigenous island and continental peoples with whom I had no cultural bond, of Natives. And on 'this side of the beach', my side as an outsider, as Stranger, I wanted to write the history of people whom the world esteems as 'little'. Not of kings and queens. Not of heroes. 'Little people.' Those on whom the forces of the world press most heavily. I wanted to celebrate their humanity, their freedom, their creativity and their dignity.[1]

These have been years of great pleasure and privilege. By rights, I should be a most humble man. Historians must be humbled by living and knowing only vicariously and distantly what their subjects of enquiry have lived and known immediately before them. Anthropologists must be humbled by the difficulty of entering another culture, one so easily known to those who belong to it. History and anthropology are both plagiarisms, replays of others' lives and living. I owe the past and the others the dignity of being able to be their own selves in my representations of them. I owe them all those dignities I expect for myself. It is I who intrude on them, not they on me.

My principal ambition – or the one I have learned to make principal in these fifty years – has been to enter into the believing selves of those whose lives I am replaying.

All humanity is believing. Across times. Across cultures. All humanity has answers to questions that can never be answered. All humanity has an ultimate metaphor for what is. That metaphor might not be explicit, on the surface of things, easy to see, but it is there. Being cross-cultural in time and space, it seems to me, means entering that ultimate metaphor, translating others' metaphors into my own metaphor. Hearing the silences of others' metaphors, so that I can hear the silences in mine. It is a very humbling thing to discover that all our ultimate metaphors are equidistant from reality. It is humbling to discover that the location of all our spiritualities – dialogic or manifest – lies in a question that has no answer other than: 'Here I am. Here is my believing self.' My believing self is not my beliefs. Beliefs are static, propositional, products of closure. Believing is actual, processual.

My believing self is my soul, my spirit. My spirit is my locating, searching self. It is not a soul that is 'saved'. Not an ethereal, wispy, ghost-buster sort that eventually escapes this body and this vale of tears. A spirit. A place of reflection where one knows oneself as is – and would be. A place of commitment – and defection; of guilt – and innocence; of love – and hatred; of truth – and lies; of believing – and knowing. My ambition always in writing ethnographical history is to locate other spirits, their searching selves where they find themselves as I do, always on the edge, in between. Giving others their otherness, giving back the past its own present, is how I respect humanity's dignity.

It was a brave new world, this world of the history of the encounters between Natives and Strangers in which I got involved fifty years ago. We were engulfed by a dozen disciplines from archaeology to zoology, their internal debates, their lateral pursuits. All the time we thought we were writing history. It was as if life were a permanent *Times Literary* crossword puzzle. It was innocent intellectuality with no responsibility other than to ourselves. In the eyes of many, this history of a Native/Stranger encounter did not have *gravitas*, though. *Gravitas* – having a seriousness, weightiness, high in cultural estimations. Ancient history and classics had *gravitas*. Renaissance and Reformation history, too. Even British history. Australian history was on the edge of being respectable in these years. The history of native peoples in their encounters with the 'civilised' certainly did not have *gravitas*. When I told my professor of history that I was heading off to Harvard to do anthropology so that I could write encounter history better, he said: 'Dening, this is the end of your academic career.' He meant that it was impolitic to engage in an area which my discipline, the university and society thought to be of little consequence. I venture to say that it is only now, at the beginning of the twenty-first century, that the pursuit of know-ledge of the otherness of indigenous peoples has the *gravitas* that it must have to seep into our life in Australian history and all its parts. Bennelong, the maverick Aboriginal mediator between his people and the convict colonists in the late eighteenth century, does not have the *gravitas* of Ned Kelly, a criminal 'bushranger' and murderer with an Irish spirit of rebellion in the nineteenth century. A massacre of First People defending their land does not yet have the consequence of 'Eureka', an armed rising of miners against what they thought was unjust taxation. We are a long way from seeing the mutual killings of First People and settlers in our past as fratricide. Healing myths will begin only when we really see their brotherhood and sisterhood in death.

For us who revelled in our innocence and looked to the respect that we thought we were owed by those we studied – our Natives – precisely because we were so beleaguered and unfashionable academically, it was like a kick in the stomach in the 1960s to be told by those whom we studied that we did not treat them with proper dignity, and never would, never could. In 1961 Frantz Fanon put it to the world that no one who in some way benefits by the power of the victors can write two-sided history. No one can mediate between the disempowered living and the voiceless dead. It seemed that in an instant the disempowered of the world heard him. The dignity the disempowered demanded was that they have their own voice to say who they were, where they had been and where they were going.[2]

For me, it was the most important lesson of my intellectual life. The past belonged to those on whom it impinged more than to those who had the skills to discover it and tell it. Those on whom it impinged were owed the dignity of being heard with their own voice. And that voice, they immediately told us, was to be found in myriad ways – in their dances, their songs, their legends, their myths, their body paint and tattoos, their carvings, their poetry, their very language. It was our responsibility to learn how to listen, they told us.

I agreed with them. It was first our responsibility to listen, even to discover the lines that joined the millennia of our First People's past to the modernity of their present. Their 'aboriginality', which joined them to their land in their believing spirits, had no language that would be accepted in the law and politics of those who had dispossessed them. If I was to write the history of the bound-together present, I would have to find a language that would both express the First People's understanding of their aboriginality and convince those who had dispossessed them of its truth.

But what the dispossessed did not have the right to say, in my opinion, was that there was no entry into their otherness by those who did not share it. That leads to nihilism. Over these past decades we have seen claims that the otherness of gender, sexuality, class, age, culture and race is inaccessible, and that any claim of accessibility is a disempowerment. That is not true. What is true is that accessibility always involves some mutual conferring of human dignity: of white to black, of black to white; of male to female, of female to male; of young to old, of old to young.

My gift to the past in the history I write is always that in the contingencies that suffuse every part of our being, I discover their true stories with all the strategies of neomodernity and all the tropes of a storyteller. That is my obligation – to make history that is true to the tropes of my times, the ideals of my disciplines, the political realities of my knowledge, the creativity of my imagination. My neomodernity has embraced all the ideals of knowledge-advancement of modernity – perspective, exhaustive research, critical dialogue, disengagement as far as is humanly possible from all that filters that knowledge with prejudice and error. These ideals demand that I sit for hours, days, weeks, months and years at desks in the archives. My extravagance with time there is rewarded with a sensitivity that comes in no other way. It is an overlaying of images one on the other. It is a realisation that knowledge of the past is cumulative and kaleidoscopic, extravagantly wasteful of my energy. This is both the cost and the benefit of my modernity. But my modernity is neo-new. It is in touch at the same time with both the possibilities and the limits of knowing; it is a modernity that is expressive of what is known and how brokenly it is known. It is a modernity that begins with the real and enlarges it with creative imagination. It is a modernity that always acknowledges my authorial presence.

My tropes are those of a storyteller, but a teller of true stories. I do not write fiction. Fiction is too disrespectful of the generations of archaeologists, anthropologists, linguists, historians and scholars of all descriptions who have helped us know what we know. Fiction is too disrespectful of the thousands of descendants of the First People who by song, dance and story have clung to the truths of their past and the metaphors of their understandings through the millennia.

I do not write 'non-fiction', either. I do not write 'non' anything, and I do not like the company I am forced to keep on the 'non-fiction' shelves in the bookstores – cookbooks, personality disorders, do-it-yourselves, ghost-written autobiographies of celebrities. I use my imagination in my writing. Of course I do. Imagination is not fantasy. Imagination is finding a word that others will hear, a metaphor that someone else will see. Imagination is catching a glimpse of that moving target, the final chapters of our books. Imagination is seeing what is absent, hearing the silence as well as the noise. Imagination is taking the cliché out of what has been said over and over again. Imagination is knowing that we read and write with our whole body and all its emotions, not just with our mind. Imagination is sculpting the shape of our books in surprising and intriguing ways.

'Historying' is a word invented by some of us involved in this creative process of writing true stories about the past. I like the word because it is the present participle first of all, or the '-ing' form, as the parsers prefer to call it these days. 'No harm in using it,' Nicholas Hudson tells us in *Modern Australian Usage*, provided that it is remembered that the '-ing' form covers two quite different phenomena – the present participle and the verb–noun, also known as the 'gerund'.[3]

Henry Watson Fowler (who lives on, I sometimes think, in the spelling and grammar tools menu on my computer) is less patient with participles, although, to do him justice, he is principally upset by unattached participles – 'as insidious as they were notorious'; fused participles – 'close to German ponderousness', 'ignorant vulgarisms'; sentry participles – editors must discipline newspaper writers of inch-long paragraphs lest they encourage 'the survival of the unfittest'. But in more accommodating mode, he writes, 'tender grammatical consciences are apt to vex themselves, sometimes with reason, sometimes without, over the -ing forms of the verb'.[4]

Tender grammatical consciences beware, then. 'Historying' is a moral act in more ways than one. 'History' – the past transformed into words or paint or dance or music or play – is our noun. 'Historying' is our verb–noun. Historying is the unclosed action of making histories. History, the noun, is closed, shaped, a product. Historying is process, never done, dialectical, and dialogic. Gossiping, explaining to the taxman, pleading not guilty to the judge, eulogies over the grave – historying actions are manifold, each with a moral dimension. Let us not go that way. Historying for those of us who are likely to be writing manifestos about it is more defined – not by topic, not by period, not by method, not by style, not by interpretive agreement. None of us is the clone of any other. None of us is the clone of our teachers. None of our students is a clone of us. Our historying is as idiosyncratic as our fingerprints. Are we joined together in our historying, though? Yes, we are, I would like to say.

Historying is not just making history. It is also educating, supervising, examining, researching, reviewing, being members of professional associations, advising governments and institutions, giving public face to scholarship in the media, sharing the burdens of administration in committees of all descriptions, applying for research grants, being paid for some of it, being freely generous with time and energy for the sake of ideals, being conscious that all this is self-interested in personal ambitions, in institutional rivalries, in the scramble for funded support. There are schemers and frauds and nastiness in such historying. But altruism and ideals suffuse it, too. There is a passion that such knowledge is public, that it be subject to critical appraisal, that it serves a good greater than the individual's fame.

Let me go to one moment in these different dimensions of historying, that moment when we engage our students in the creative act of making history. Let us say we are educating our graduate students, when we relieve them of the grind of lectures and tutorials to have the time and freedom to enjoy the pleasures and endure the pains of our craft, our art, our science. It is a time when we expose them to all the advantages of knowledge-advancement that modernity has given us, and how this modernity is renewed with the experience of both the possibilities and the limits of knowing, a confidence in our ability to know, but a sense of how brokenly we know, an ear for the different voices of our authorship, an understanding that no matter how local the topic of our historying, we are joining a conversation that is global.

I tell these young people that they must be a number of things in their historying. 'Be mysterious,' I tell them. 'Mystery', 'mysterious' are words layered with thousands of years of meaning. At the heart of these meanings is an understanding that a mystery is a most complicated truth clothed in story or play or sacramental sign. Being mysterious means that there is work to be done – not just by the storyteller, not just by the author, not just by the priest, but by the audience, the reader and the believer as well. There is no closure to mystery, only another story, another translation. I think that a writer should liberate the readers to go where they want. It is their conversation we are joining. There is a certain abruptness or directness in being mysterious. We have to have the confidence that readers have instantaneous skills in being where we take them.

Be experiential. Write as observers, not as spectators, with cultural antennae at full extent, seeing the multivalence in every word. Make every experience 'an experience' as John Dewey advised, reflected on, joined to all the dangerous memories of living. Suffuse it with our believing selves, letting the reader sense and share our vulnerability. That is our dialogic gift.

Pursue metaphor, not model. Write as if everything is in the present tense. Give back to the past its own possibilities, its own ambiguities, its own incapacity to see the consequences of its action.

Culture is talk. Living is story. Culture is talk. I hear this talk in all its multivalence, with all its conditions of person and place and occasion. Living is story. I hear these stories in all the tropes with which they are told to me – their metaphors, their metonymies, their ironies. In my turn I tell my true stories as artfully as I can. My true stories won't clone theirs either in their pastness or their otherness. There will always be part of me as well as part of them in my true stories. My histories won't have the closure of hindsight. There is nothing so undignified and mocking of the past as hindsight. My stories won't freeze them in any one moment of their living. That is what the Terror wants, Jean-François Lyotard has told us, 'to arrest the meaning of words', to put a template on living.[5] The Terror: the terror of fundamentalism, the terror of *auto-da-fé*, the terror of science in the service of power.

All reification is a process of forgetting is how Herbert Marcuse put his slant on this notion of Terror: 'All reification – the transformation of lived experience into things – is a forgetting.' 'Art fights reification', Marcuse goes on, 'by making the petrified word speak, sing, perhaps dance.'[6] Yes! I give the past the dignity it is owed with my artfulness and my compassion.

In a world as monstrously without compassion as ours is, it is not surprising that its victims turn to words with the deepest reflective meaning. All over the Pacific, in all the towns and camps and ghettos of Aboriginal Australia, there are poets. An inner dignity demands the intensity of a poem.

Perhaps my true stories should be poems to be truly compassionate. I wish I had the courage to write them. But I have to leave it to others, like my closest anthropologist friend, Ivan Brady, who does have the courage to write his ethnographies as poems.[7]

These fifty years have gone quickly. In their very first moments I was engaged in trying to understand how the islanders – I called them Polynesians then, Sea People now – inhabited the vast space of their ocean – I called it the Pacific then, Sea of Islands now. If I had the arrogance in those early years to think that it would be I who would give them their history, I have had the pleasure in these later years to hear their many different voices telling their stories with metaphors that reach into their believing selves much more directly than mine. But I have always had the ambition to tell the story of the Sea People's voyaging to the farthest point of their Sea of Islands two thousand years ago in such a way that embedded in that story was all the knowledge that I had acquired in those fifty years, together with the inspiration given me by the great scholars who have suffused my understanding with their wisdom. It is only recently that I have found the confidence and the courage to write that story in a way that displays the certainties of my factual knowledge, the probabilities of my understanding and the possibilities of my interpretation together with a compassion that the Sea People's identity and pride deserve.[8]

The Pleiades have risen. The Mataiki – 'Little Eyes' – are into the second of their four-month stay in the sky. The season of plenty is in harvest. The west winds are reaching further into the east against the prevailing north and south easterlies. The voyaging time has begun. They are well ready.[9]

One hundred and fifty generations ready. Three millennia ready. For three thousand years this Sea People has lived on the eastern edge of a forty-millennia movement of people from the west down a corridor of islands into the ocean they call Moana, the Great Ocean. For three thousand years this Sea People has made a sea of islands their own. Samoa, Tonga and Fiji enclose that sea. The Sea People sail the circuit of the sea with confidence. They trade. They raid. They adventure. They are blue-water sailors. Their bodies have responded to the sea's demand on them. They are the largest humans on earth. They are survivors in wet and cold. They are at home on the sea, day and night and in all seasons. They have learned that with the horizon all around them and a vessel in motion, the old land order no longer prevails. Night and day there must be someone responsible for all the tasks necessary to keep the vessel on its course. All the activities of living – sleeping, eating, working, playing – are on a different cycle at sea.

Above all, the millennia have given this Sea People an artefact of cultural genius, their *va'a*, their canoe. Their *va'a* is a thing imprinted with millennia of experience as generations find the woods, the fibres, the resins that pull and strain, resist work fatigue and rotting, seal. Their *va'a* is a thing of very precise design – of curves that give strength, of asymmetric shapes that play wind and water against one another, of structured balances that avoid congestion of strain, of aerodynamics that free it to fly along the wind.

It is the way of such artefacts of cultural genius that the real genius lies in simplicity. For the *va'a* three things made it unique in the inventiveness of humankind in mastering the sea environment. A lug. A triangular sail. An outrigger. The lug, a projection on the inside of the hull, perforated so that cordage could be pulled through, makes it possible to compress all parts of the *va'a* together. The triangular sail, without masts or stay, pivoting on its head, held high by a prop, creates a self-steering vessel without need of rudder or pulleys. These days we see windsurfers exploiting its simplicity and speed.

The outrigger on the windward side, fitted to the hull by means of the lug, gives stability and manoeuvrability. The double *va'a, va'a tauna*, removed the need of the outrigger and by means of a platform over the two hulls, perhaps four metres wide and thirteen metres long, allows the vessel to carry fifty to eighty people, a shelter, a sand fire-pit and cargo of up to thirty thousand kilograms.

With Mataiki's rising come also Na Kao (Orion's brightest star) and Muri (the Follower of Pleiades). All these stars beckon to the north-east. In the west on the opposite horizon Metau-o Maui (Scorpius) and Maitiki (Sagittarius) are setting. So there is an arc of light over the corridor of warm waters to the north-east. The sea experts among them know every step and stage of that arc, especially the stars that stand in zenith over their homeland. The zenith stars would be like beacons beckoning them back.

Through the millennia they had sailed eastward on exploring voyages for days, perhaps weeks, at a time, confident that the wind would bring them home. The southerly tack takes them to cooler waters, the northerly to warmer waters. The risks are less in the warm waters. When they make the decision to seek new lands to settle, they know that they will have to go farther than they have ever gone. That there is land out there to the east they are sure. Its signs are in the flotsam that comes to their shores. They are always confident that that they will make a landfall on that land to the east. The land-nesting birds and the myriad other birds will guide them, as will the phosphorescence beneath the surface in the lee of islands. Lagoon reflections in the clouds, shadows of islands in the ocean swells, there is land to the east and they are confident that one day they will reach it. They know the annual monsoonal cycles that drive the west winds. There are other cycles, also, every four or seven years. The temperature of the sea drops. Fish change their habits. Birds change their migratory lines. In these cycles the west winds win out more easily over the east winds. Their *tuhuna pu'e*, sea experts, know that these are the seasons of discovery.[10]

I tease you with an unfinished story. I am being mysterious. How can there be any closure in a few hundred words on an issue so important or so serious as performing cross-culturally? We don't learn truths by being told them. We learn truths by experiencing them in some way – in theatre, in ritual, in story. My story of the first crossing of the Sea of Islands two thousand years ago is my cross-cultural performance. If I have told it well, then you may be tempted to find out how it ends. But in fact it doesn't matter if you never find out how it ends. I honour these 'little people' on the 'other side of the beach' with describing some of the skills and knowledge with which they accomplished perhaps the most remarkable voyage in all humankind's history. That is my gift to them and to those who can discover themselves in metaphors that take them back through the millennia.

Well, a friend said to me, writing stories is like dropping a rose petal into the Grand Canyon and waiting for the bang.

Notes

1 My writings on encounter history are to be found in such publications as: *Islands and Beaches: Discourse on a Silent Land, Marquesas 1774–1880* (Honolulu: University Press of Hawaii, 1980); *The Death of William Gooch: History's Anthropology* (Melbourne: University of Melbourne Press, 1995); *Performances* (Chicago: University of Chicago Press, 1996); *Beach Crossings: Voyaging across Times, Cultures and Self* (Philadelphia: University of Pennsylvania Press, 2004).

2 Frantz Fanon, *The Wretched of the Earth* (Harmondsworth: Penguin, 1963).

3 Nicholas Hudson, *Modern Australian Usage* (Melbourne: Oxford University Press, 1993): 202.

4 H. W. Fowler, *A Dictionary of Modern English Usage* (Oxford: Oxford University Press, 1965): 254, 438.

5 Jean-François Lyotard, *Rudiments Païens*, quoted in Michel de Certeau, *The Practice of Everyday Life* (Berkeley: University of California Press, 1988): 165.

6 Herbert Marcuse, quoted in Michael T. Taussig, *The Devil and Commodity Fetishism in South America* (Chapel Hill: University of North Carolina Press, 1980): 54.

7 Ivan Brady, *The Time at Darwin's Reef: Poetic Explorations in Anthropology and History* (Walnut Creek: Rowman and Littlefield, 2003).

8 Epeli Hau'ofa inspired the name 'Sea of Islands' for the Pacific (*A New Oceania: Rediscovery of Our Sea of Islands* (Suva: University of the South Pacific, 1993)). Those who write of the Sea of Islands from outside are happy to use the name. It gives a sense of identity to those who are the descendants of the great voyages that peopled this vast ocean space. Houston Wood has reviewed this indigenous search for a metaphor of identity in his article 'Cultural Studies for Oceania', *Contemporary Pacific* 15 (2003): 340–74.

9 The archaeological/anthropological/historical/cultural studies scholars Patrick Kirch and Roger Green have led us all in their studies of ancestral 'Polynesia'. Their most recent contribution is *Hawaiki, Ancestral Polynesia* (Cambridge: Cambridge University Press, 2001). Patrick Vinton Kirch, *On the Roads of the Winds: An Archaeological History of the Pacific Islands before European Contact* (Berkeley: University of California Press, 2000) offers a comprehensive study of the Sea People's voyaging. The studies of Andrew Parley, Malcolm Ross and Darrell Tyron on comparative linguistics and of Adrian Porridge on the Sea People's *va'a* in Peter Bellwood, James J. Fox and Darrell Tyron (eds), *The Austronesians* (Canberra: ANU Department of Anthropology, 1995) make the foundations on which I build the voyaging story. Geoffrey Irwin, *The Prehistoric Exploration and Colonisation of the Pacific* (Cambridge: Cambridge University Press, 1992) offered the insight that regular counter-winds will inspire adventurous discovery voyages because the counter-winds always promised the sailor a means to come home. Philip Houghton, *People of the Great Ocean: Aspects of Human Biology of the Early Pacific* (Cambridge: Cambridge University Press, 1996) describes the environmental and biological conditions that made voyaging to remote Oceania possible.

10 Ben Finney tells the story of the intellectual debate and cultural achievements of the voyaging canoes re-enactments in *Voyage of Rediscovery: A Cultural Odyssey through Polynesia* (Berkeley: University of California Press, 1994). Finney's most comprehensive study of traditional navigation is to be found in his 'Nautical Cartography and Traditional Navigation in Oceania', in *The History of Cartography*, Vol. II, Book Three: *Cartography in the Traditional African, American, Arctic, Australian and Pacific Societies*, ed. David Woodward and G. Malcolm Lewis (Chicago: University of Chicago Press, 1998): 448–92. His latest word on these matters is to be found in his *Sailing in the Wake of the*

Ancestors: Reviving Polynesian Voyaging (Honolulu: Bishop Museum, 2003). Thomas Gladwin's *East is a Big Bird: Navigation and Logic on Pulawal Atoll* (Cambridge, Mass.: Harvard University Press, 1970) and David Lewis's *We the Navigators: The Ancient Art of Landfalling in the Pacific* (Canberra: ANU Press, 1972) have inspired me over the years, as has Edward Dodd's study *Polynesian Seafaring* (New York: Dodd, Mead and Company, 1972). My own contribution to the debate about the Sea People's navigation coming out of research fifty years ago was 'The Geographical Knowledge of the Polynesians and the Nature of Inter-Island Contact', in Jack Golson (ed.), *Polynesian Navigation: A Symposium on Andrew Sharp's Theory of Accidental Voyages* (Wellington: A. H. and A. W. Reed, 1972): 102–58. Will Kyselka, *An Ocean in Mind* (Honolulu: University of Hawai'i Press, 1987) tells the story of the actualities of sailing a *va'a tauna*. My story of the first crossing of the Sea of Islands is completed in *Beach Crossings*, cited above.

9 Historical fiction and the future of academic history

David Harlan

The historian Peter Burke recently argued that 'Western historical thought' (by which he meant Western academic history) has now achieved worldwide hegemony, that its central beliefs and assumptions, its mental habits and institutional procedures have become the basis for 'a global community of professional historians with similar if not identical standards of practice'.[1] But as Jörn Rüsen pointed out in a preface to Burke's essay, the dominance of professional academic history has occurred at precisely the moment when popular history – historical novels, Hollywood films, museums, historical comics, online websites and so on – has returned 'with a vengeance'.[2] It is not professional history that will shape historical consciousness in the future but the yet-to-be-defined relationship between its own highly specialised representational strategies and the unconstrained profusion of popular histories that are being thrown up by various indigenous cultures around the world. Or to put it differently, the history of history through the end of the twentieth century may indeed be a narrative describing the rise of academic history to global hegemony, but it will now and necessarily become something very different: a history of the periodic accommodations that local academic communities have managed to forge with the various historical cultures that surround them. Dipesh Chakrabarty has described this coming process of conflict and accommodation as clearly as anyone:

> To the degree that the media and other institutions of popular culture today (such as films, television, internet, museums, and so on) challenge the hegemony of the university as the producer and disseminator of research and knowledge by setting up parallel institutions that, socially speaking, serve the same function with respect to the past, narratives about the past will have many different sources authorizing them. In the contestation of faculties that takes place in the cultural turmoil of mass-democracies . . . universities may very well seek different kinds of accommodation with popular culture in different social and national contexts. Out of that process may emerge a global culture of professional history that will not be identical all over the world.[3]

What might this newly emerging relationship between academic history and popular, mass-media history look like in the United States? It is hard to tell, of course, because academic historians are only beginning to acknowledge popular history's claims to legitimacy. But it is worth a try. I have elsewhere described the profession's response to the rise of historical documentaries; here I want to discuss its response to historical novels, and what their increasing popularity might mean for the future of the profession.

'. . . a new golden age of historical popularization'[4]

In the last twenty years we have witnessed a worldwide florescence of popular interest in the past, perhaps nowhere more so than in the United States. Indeed, Americans seem more deeply interested in history now than they have ever been. Most of the museums in this country were built in the last quarter-century and they are packed with visitors, day after day, week after week.[5] The Holocaust Museum in Washington, D.C., has become a major tourist destination, with long lines snaking around the block and people standing in line for hours. Hollywood used to make two or three big-budget historical dramas a decade; now they turn out three or four a year, many of them very good movies by any standard. Even historical documentaries are reaching a mass audience, as the remarkable career of Ken Burns so richly demonstrates. Indeed, a career like Burns' would have been inconceivable twenty years ago. And historical fiction has become immensely popular; you would have to go all the way back to the first half of the nineteenth century to find a time when Americans read historical novels as eagerly as they do now. *Cold Mountain* (1997), a dense, five-hundred-page historical fiction set in the backwoods of North Carolina in the autumn of 1864 was the most commercially successful novel in recent memory.[6] When it won the National Book Award in 1997 it edged out other historical novels by such well-known writers as Don DeLillo, Thomas Pynchon and Caleb Carr. And there were more the following spring, by Elmore Leonard, Jane Smiley, Gore Vidal, T. C. Boyle, Charles Johnson, Peter Carey, Russell Banks and others.[7] Six of the last thirteen National Book Awards and seven of the last thirteen National Book Critics Circle Awards have gone to historical novels. Even historical comics are enjoying a florescence. As the Princeton historian Sean Wilentz recently pointed out, we are living in the 'new golden age' of popular history.[8]

We academic historians have not known quite what to make of all this. We are delighted to see so many people drawn to the past, of course, but we tend to think that most of the films they are watching and the novels they are reading (to say nothing of the comics) are little more than historical melodramas, long on misty nostalgia and short on critical analysis.[9] The mainline journals review a handful of historical films now but historical novels very rarely show up on their radar screens. When they do, the reviewer almost never ventures beyond the most obvious questions of factual accuracy.

As James Goodman recently explained: 'Historians are not, by and large, interested in what most interests novelists: the sound of words, imagery, the shape of the story, voice. They approach fiction no differently than they approach history, discussing what the novelist got right and what he or she got wrong, the analytic ends but not the literary means, the content but not the form.'[10]

Six years ago, Sean Wilentz wrote a cover essay for the *New Republic* titled 'America Made Easy: Adams, McCulloch and the Decline of Popular History'.[11] But Wilentz was worried not about the decline of popular history so much as its re-emergence: historical amateurs flooding the country with Hollywood docu-dramas and comic books posing as history books. As Wilentz sees it, most of these new histories are little more than a sticky-sweet compound of cheap sentimentalism and soppy-eyed spectacle: appreciative rather than critical, descriptive rather than analytical, reassuring rather than demanding – and worst of all, intellectually debilitating. It is a conformist history that does little more than regurgitate and reconfirm the petty platitudes and self-serving mythologies of the dominant culture – in other words, it is a perversion of the real thing (i.e., of the academic history).[12] We may be witnessing 'a new golden age of historical popularization', but for Wilentz (and how many others?), that golden age has produced little more than a vacant lot heaped with rubbish.

All of which raises three obvious questions. First, is this new popular history really history? Some of the best historical films and novels may convey what the historian John Demos calls 'the inner feel, the specific textures of experience' of a particular period, but in what sense and by what criteria can they be considered real histories? Second, does popular history have some-thing to tell us that academic histories cannot, or for some reason do not? Do its practitioners have privileged access to some particular precinct of the past? In other words, what can we learn from a historical novel or a historical film that we cannot learn from a historical monograph? And third, what does the growing popularity and increasing sophistication of this new popular history mean for the future of academic history? Are historical monographs about to be replaced by films, novels and comics? Should academic historians take a collective sabbatical and enrol in the Iowa Writers Workshop? Probably not (most of us could not get in anyway) but novelists, film directors and comic-book artists are making increasingly sophisticated claims to intellectual legitimacy, claims that can no longer be dismissed with the sort of smug and sweeping contempt that Henry James and Sean Wilentz thought sufficient.[13] Brian Fay, the long-time editor of *History and Theory*, may be closer to the mark when he claims that such 'unconventional histories' have the capacity both to deepen and enrich academic history.[14] I have discussed the implica-tions of history-on-film's surging popularity elsewhere; here, I want to discuss historical novels, particularly what their growing number and increasing sophistication suggest about the future of academic history.[15]

Geörg Lukács, Alfred Kazin and the eclipse and re-emergence of literary realism

Neither academic historians nor literary critics paid much attention to historical fiction until 1937, when the Hungarian historian and literary critic Geörg Lukács published *The Historical Novel*.[16] Lukács argued that it was the French Revolution and its aftermath – the revolutionary wars and the subsequent rise of Napoleon – that created the material grounds for the historical novel, and that they did so by turning history into a mass phenomenon. For the first time, Lukács claimed, ordinary men and women came to think of their lives as historically conditioned, the products of an ongoing, yet-to-be-completed process. For the first time, they saw their history as a *human creation* rather than a natural process or the result of divine intervention. And if history was created by human beings it was (at least in theory) subject to human control. History became a power the people themselves might seize and direct.[17]

Lukács went on to argue that it was Sir Walter Scott, writing about the time of Napoleon's collapse and searching for some way to express the new historical consciousness he saw emerging in France, who invented the modern historical novel. Earlier writers had written novels about the past, of course, but they were not what Lukács thought of (and taught us to think of) as *historical* novels, mainly because their characters were not seen to be the products of a particular historical period – they did not derive their individuality from 'the historical peculiarity of their age'.[18] But beginning with *Waverley* (1814), Scott created protagonists – the Waverleys themselves, of course, but later the Mortons, the Osbaldistons and others – whose mental and emotional lives clearly *were* shaped by the age in which they lived. They took their task – and for Lukács this became the central work of the historical novel after Scott[19] – as coming to terms with the historically determined contradictions and conflicts that were threatening their societies. As Lukács explains:

> It is their task to bring the extremes whose struggle fills the novel, whose clash expresses artistically a great crisis in society, into contact with one another. Through the plot, at whose centre stands this hero, a neutral ground is sought and found upon which the extreme, opposing social forces can be brought into a human relationship with one another.[20]

But finding themselves at the historical crossroads, Scott's protagonists typically falter. Rather than trying to channel the tidal movements of history, they stand aside or turn away, baffled and confused; rather than acting with imagination and resolve, they waver and vacillate. Nevertheless, Lukács is undoubtedly right when he claims that 'the typically human terms in which great historical trends become tangible had never before been so superbly, straightforwardly and pregnantly portrayed. Never before had this kind of portrayal been consciously set at the centre of the representation of reality.'[21] *Waverley* broke new ground for the historical novel by expanding its focus to include not only the determining conditions of a historical era but how those conditions shaped the mental and emotional lives of the people who lived through them – and how they responded (or failed to respond). In *Waverley* and the works that followed it, underlying historical conditions are reflected in the intellectual and emotional make-up of the characters. We are brought to see, for example, that Fergus MacIvor – the young Highland chieftain, ardent Jacobite and central figure in *Waverley* – would have been a very different person had he been born sixty years earlier (or sixty years later, for that matter).[22] As Lukács puts it, readers 're-experience the social and human motives which led men to think, feel and act just as they did in historical reality'.[23] For Lukács, historical fiction is fiction that takes history itself as its subject.

Lukács' great contribution was to rescue the historical novel from the Romantics (mainly by showing us how to read Scott as a realist). But this was part of a larger project: the resurrection of literary realism itself.[24] It was Lukács who had led the opposition to literary modernism in the 1920s, attacking Joyce, Kafka and the other great modernists for (as he saw it) transforming the novel into a purely aesthetic experience, the literary equivalent of art for art's sake. For Lukács, realism was not just a literary style; it was 'the basis of all literature'. As late as 1970, just a year before his death, he was still insisting that 'the goal of art is to provide a picture of reality in which the contradiction between appearance and reality, the particular and the general, the immediate and the conceptual, etc., is so resolved that the two converge into a spontaneous integrity'.[25] In the historical novel as Lukács redefined it, this convergence manifests itself in the characters' struggles to understand themselves in time.

The Russian Communist Party responded to this with all the boorish and brutal belligerence for which it had already made itself infamous. *History and Class Consciousness* (1923), the book for which Lukács is most widely known, was savagely attacked by the Soviet literary establishment, and even by the Party itself. In 1930, seven years after it had first appeared, Lukács was forced to repudiate the book publicly and confess to various ideological crimes – an act which may have saved his life but which also sent *History and Class Consciousness* into what must have seemed at the time like permanent exile.[26] But in the 1960s a new generation of readers rediscovered Lukács, finding unexpected inspiration in his passionate response to Stalinism.[27]

The Historical Novel, Lukács' great manifesto of literary realism, appeared in 1937; five years later, Alfred Kazin published *On Native Grounds*, the most beautifully written and broadly influential defence of literary realism yet written by an American. Like Lukács before him, Kazin celebrated literature that positioned itself at the crossroads of history and character, literature that depicted not only the transformation of the old order but the wild enthusiasm and flint-like determination with which the disinherited grasped its possibilities and wove them into a new cultural inheritance. Kazin read American literature as if it were a single continuous narrative depicting the struggle of ordinary men and women to transcend the historical moments in which they found themselves and bring forth something new – in this case, the moral transformation of American society in the first third of the twentieth century.[28] It was Kazin, more than anyone else, who brought about the return of historical realism to American literary criticism.

But it was a short-lived return: eight years later, in 1950, Lionel Trilling published *The Liberal Imagination* and everything changed. Where Kazin had looked to immigrants and working people for inspiration, Trilling turned to the educated classes; where *On Native Grounds* was informed and inspired by Theodore Drieser and John Dos Passos, *The Liberal Imagination* took its counsel from the likes of Matthew Arnold, Irving Babbitt and Paul Elmer More; where *On Native Grounds* was 'a belligerent expression of hope', *The Liberal Imagination* found its wisdom in the tragic sensibility of *Civilization and its Discontents*.[29] Together with the literary formalisms that followed it (the new criticism, structuralism, poststructuralism, decon-struction), this deracinated, Anglo-oriented and culturally conservative criticism dominated literary thought in the United States for over thirty years, from the early 1950s through to the early 1980s. There were differences between Trilling and the later formalists, of course, but they all shared a reluctance to associate literary works with the historical conditions and cultural systems out of which they had emerged. During the sixties and seventies and into the early eighties literary formalism – humanist and other-wise – drove historicist criticism and literary realism to the very margins of American thought.

Like criticism, fiction turned in on itself in the 1970s, seemingly content to ponder (and subvert) not only the nature and conditions of its own epistemology but the very possibility of historical knowledge itself. Some of the most prominent writers in the country – John Barth, Donald Barthelme, Robert Coover, William Gaddis, William Gass and others – were turning out historical novels during these years but they were not much interested in the past. They *were* interested in the nature and validity of the claims they were making *about* the past.[30] This was historical fiction in its formalist phase – what the critic Linda Hutcheon so aptly termed 'historiographical meta-fiction': highly self-referential historical novels that simultaneously deployed and undermined not only their own sources but their own explanations of those sources.[31]

If the *monologue interieur* was the hallmark of the modernist novel, and if, as Frank Ankersmit has suggested, historical writing can be thought of as Western civilisation's *monologue interieur* about the past from which it originated, then the postmodern historical novel might be said to have constituted that *monologue interieur*'s Pyrrhonian moment, when the culture looked at its own creation, winced, drew back and strung together a series of literary exercises in order to demonstrate that we do not *need* a past, literary or otherwise.[32]

But by the late 1970s historiographical metafiction was coming under increasingly hostile criticism, from both left and right. In 'Postmodernism, or, The Cultural Logic of Late Capitalism' (1984) the Marxist critic Fredric Jameson claimed that historiographical metafiction had reduced 'real history' – by which he meant 'the traditional object, however it may be defined, of what used to be the historical novel' – to a 'depthless pastiche', a proliferation of meaningless but marketable images that have been absorbed into and become a functioning element of what Jameson called 'the cultural logic of late capitalism'.[33] Five years later, in 'Stalking the Billion-Footed Beast: A Literary Manifesto for the New Social Novel', the conservative novelist and literary critic Tom Wolfe lashed out at American writers for their epistemological navel-gazing, urging them to saddle up and 'head out into this wild, bizarre, unpredictable, Hog-stomping Baroque country of ours and reclaim it as literary property'.[34]

It was at this very moment – when the introverted and introspective (not to say self-absorbed and narcissistic) historiographical metafiction of the sixties and seventies, under attack from left and right and clearly exhausted – that the realist novel came roaring back. To go from the highly parodic, self-mocking and sometimes bitter fiction of Robert Coover, William Gaddis and Donald Barthelme to the intensely earnest novels of Russell Banks, Don DeLillo and Toni Morrison is to go from fiction that is overly formalist, wildly allegorical and bitingly satirical – fiction in which the past has become little more than a playful artifice – to fiction that is obsessed with the past, determined 'to figure out how [America] works and what went wrong and how to fix it'.[35] This is fiction deeply rooted in the world, anchored in it, tugging at it, pulling against it. Literary realists like Russell Banks don't worry about the deceptions of textuality or the mnemonic nature of recorded history; rather they worry, as Banks himself put it in 1993, that 'we are facing the death of our culture and the atomization of human beings in it. One of the quests of my own work is to identify the possibilities of resistance to that atomization.'[36] To be sure, the realist historical novels that emerged in the late seventies and early eighties still bear the cross of scepticism that they inherited from their postmodern predecessors (more on that below), but the best of them are also driven by a deep-rooted, almost visceral sense of outrage – and a hard-boiled, single-minded determination to 'destroy the world as it is'. 'It's not memory you need for telling this story,' the narrator of Banks' *Continental Drift* warns. 'It's clear-eyed pity and hot, old-time anger . . . and a proper middle-class American's shame for his nation's history.'[37] *Continental Drift* ends four hundred pages later with a benediction worthy of Father Mapple himself:

> Good cheer and mournfulness over lives other than our own, even wholly invented lives – no, especially wholly invented lives – deprive the world

as it is of some of the greed it needs to continue to be itself. Sabotage and subversion, then, are this book's objectives. Go, my book, and help destroy the world as it is.[38]

It is, as Banks insists, 'a very interesting and fruitful period in American fiction'.

> You've got at least two generations of writers – and who knows what the next generation coming along will do? – who are making realism viable again by absorbing into it new strands that come out of the Latin American tradition, out of García Márquez or Carpentier, out of the African-American tradition, and even out of a European tradition that DeLillo and others have brought into American fiction. It is a rich and wonderful time for American fiction writers.[39]

The metahistorical romance, the historical sublime and the voices of the dead

Over the last several years the literary critic Amy Elias has emerged as one of the most interesting and insightful guides to this new literary realism. In one big book and a steady stream of articles she has charted the evolution of historical fiction from the historiographical metafiction of the 1960s and 1970s to what she calls the 'postmodern metahistorical romance' of the 1980s and 1990s. Elias thinks this entire literature, from the early sixties through to the late nineties, has been driven by 'the cult of the historical sublime', that is by a fascination with our obstinate and utterly intractable need to know the past – not just a particular precinct or portion of the past but the past itself, History with a capital H, History as the guarantor of ultimate meaning and ontological order – coupled with an acute awareness that this kind of knowledge is, in fact, quite beyond the realm of the possible, that it inhabits some Lyotardian lacuna beyond all knowing and representation, 'a desired horizon that can never be reached but only approached'.[40] The 'postmodern metahistorical imagination' faces the chaos of the past – what Friedrich Schiller called the 'moral anarchy' of history and what Hayden White calls its 'terror' – yearning for form and meaning, sense and sequence, but knowing that such pleasing illusions have all the texture and substance of smoke. This is pretty much what White had in mind over forty years ago when he described 'the burden of history' – and perhaps what he had in mind just a couple of years ago when he wrote that academic history

> continues to fascinate us moderns but always fails finally to satisfy our curiosity about the objects of study to which it draws our attention. The dead can be studied scientifically but science cannot tell us what we desire to know about the dead. Or rather, those aspects of the past that can be studied scientifically do not yield the kinds of information or knowledge that drive us to the study of the past in the first place.[41]

The past for White is 'a place of fantasy we confront with anxiety'. Elias thinks it was the historicism of Michel Foucault and Jean-François Lyotard that provoked the recent resurgence of this cult of the sublime. This is not the sublime of the Romantics, of course: for Lyotard and Foucault, as for Freud before them, what is significant about the sublime is not its turbulent, chaotic or horrific nature but its unrepresentability – and the fear, even terror, that an unknowable, unrepresentable past seems to evoke.[42] This was the conceptual sensibility that underlay and informed Elias's analysis of 'post-modern metahistorical fiction' in *Sublime Desire: History and Post-1960s Fiction* (2001). As she later explained: 'The whole argument hinged on the idea that the postmodern, metahistorical imagination faces the chaos of history and yearns for something more, thus continually struggling to make sense of history but in its heart of hearts convinced that such surety is an impossible, rationalist dream.'[43] She revised and extended that argument, suggesting that our need for History with a capital H – History as an inexor-able need that pulls us down into the past as if by some deep-running tidal current – might be more usefully read not as a need for ultimate meaning but as the need to transcend ourselves, to reinvent ourselves by engaging the dead in a conversation about what we should value and how we should live. And here she drew (quite unexpectedly, at least for readers familiar with her earlier work) from Martin Heidegger's well. As Elias reads him, Heidegger had argued that the meaning of a dialogue differs from what either party intended. It is still subject to the slippage between signifier and signified, of course, but this is not the sort of endless play that once led us down Derrida's secret path to nothingness. And the reason for that is that Elias's Heidegger thinks language provides author and reader with a 'hint' about the meaning of their dialogue, a glimmering that emanates from the linguistic structure of the dialogue itself, a literally unspeakable intuition that lies 'at the borders of conscious perception'. With language thus serving as both medium and guide, the dialogue becomes 'the interaction of human con-sciousness with language to form a meaning, a discourse, that is more than the sum of its parts and to some extent beyond the control of its interlocutors *but emerging from their speech and interaction*'.[44]

The Heideggerian dialogue thus occupies a middle ground, somewhere between the direct, unmediated expression of authorial intention and the open-ended (not to say downward-curving) free-play of Derridean decon-struction.[45] Elias is thereby able to claim that it is in the shaping reciprocity of a dialogue with 'the other' – in this case, the dialogue between the reader and the voice(s) she finds in the text – that we can hope to break through our polar privacy and enlarge the range of our self-centred sympathies, to liberate ourselves from our habitual ways of responding and become the unfinished persons Nietzsche knew us to be.[46] As Elias puts it, 'We return to the past again and again seeking not closure but creative openness, dialogue with the voices we hear there; we return seeking the creative living utterance that we need for self-formation.'[47]

In other words – as any and every reader already knows – it is the voices we hear in historical novels that draw us to them, not the information we may acquire about the lives and times of their famous or not-so-famous protagonists. We read Styron's *Confessions of Nat Turner* to hear the voice of Nat Turner, Atwood's *Alias Grace* for the voice of Grace Marx, DeLillo's *Libra* for the voice of Lee Harvey Oswald, Louise Erdrich's *Tracks* for the voices of Nanapush and Pauline, Faulkner's *As I Lay Dying* for the voice of Darl Bundren. Voice is primary; everything else – life and times, setting and background, motive and reason, sense and sensibility – is driven by and follows from the voices we hear in the novels we read. DeLillo has been quite explicit about this:

> Once I found Oswald's voice – and by voice I mean not just the way he spoke to people but his inner structure, his consciousness, the sound of his thinking – I began to feel that I was nearly home free. Once you find the right rhythm for your sentences, you may be well on your way to finding the character himself. And once I came upon a kind of abrupt, broken rhythm both in dialogue and narration, I felt this was the prose counterpart to not only Oswald's inner life but Jack Ruby's as well. And other characters, too. So the prose itself began to suggest not the path the novel would take but the deepest motivation of the characters who originated this prose in a sense.[48]

The historian John Demos says he reads historical fiction for the 'inner feel' of a particular historical period but this too emanates from the voices of the characters. Voice is the writer's North Star that guides him through his labours and the promise that keeps the reader reading. It is the voices of his characters that the writer must find in the records and recreate in his book and those voices are the only historical truth to which he can ever lay claim. Russell Banks' *Cloudsplitter* is a fictional biography of Owen Brown, son of the abolitionist John Brown. As Banks recently explained, his novel

> would become his [Owen Brown's] chance to tell his story. And I would become, in a sense, merely his mouthpiece, so that, for a reader, Owen Brown's voice would be the voice of history in my work of fiction. His language, from my ear to the page, would be its language. And in the writing of my novel, that is all I would be true to . . . That is the voice of history . . . Thus, any reader who went there for anything other than that voice and the story it told would be either disappointed or seriously misled, and misled, might criticize my novel for failing to be true to the 'facts'.[49]

No one, of course – least of all Russell Banks – thinks it is the real Owen Brown who speaks to us through the pages of *Cloudsplitter*. Even in a historical novel as good as this, the past is not given to us as a possession, radiant with presence; even in *Cloudsplitter* we experience the past as loss (the text being, after all, the scene of the trace). In fact, it is in the experience of listening to the voices of the dead that we experience that loss in one of its most intense forms. Frank Ankersmit has described this as poignantly as anyone:

> Loss here is epistemological rather than metaphysical; it expresses a despair about our relationship to the world, to the past, about their unattainability *at the moment when the world and the past seemed nearer to us than ever before* . . . This feeling of despair is all the more intense, for although it may have been occasioned by a work of art, a poem, or by what has provoked a historical experience, all of these are at the same time experienced as a reminder of the unattainability of all of the world and the past. These objects then exemplify this sad feature of our condition humaine, and with the unfulfilled promise of this painting, of this poem, we weep the loss of all the world and of all that the world had promised us when it presented itself to us in its attire of sublimity.[50]

Not the voice of Owen Brown, then, but close enough to evoke both promise and loss, the hope of incipient transubstantiation and the downward curve of deferral. Close enough, in other words, to engage us heart and mind.

Novels are aesthetic objects, not unlike paintings or symphonies. Just as the meaning of a painting lies in the experience of viewing it, and a symphony in the experience of hearing it, so the meaning of a novel lies in the experience of *reading* it, the experience of hearing the voice of another resonate deeply within us (rather than in whatever 'facts' we may carry around from our reading). This experience brings us face-to-face with the echoing emptiness of our own dreams and schemes and routine rambling thoughts, the crimped and cramped circumference of our own imaginations, the cast-iron borders of our own slender sympathies. I take this to be what Elias was getting at when she wrote that what we seek in novels is not closure but creative openness, not a confirmation of who we are but an incitement to self-interrogation and an inducement to grow less sentimental about ourselves.

But why *historical* novels? What can we find in historical novels that we cannot find in novels set more or less in the present? What can we find in Styron's *The Confessions of Nat Turner* that we cannot find in one of his novels set in more contemporary times – say, *Set This House on Fire*? The answer lies, first, in the fact that Styron knows the colonial South as well as anyone; his representation of racial slavery in eighteenth-century Virginia rings true to everything we already know about that dark and dreary subject. And just as important, as we read our way into *The Confessions* . . . 'its innumerable, tiny pieces fit together; they even multiply within and upon themselves, like cells in a maturing body. They acquire a density, a dimensionality, that we could scarcely have imagined on setting out.'[51] So we suspend our disbelief and become willing readers, attentive to and eventually enthralled by what we eagerly accept as the voice of Nat Turner. Like the voice of Banks' Owen Brown, the voice of Styron's Nat Turner becomes 'the voice of history', carrying us through the novel from beginning to end.

Second, as we imagine ourselves slipping into Nat Turner's skin, inhabiting his interior world but simultaneously making him grow in our minds, we gradually find that some of his ways of thinking, some of his moods and feelings, have bled into our own, have become part of our own mental and emotional repertoire. All this is deeply problematic, of course, not least because any historical character worth spending time with will almost always resist our attempts to appropriate him. But over the years you simply find that a historical character with whom you have spent a great deal of time, a historical character whom you have come to know well – someone whose way of grasping life you have come to admire, someone whose sensibility you would like to cultivate – has stayed with you, has shaped and now become part of your own internal patterns of perception and reflection.

All of which is not unlike what Hayden White once called 'retrospective ancestral substitution':

> The historical past is plastic in a way that the genetic past is not. Men range over it and select from it models of comportment for structuring their movement into their future. They choose a set of ideal ancestors which they treat as genetic progenitors. This ideal ancestry may have no physical connection at all with the individuals doing the choosing. But their choice is made in such a way as to substitute this ideal ancestry for their actual.[52]

Lenin consolidated the Russian Revolution by 'imposing a completely new set of ancestral models on Russian society'; Luther sparked the Protestant Reformation by 'bestowing ancestry on a group which had lost it during the course of the Middle Ages'; the Roman Empire collapsed because 'men ceased to regard themselves as descendants of their Roman forebears and began to treat themselves as descendants of their Judaeo Christian predecessors'.[53] In each case it was the creative reinterpretation of the past that broke the back of the present: it was 'the constitution of a fictional cultural ancestry' that splintered the medieval Church, destroyed the Roman Empire, and consolidated the Russian Revolution.

It is only by thinking of ourselves as the latest in a long line of such predecessors that we can hope to see ourselves as historical actors, bound and defined by the responsibilities and expectations of a tradition that we ourselves have constructed and populated. Trying to figure out what all these chosen predecessors may or may not have in common, trying to perceive affinities and attractions between them, trying to arrange them in chronological order so we can think of ourselves as the latest in a long line of such thinkers – this is how history comes into its own as a mode of moral reflection, a way of curing up life into meaning. That historical novels are better tools for doing this than historical monographs is probably obvious. What that fact means for the *future* of academic history may not be.

From practitioners to critics: the coming crisis of academic history

In *Possessed by the Past: The Heritage Crusade and the Spoils of History* and several other books, the historian David Lowenthal has argued that while real history reconstructs the past as a foreign country, a place where they do things differently, popular history (what he calls 'heritage') reconstructs the past as a theatre of the present, a costume-drama filled with people you already know, people you can relate to, people like Bob and Jane next door. Lowenthal thinks 'Heritage' is the abyss into which 'history' is disappearing. He thinks we have become a hopelessly retro-chic culture, our newfound interest in the past no more than a fascination with collectables. What remains of the historical imagination is utterly awash in the waste products of the mass media.[54]

Possessed by the Past was a jeremiad *cri du coeur* sent up in the late 1990s to lament what Lowenthal could see only as an impending millennial disaster. But Lowenthal is hardly the only one weeping in his beard. As we have seen, Sean Wilentz, the Princeton historian, also thinks popular history has fallen into the gravitational pull of what he calls 'the universe of entertainment'.[55] It has become a fascinating but essentially passive spectacle, a neon epic of mind-numbing nostalgia, a compound of melancholy and yearning that refuses to challenge its viewers or force them to confront the pleasing platitudes of American culture, or contemplate its darker possibilities. It is a seductive and captivating history that opens the heart but castrates the intellect.[56] Dan Carter is the William Rand Kenan University Professor at Emory University in Atlanta, Georgia. He has decided to swear off popular history altogether. In a dismissive and condescending review of John Frankenheimer's taut and fascinating film, *George Wallace: Settin' the Woods on Fire*, he charged that historical documentaries are little more than 'soap opera substitutes for real engagement with the past'. They have become enormously popular, of course, and enormously seductive, with their huge audiences and equally huge royalties. But like Nancy Reagan, Carter has steeled himself against temptation: 'When asked to become a part of such productions, the greatest contribution [academic] historians can make is to take the advice of a former First Lady: "Just say No". I've taken the pledge.'[57]

If we follow the Lowenthals and Wilentzes and Carters of the world we will entomb ourselves in a pyramid of irrelevance. After all, it is academic historians who are in danger of becoming a priestly caste, not popular historians. We like to think of ourselves as 'practitioners', members of a first-order discipline engaged in the professional production of original and reliable knowledge about the past (as opposed to those pinched and timid souls in the English department who content themselves with commenting on other people's work).[58] We assume that our primary responsibility is to convey this professionally certified knowledge to our undergraduates, and the techniques for producing it to our graduate students. In other words, we teach them how to read and write academic history. But a new history is being produced, outside the academy, by novelists, memoirists, autobiographers and film-makers. If we intend to meet the challenge of this new history, if we want our students to develop historical imaginations that are morally sustaining and politically relevant, we must teach them to be thoughtful, reflective and resourceful readers of *all* the forms in which their society represents the past to itself. Academic history is one of those forms, of course, but it is only one, and it is neither the most interesting nor the most important.

What we need now is a map that would delineate the various forms of historical representation which constitute the historian's newly enlarged territory. Such a map would be enormously helpful, first and most obviously, in identifying the major forms of historical representation and describing the particular realm over which each of them presides. For example, historical novelists typically recreate a portion of the past by (among other things) recovering the details of everyday life – details that are often so minute, so finely grained, that academic historians usually overlook them. Here is Margaret Atwood describing the kinds of historical material she needed in order to recreate the lost world of Grace Marks, one of the most notorious and enigmatic women of nineteenth-century Canada:

> [Academic] history is frequently reluctant about the now-obscure details of daily life . . . Thus I found myself wrestling not only with who said what about Grace Marks but also with how to clean a chamber pot, what footgear would have been worn in winter, the origins of quilt pattern names, and how to store parsnips.[59]

The historical novelist creates a historical world so fully realised that her readers find themselves actually living in it, usually for days at a time. To do that she puts down layer upon layer of tiny, now almost totally obscure details: how bedpans were emptied, how turnips were stored, how bodies were cleaned. And since academic history is usually silent about such minutiae, the historical novelist has to gather the facts herself. So when she goes to the archives she finds herself – as Margaret Atwood did – working in a historical realm all her own. The same goes for the cinematic historian. When Ken Burns begins working on a new film he searches the archives for images. Images are for the creator of historical documentaries what details are for the writer of historical novels. All of which is simply to say that each form of historical representation has its own particular region of the past, its own realm or province – and its own criteria for determining what counts as a fact, its own research procedures and its own criteria of evaluation.

So our map – let us call it 'The Territory of the Historian' – should, first of all, identify these realms or provinces and describe the powers, the limitations and the responsibilities peculiar to each of them. Second, it should describe the codes and conventions that govern representation and evaluation in each realm. This would have the great advantage of demonstrating what we already know but constantly forget: that the criteria for evaluating any representation of the past must be both media-specific and genre-specific. We simply do not have a set of generic meta-criteria that can be applied to any and every form of historical representation. The criteria that we have developed for evaluating written history, for example, just do not apply to history-on-film, at least not without a lot of compromises and adjustments. That is not to say that anything goes in that particular realm but rather that like every other realm, it has its own areas of expertise, its own methods of representation and its own criteria for determining what counts as good history and what does not – its own ways of explaining, for example, why Oliver Stone's *Nixon* is good history and Alan Parker's *Mississippi Burning* is not.

Third, how should we understand the relationships *between* the culture's various modes of historical representation? How, for example, should we understand the different forms of meaning and understanding generated by Edward Zwick's film *Glory* (1989) and Peter Burchard's book, *One Gallant Rush: Robert Gould Shaw and His Brave Black Regiment*?[60] Both offer interesting, informative and even insightful accounts of the Fifty-fourth Massachusetts Regiment and of the nature and persistence of racial prejudice during and after the Civil War. But they have very different things to tell us about their common subject and they tell them in very different ways. What can we learn from the one that we cannot learn from the other? What can we learn from films that we cannot learn from historical novels and monographs? And vice versa? And how are we to understand the relationship between them? Historical novels and histories-on-film are not about to replace historical monographs. Nor is film merely a supplement to written history. Film rather stands *adjacent* to written history, at a location whose co-ordinates are yet to be specified.[61] Hence the third thing we would like our map to do: delineate and describe the relationships between the primary modes of historical representation.

And with this we finally arrive at the heart of the matter: the nature of the historical imagination in a media-saturated culture that, mercury-like, has been spilled into drops that cannot be gathered. If our students are to become thoughtful and resourceful readers of the past in a culture as dispersed and eclectic as this one, they will have to become adept at finding their way between competing but equally valid truth claims made in distinct and often divergent modes of historical representation. They will have to become *bricoleurs*, sophisticated multimedia rag-pickers, quick, shrewd and witty readers of *all* the forms in which their culture represents the past, shuttling back and forth, to and fro, cutting and pasting, weaving and reweaving interpretive webs of their own devising. For only thus can they hope to develop a historical imagination that is morally coherent and politically effective – a historical imagination that can help them say, 'This is how we mean to live but do not yet live; this is what we mean to value but do not yet value.'[62]

Notes

1 Peter Burke, 'Western Historical Thinking in a Global Perspective – 10 Theses', in Jörn Rüsen (ed.), *Western Historical Thinking: An Intercultural Debate* (New York and Oxford: Berghahn Books, 2002): 17. *Western Historical Thinking* includes responses to Burke's thesis by historians and philosophers of history from around the world.

2 Rüsen, 'Preface to the Series', in *Western Historical Thinking*, p. vii. But see also p. xii, where Rüsen acknowledges the emergence of 'other cultural, but non-academic, practices of "sense formation" as being equally important forms of human orientation and self-understanding (in their general function not much different from the efforts of academic thought itself)'.

3 Dipesh Chakrabarty, 'A Global and Multicultural "Discipline of History"?', *History and Theory* 45 (February 2006): 109.

4 Sean Wilentz, 'America Made Easy: McCulloch, Adams, and the Decline of Popular History', *New Republic*, 225:1 (2 July 2001): 36.

5 As the historian Neil Harris as quoted in 'A Glance at the Summer Issue of *Daedalus*: Crossroads for American Museums', *Chronicle of Higher Education: Magazine and Journal Reader* (13 September 1999). No volume number; available online at http://chronicle.com/daily/99/09/990913olj.htm.

6 *Cold Mountain* sold over 1.5 million copies in its first nine months and went through twenty-five printings in its first year (Bruce Cook, 'Peeps Into The Past', *Washington Post*, 18 July 1999, p. X4).

7 The same thing is happening in Great Britain – with the same surprising intensity. See Richard Evans, 'How History Became Popular Again', *New Statesman*, 5 March 2001.

8 Wilentz, 'America Made Easy'.

9 See, for example, the selections in Robert Brent Toplin (ed.), *Ken Burns's Civil War: The Historians Respond* (New York: Oxford University Press, 1996).

10 James Goodman, review of Mark C. Carnes (ed.), *Novel History: Historians and Novelists Confront America's Past (and Each Other)* (New York: Simon and Schuster, 2001), in *American Historical Review* 107:2 (April 2002): 502.

11 Wilentz, 'America Made Easy'.

12 Even more remarkable than Wilentz's condescending attitude towards popular history is the gendered nature of the oppositions he employs to describe it. Popular history is 'passive', 'nostalgic', 'sentimentally descriptive', 'fascinating but undemanding', 'passive nostalgic spectacle', and so on. Popular historians 'simplify', 'sensationalize' and basically 'gossip about the past'. Their books offer 'forms of reassurance' and 'sentimental appreciation rather than critical analysis'. Academic history, on the other hand, is distinguished by its 'love of historical facts'. It is 'meant to rattle its readers' by 'the advancing of strong, even heretical personal judgments' and 'a remorseless reexamination of the nation's past'. It is a 'historiography of national self-reckoning' rather than self-congratulations.

13 Or perhaps, as Hayden White suggests, we should take to writing 'modernist anti-narratives', at least for what he calls 'the modernist event' (he is thinking

of those uniquely violent and literally unrepresentable events that have come to characterise the twentieth century – the Holocaust in particular). 'What I am suggesting is that the stylistic innovation of modernism . . . may provide better instruments for representing "modernist" events . . . than the storytelling techniques traditionally utilized by historians for representation' (White, 'The Modernist Event', in V. Sobchack (ed.), *The Persistence of History: Cinema, Television and the Modern Event* (New York: Routledge, 1996): 17–38; the quoted passage appears on p. 32. 'The Modernist Event' is also available in White, *Figural Realism: Studies in the Mimesis Effect* (Baltimore: Johns Hopkins University Press, 1999).) For three interesting commentaries on White's notion of 'the modernist event' – and more generally on his belief in the continuing relevance of modernist literature and contemporary literary theory (by which he tends to mean the tropology of neoclassical rhetoricians) for the writing of history – see: Richard T. Vann, 'The Reception of Hayden White', *History and Theory* 37:2 (May 1998): 143–62; F. R. Ankersmit, 'Hayden White's Appeal to Historians', *History and Theory* 37:2 (May 1998): 182–94; and Noël Carroll, 'Tropology and Narration', *History and Theory* 39:3 (October 2000): 396–405, particularly 397 and 402. Joseph Mali suggests something similar in *Mythistory: The Making of a Modern Historiography* (Chicago: University of Chicago Press, 2003): 'I define modernism as a cultural movement that consists in the "recognition of myth", and I define modern historiography in those terms as well. Recall the famous words of Claude Lévi-Strauss – that his aim was "to show not how men think in myths, but how myths operate in men's minds [*les mythes se pensent dans les hommes*] without their being aware of the fact . . . This is the common interpretation of Stephen Dedalus's famous cry that history is the nightmare from which he is trying to awake' (pp. 18, 12). See pp. 1–35 in particular for a discussion of the relationship between literary modernism and contemporary historiography. For two intriguing experiments that explore what modernism as a literary form (especially its tendency to collapse the traditional subject/object dichotomy) might mean for historical writing, see Simon Schama's *Dead Certainties* (New York: Knopf, 1991) and his later, more interesting *Landscape and Memory* (New York: Knopf/Random House, 1995).

14 In his introduction to a special issue of *History and Theory* devoted to 'unconventional' histories, Brian Fay wrote that the best of them 'can reveal new conceptual resources and novel forms of representation that might be useful in deepening the possibilities of history as a discipline' (Fay, 'Unconventional History', *History and Theory* 41 (December 2002): 2–3).

15 David Harlan, 'Ken Burns and the Coming Crisis of Academic History', *Rethinking History* 7:2 (2003): 169–92.

16 There is a certain irony here, for Lukács denied the identity of the historical novel, arguing that *all* literature is historical, much like the New Historicism of the 1980s. For an interesting discussion, see David Cowart, *History and the Contemporary Novel* (Carbondale: Southern Illinois University Press, 1989): 4–5.

17 Geörg Lukács, *The Historical Novel* (Boston: Beacon Press, 1963): 23–4.

18 Ibid., p. 19; see also p. 31.

19 Ibid., p. 34.

20 Ibid., p. 36.

21 Ibid., p. 34.

22 Harry E. Shaw, 'Is There a Problem with Historical Fiction (or with Scott's Redgauntlet)?', *Rethinking History* 9:2–3 (June 2005): 176.

23 Lukács, *The Historical Novel*, p. 42.

24 Lukács' own term was 'critical realism', which he coined in order to distinguish his aesthetics from the Soviets' 'socialist realism'.

25 Lukács in *Writer and Critic* (1970), from Terry Lovell, *Pictures of Reality: aesthetics, politics and pleasure* (London: British Film Institute, 1980): 35.

26 Lukács has often been criticised for 'refusing the way of the martyr' but his later writings – most obviously *Existentialisme ou Marxisme*, his 1948 polemic against Sartre – suggests an enduring commitment to Marxism.

27 It was also about this time – the late 1960s – that Lukács discovered Alexander Solzhenitsyn. Solzhenitsyn was a bred-in-the-bone conservative, of course; he thought the only hope lay in abandoning Western materialism and returning to the virtues of Holy Russia. But Solzhenitsyn's early novels contained just the sort of historical realism for which Lukács had been searching. This was not as surprising as it might seem. After all, Solzhenitsyn had always been a politically committed writer; his novels had always depicted ordinary people wrestling with the sorts of social conflict that typically emerge during periods of historical transition. Moreover, had Lukács lived only a few more years – he died in 1971 – he would have been absolutely delighted with the combative humanism of Solzhenitsyn's later work, especially *The Gulag Archipelago* (1974).

28 Kazin was also a man of his times; indeed, he was perhaps the last major American critic to have been shaped by the struggles of the Depression and the Second World War. Andrew Delbanco recently offered a fitting anecdote: his own copy of *On Native Grounds* is 'an English edition printed in accordance with wartime production standards on cheap paper and bound in boards not much more rigid than matchbook covers. It was bought by my mother in a London bookstall in 1943, the year the German army was stopped at Stalingrad and expelled from Africa by Montgomery and Patton.' Kazin was also, perhaps, the last major American literary critic who could plausibly write that Sherwood Anderson and Carl Sandburg, those stout-hearted voices from the American heartland, had 'brought home the Middle West to me as the valley of democracy and the fountainhead of hope' (Delbanco, 'On Alfred Kazin (1915–1998)', *New York Review of Books* 45:12 (16 July 1998): 23.

29 The website www.IntellectualConservative.com lists Trilling's *Liberal Imagination* as number 14 on its list of the 'Top 25 Philosophical and Ideological Conservative Books' of all time, even going so far as to suggest that 'in disposition, if not political convictions, Trilling was the first Neoconservative'.

30 Though this could hardly have come as a surprise, since literary theorists and philosophers of history were all insisting that history is simply another literary form, that instead of discovering the past, historians constitute it by constructing their own systems of signification. But a word of caution is probably in order here, for it is all too easy to exaggerate the extent of this apparent 'retreat from realism'. For a more thoughtful and balanced consideration, see Robert Towers, 'The Flap over Tom Wolfe: How Real is the Retreat from Realism?', *New York Times Book Review*, 28 January 1990: 15–16.

31 'In the words of *Waterland*'s history teacher, the past is "a thing which cannot be eradicated, which accumulates and impinges". What postmodern discourses – fictive and historiographic – ask is: how do we know and come to terms with such a complex thing' (Linda Hutcheon, *A Poetics of Postmodernism: History, Theory, Fiction* (New York: Routledge, 1988): 123).

32 It was the Pyrrhonians who developed the tropes as a series of skeptical reasonings designed to lead one, almost inexorably, to an *epochē*, or suspension of belief on matters not immediately evident to the senses. But it was Montaigne – that most sceptical of believers – who best described the downward curve of all such thinking:

> To judge the appearances that we receive of objects, we would need a judi-catory instrument; to verify this instrument, we need a demonstration; to

verify the demonstration, an instrument: there we are in a circle. Since the senses cannot decide our dispute, being themselves full of uncertainty, it must be reason that does so. No reason can be established without another reason: there we go retreating back to infinity.

(Montaigne, 'Apology for Raimond Sebond', in *Complete Works of Montaigne: Essays, Travel Journal, Letters,* trans. D. Frame (Stanford: Stanford University Press, 1967): 454)

On history as 'the *monologue interieur* of contemporary Western civilization', see F. R. Ankersmit, 'Hayden White's Appeal to Historians', *History and Theory* 37:2 (May 1998): 190:

> For is not the historical discipline, when considered as a whole, the *monologue interieur* of contemporary Western civilization about a past from which it originated? Is our civilization not 'writing itself' by means of historical writing in the way Barthes meant; is historical culture not how our civilization, so to speak, writes itself in the style of the middle voice; are history and historical writing not the place where our civilization becomes conscious of itself and of its own nature and, as Jörn Rüsen has emphasized, where our civilization achieves and becomes aware of its identity? . . . This is, needless to say, one of the main insights developed in Rüsen's trilogy. See, for example, J. Rüsen, *Vernunft* (Gottingen, 1983): 57, where Rüsen writes 'das historische Erzahlen ist ein Medium der menschlichen Identitatsbildung' ['human individuals conceive of their identity in terms of the historical narratives that they tell themselves about their past'].

33 Fredric Jameson, *The Jameson Reader,* ed. Michael Hardt and Kathi Weeks (Oxford: Blackwell, 2000): 205. (An earlier version, bearing the same title, was published in 1984.) See 'Postmodernism, or, The Cultural Logic of Late Capitalism', in ibid., pp. 188–232. See especially the section of that essay titled 'The Postmodern and the Past', beginning on p. 201.
34 Tom Wolfe, 'Stalking the Billion-Footed Beast: A Literary Manifesto for the New Social Novel', *Harper's,* November 1989, p. 46. See also the critical responses from Philip Roth, Walker Percy and others in ibid., February 1990. The most trenchant criticism of Wolfe's essay is probably Towers, 'The Flap over Tom Wolfe'.
35 Amy Elias, 'Metahistorical Romance, the Historical Sublime, and Dialogic History', *Rethinking History* 9: 2 and 3 (June–September 2005): 165.
36 Russell Banks as quoted in Don Lee, 'About Russell Banks: A Profile', *Ploughshares* (Winter 1993–4). Available at: <http://www.pshares.org/issues/article.cfm?prmArticleid=3624>.
37 Russell Banks, *Continental Drift* (New York: HarperCollins, 1985): 1–2.
38 Ibid., p. 410.
39 Russell Banks, 'Reinventing Realism: An Interview with Russell Banks', *Michigan Quarterly Review* 39:4 (Fall 2000): 740.
40 Amy Elias, *Sublime Desire: history and post-1960s fiction* (Baltimore: Johns Hopkins University Press, 2001): xviii, 26. For an interesting and comprehensive discussion of the historical sublime, see Frank Ankersmit, *Sublime Historical Experience* (Stanford: Stanford University Press, 2005). Ankersmit wants to shift the focus of contemporary philosophy of history from issues of truth and representation to those of experience, specifically 'the sublimity of historical experience'. In *Sublime Historical Experience* he explains why 'historical experience always essentially is . . . an experience of loss'. He thinks this loss originates in the slippage between language and reality; more important, he thinks our experience of loss *is* our experience of the historical:

The past does not exist prior to this sublime indeterminacy [i.e., the slippage between language and the reality it purports to describe], the past does not *cause* this indeterminacy – the past *is* this indeterminacy, the past *constitutes* itself in this indeterminacy; temporal distance is therefore a merely accidental and additional property of what we experience as a past . . . Loss here is epistemological rather than metaphysical; it expresses a despair about our relationship to the world, to the past, about their unattainability at the moment when the world and the past seemed nearer to us than ever before, and not a despair about our loss of part of the world or of the past that formerly used to be our securest possession. Indeed, sublimity is an epistemological rather than a metaphysical notion. And this feeling of despair is all the more intense, for although it may have been occasioned by a work of art, a poem, or by what has provoked a historical experience, all of these are at the same time experienced as a reminder of the unattainability of all of the world and the past. These objects then *exemplify* this sad feature of our *condition humaine*, and with the unfulfilled promise of this painting, of this poen, we weep the loss of all the world and of all that the world had promised us when it presented itself to us in its attire of sublimity.

(Ibid., pp. 176–8)

See also Ankersmit, 'The Sublime Dissociation of the Past: Or How to Be(come) What One Is No Longer', *History and Theory* 40:3 (October 2001): 295–323 (reprinted with some emendations as 'Sublime Historical Experience', in Ankersmit, *Sublime Historical Experience*, pp. 317–68); and Ankersmit, 'Invitation to Historians', *Rethinking History* 7:3 (Winter 2003): 412–34, especially Section 7, 'Experience', pp. 427–32. For an earlier statement of the historical sublime as 'particular to historical writing and rooted in its cognitive function', as deriving 'directly from the cognitive enterprise which defines historiography, that is to say, from historians' engagement with an object outside their texts', see Ann Rigney, 'The Untenanted Places of the Past: Thomas Carlyle and the Varieties of Historical Ignorance', *History and Theory* 35:3 (October 1996): 338–57. The quoted passages appear on p. 338 and pp. 352–3, respectively.

41 Hayden White, 'The Public Relevance of Historical Studies: A Reply to Dirk Moses' *History and Theory* 44:3 (October 2005): 333. In 'The Politics of Historical Interpretation: Discipline and De-Sublimation', *Critical Inquiry*, 9:1 (1982) (see extract source below) White went so far as to argue that at bottom it is their response to the historical sublime that differentiates eschatological, ideological and progressive politics:

It seems to me that the kind of politics that is based on a vision of a perfected society can compel devotion to it only by virtue of the contrast it offers to a past that is understood in the way that Schiller conceived it, that is, as a 'spectacle' or 'confusion', and 'uncertainty'. Surely this is the appeal of those eschatological religions that envision a 'rule of the saints' . . . Modern ideologies seem to me to differ crucially from eschatological religious myths in that they impute a meaning to history that renders its manifest confusion comprehensible to either reason, understanding, or aesthetic sensibility. To the extent that they succeed in doing so, these ideologies deprive history of the kind of meaninglessness that alone can goad living human beings to make their lives different for themselves and their children, which is to say, to endow their lives with a meaning for which they alone are fully responsible.

(White, *The Content of the Form: Narrative Discourse and Historical Representation* (Baltimore: Johns Hopkins University Press, 1987): 72. Originally published in *Critical Inquiry* 9:1 (1982))

42 Though see Ankersmit, who describes his *Sublime Historical Experience* as 'a rehabilitation of the Romanticist's world of moods and feelings as constitutive of how we relate to the past. How we *feel* about the past is no less important than what we *know* about it – and probably even more so. "Sentir, c'establish penser", as Rousseau like to say, and this is where I fully agree with him. So I invite the reader of this book to enter the dark and sometimes even sinister Romantic world of the profoundest and quasi-existentialist layers in our relationship to the past' (Ankersmit, *Sublime Historical Experience*, p. 10). But see also the discussion of 'Experience, Truth and Language' on pp. 222–39: 'This may, again, be interpreted as a plea in favor of a Romanticist conception of our relationship to the past – a conception seeing in moods, feelings, and the experience of the past the highest stage of historical consciousness. This is, finally, where and why it surpasses the Enlightened rationalism of contemporary "Theory", whose arid abstractions have so much dominated historical thought in the last decades; this is where it can, at least, be seen as a correction of all the hermeneuticist, (post-)structuralist, tropological, or narrativist theories of history and in terms of which we used to conceive of the past and of what it must mean to us' (pp. 231–2).

43 Elias, 'Metahistorical Romance', p. 165.

44 Ibid., my emphasis, p. 167.

45 See the second half of ibid. The Heideggerian 'middle ground' as she describes it should not be confused with Roland Barthes's 'middle voice', which he introduced in his well-known essay, 'To Write: An Intransitive Verb' (included, with a discussion, in *The Structuralist Controversy: The Languages of Criticism and the Science of Man*, ed. R. Macksey and F. Donato (Baltimore: Johns Hopkins University Press, 1972): 134–56). Hayden White later claimed that the middle voice may be the only mode of representation appropriate for such extreme events as the Holocaust. See White, 'Historical Employment and the Story of the Truth', in Saul Friedlander (ed.), *Probing the Limits of Representation: Nazism and the 'Final Solution'* (Cambridge, Mass.: Harvard University Press, 1992): 37–53, and White, 'Writing in the Middle Voice', *Stanford Literary Review* 9:2 (Fall 1992): 179–87. White's appropriation of the middle voice has encountered a mixed reception from historians. Dominick LaCapra has been particularly critical. In *Writing History, Writing Trauma* he refers to 'the particularly difficult and knotty twist in White's argument represented by his appeal to the middle voice, which he takes as the appropriate way to write trauma'. See LaCapra, *Writing History, Writing Trauma* (Baltimore: Johns Hopkins University Press, 2001): 8–18 for his criticisms of White's position generally and pp.19ff. for his criticism of White's appropriation of the middle voice as a solution to the problem of representing the Holocaust. With regard to the latter, LaCapra claims that the middle voice tends to blur the distinction between perpetrator and victim (though he has also suggested that 'it is most warranted and perhaps even necessary in treating empathically the most equivocal and internally divided dimensions of history'. See LaCapra, 'Tropisms of Intellectual History', *Rethinking History* 8:4 (December 2004): 499–530. More generally, he criticises White, Ankersmit and others for promoting what he sees as 'a radically constructivist identification of history with fictionalisation, rhetoric, poetics, performativity, or even self-referential discourse'. LaCapra charges that this 'radical constructivism . . . presents the human being as "endowing" the past or the other with meaning and value. Radical constructivism might be interpreted as a form of secular creationism in which the human being becomes an ultimate foundation and the displaced repository of quasi-divine powers' (ibid., p. 8 and p. 57 n. 16, and see p. 197, where he dismisses 'radical constructivism' as 'the negative mirror image' of a traditional positivist or documentary approach). Martin Jay, on the other hand, criticises White's employment of the middle voice because it 'undercuts

what is most powerful in his celebrated critique of naïve historical realism', i.e., he celebrates it for precisely the strong textual formalism to which LaCapra objects. See Martin Jay, 'Of Plots, Witnesses and Judgments', in Saul Friedlander (editor), *Probing the Limits of Representation: Nazism and the 'final solution'* (Cambridge, MA: Harvard University Press, 1992): 97–107, but especially 97. For a more nuanced critique of White and the middle voice from a position he himself elsewhere describes as 'empiricist', see F. R. Ankersmit, 'White's Appeal to Historians', *History and Theory* 37:2 (May 1998): 182–93, but especially 189–92.

46 White, of course, had already been here. Under the influence of an early (and persistent) existential humanism he had come to think that the past was most significant for what it did not yet contain, almost as if it were emptiness itself that stokes the fires of the historical imagination. As he put it in 'The Politics of Historical Interpretation: Discipline and De-Sublimation' (p. 72), history presents us with 'the kind of meaninglessness that alone can goad living human beings to make their lives different for themselves and their children, which is to say, to endow their lives with a meaning for which they alone are fully responsible'. See also pp. 68–70, 72–4 and 80.

47 Elias, 'Metahistorical Romance', p. 169.

48 DeLillo as quoted in *Introducing Don DeLillo* (Durham, NC: Duke University Press, 1991): 55.

49 Russell Banks as quoted in Mark C. Carnes (ed.), *Novel History: Historians and Novelists Confront America's Past and Each Other* (New York: Simon and Schuster, 2001): 75; my emphases.

50 Ankersmit, *Sublime Historical Experience* p. 178; my emphasis.

51 The historian John Demos writing in a slightly different context. See Demos, 'Notes from, and about, the History/Fiction Borderland', *Rethinking History* 9:2 and 3 (June–September, 2005): 331.

52 Hayden White, 'What is an Historical System?' in Allen Breck and Wolfgang Yourgrau (eds), *Biology, History and Natural Philosophy* (New York: Plenum Press, 1972): 239. White made this point again, ten years later, in 'Getting Out of History: Jameson's Redemption of Narrative', *Diacritics* 12 (Fall 1982): 2–13. And he made it again twenty years after *that* when he argued that 'Western historical thought' emerged as 'a consequence of a retrospective choice by cultural groups or their representatives to treat themselves as descendants and heirs of earlier ones and to tailor their discourses to the standards and values of those old Greeks and Romans for specific ideological purposes'. See Hayden White, 'The Westernization of World History', in Rüsen (ed.), *Western Historical Thinking*, p. 114.

53 White, 'What is an Historical System?', pp. 238–9, emphasis in original.

54 David Lowenthal, *Possessed by the Past: The Heritage Crusade and the Spoils of History* (New York: Free Press, 1996).

55 Wilentz, 'America Made Easy'.

56 See n. 12 above and Wilentz, 'America Made Easy', *passim*.

57 Dan Carter, 'Fact, Fiction, and Film: Frankenheimer's George Wallace', American Historical Association, *Perspectives* (January 1998). Available at: <http://www.theaha.org/Perspectives/issues/1998/9801/9801FIL.CFM>. Carter's most recent books are *The Politics of Rage: George Wallace, the Origins of the New Conservatism and the Transformation of American Politics* (New York: Simon and Schuster, 1995) and *From George Wallace to Newt Gingrich: The Role of Race in the Conservative Revolution, 1963–1994* (Baton Rouge: Louisiana State University Press, 1996).

58 I have borrowed the distinction between 'first-order disciplines' and 'second-order disciplines' from Mortimor J. Adler, 'Philosophy's Past' in his *The Four*

Dimensions of Philosophy (New York: Macmillan, 1993). Adler writes that 'first-order disciplines' employ a common methodology to produce empirical knowledge about a specifically defined subject matter. 'Second-order disciplines' concern themselves with the critical examination of concepts, methods and assumptions used by first-order disciplines. That is not to say that they presume to resolve disputes within first-order disciplines; they are more like midwives. (The analogy is Wittgenstein's.)

59 Margaret Atwood, 'In Search of *Alias Grace*: On Writing Canadian Historical Fiction', *American Historical Review* 103:5 (December 1998): 1514.

60 New York: St Martin's, 1965.

61 I am indebted to Robert Rosenstone for this formulation, as for so many other insights. See Rosenstone's important statement, 'The Historical Film as Real History', *Filmhistoria* 1:1 (1995): especially 21–2. For a popular expression of the idea that film and video are replacing the written text, see Sven Birkerts, *The Gutenberg Elegies: The Fate of Reading in an Electronic Age* (New York: Fawcett, 1995). For a deeper, more interesting (and enthusiastic) analysis by a partisan of what he interprets as the 'video revolution', see Mitchell Stevens, *The Rise of the Image, the Fall of the Word* (New York: Oxford University Press, 1998). I read Rosenstone as a much-needed corrective to Birkerts' all-too-fashionable despair and Mitchell's all-too-easy optimism.

62 I borrowed this phrase from Michael Walzer, *The Company of Critics: Social Criticism and Political Commitment in the Twentieth Century* (New York: Basic Books, 1988): 230.

10 Alternate worlds and invented communities

History and historical consciousness in the age of interactive media

Wulf Kansteiner

According to conventional academic wisdom, the Western utopian tradition began in 1516 with the publication of Thomas More's *Utopia*. Since that point, utopian writings in the West have followed a curiously sensible path. Despite occasional flights of fancy, literary explorations of alternate worlds have generally stayed within the realm of the possible. The descriptions of the good life in the rational, egalitarian societies anticipated by More, Wells and Marx as well as the dystopian visions of persistent human irrationality and imminent self-destruction predicted by Swift, Huxley and Orwell always 'displayed a certain sobriety, a certain wish to walk in step with current realities'.[1] Utopian writers have foreseen the kinds of technological wonders, totalitarian systems and ecological disasters that had not yet occurred but appeared likely to occur soon, given the conduct of contemporary societies and elites.

Unfortunately, the Western utopian tradition of thinking on the cusp of new developments has encountered two significant roadblocks. The collapse of communism has aborted the most productive and ambitious strand of modern utopian thinking and other utopian traditions have not fared much better. It has become increasingly difficult, for example, to imagine the scientific breakthroughs of tomorrow. By the time our utopian fantasies appear in print they have already been outdated by the rapid development of contemporary computer and communication technologies. Utopia has been undermined by widely shared derision for egalitarian social fantasies and the astonishing technological dynamics of neo-liberal consumer culture.

The following reflections will hopefully avoid this fate by shifting the focus of utopian enquiry even further away from writing about possible alternate worlds, and reporting instead on very likely, imminent cultural developments. This chapter does not present a large-scale social vision and engages only with a very narrowly circumscribed aspect of modern technology. I relate research about the formation of historical consciousness to analyses of contemporary video-game culture because the latter has reached a stage of development that, among many other important consequences, will change how people acquire a sense of history. As a result of technical advances and artistic achievements, video-game culture, since its inception intriguingly interactive, is poised to reach a level of narrative complexity that will allow games fully to displace traditional linear narrative media like books, films and television. For the first time, narrative competency and historical consciousness will be acquired through fully interactive media which will provide consumers of history products with an unprecedented degree of cultural agency.[2] Historical culture can and will be radically rewritten and reinvented every time we turn on our computers. Once we pass this threshold, which I fully expect to happen before these lines are published, our collective memories will assume a new fictitious quality.

We have known for a long time that collective memories are psychologically and politically useful fabrications, but in the past these memories were invented through mediated or face-to-face communication and were therefore, in important respects, beyond our control. We could turn off our televisions and refuse to talk to our grandparents but sooner or later we would find ourselves involved in discussions about the past with colleagues or family members or encounter representations of the past in the media, and we would use these discussions and representations to orient ourselves in the world. We needed others to acquire a sense of history and a sense of self. Scholars have exploited this fact. They assumed correctly that while the content of our invented traditions could be completely fictitious, these traditions nevertheless, at least for most healthy individuals, revealed insights into their real group identities. Consequently, in research about collective memories, not the memories but the collectives were the targets of our scholarly ambition.

In the age of interactive media these scholarly assumptions and conclusions will gradually no longer apply. New digital technologies and formats will allow us to invent the content of our memories *and* the collectives which sustain them in such a compelling fashion that we will no longer need others to develop a psychologically functional sense of self. This development will undermine the axioms of collective memory studies but that should be the least of our concerns. As collective memories become private concoctions with regard to content and social foundation one of the most important platforms for social exchange, which has played a decisive role in the reconstitution of Western democracies since the Second World War, will cease to exist and will have to be replaced with other sources of democratic legitimacy. After 1945 and again after the collapse of the Berlin Wall, European societies engaged in processes of self-reckoning to craft new collective identities for the post-fascist and post-communist worlds, and at least during some periods these efforts of coming to terms with the past had considerable social depth.[3] Such processes are unlikely to repeat themselves in a thoroughly interactive cultural environment in which individuals no longer depend on centralised institutions of cultural production like film and television to develop their collective memories. Why would you and your friends get excited about a TV series like *Holocaust*, let alone engage in intergenerational discussions about such a production, if you had already had a chance to craft and manipulate at will a wide range of factual and counter-factual scenarios about the history of the Second World War and the Nazi crimes?

Historical consciousness

Professional historians have been primarily concerned about the proper reconstruction of past events and have been largely indifferent about the precise effects of their writings on lay readers. That lack of curiosity about the empirical origins and characteristics of historical consciousness did not prevent them from inventing authoritarian visions of national solidarity for European nation states of the nineteenth century. German historians were particularly ambitious in this regard. Having brought the blessings of a professional ethos to the study of the past, they were eager to share the fruits of their invention with their German brethren and designed top-down, authoritarian visions of national history for the citizens of the Prussian Empire.[4] After 1945 the German historical profession reluctantly abandoned its fantasies of national grandeur. Attempts to influence the popular German historical imagination were now pursued with considerably more humility and, after a generational turnover in the 1960s, the traditionally very conservative historiographical establishment even came to appreciate the virtues of democratic debate. Two opposing political camps and visions of history competed with each other. The majority faction of conservative politicians and academics worried about an identity vacuum that West Germans allegedly faced after the collapse of Nazism. Their political concept of antitotalitarianism became a great success, but they failed in their efforts to develop a compelling new national historical identity for the Cold War era. Some of their colleagues on the left of the political spectrum drew more radical conclusions from the Nazi catastrophe. They assumed that the challenges of having to explain the origins of fascism to younger generations and finding the basis for a new democratic identity might involve a fundamental revision of some tenets of German historicism. In the context of these efforts they returned to Enlightenment traditions, hoping that they would find liberal inspiration in the writings of the luminiaries and scions of German idealism.[5]

Since historicist hubris and belated liberal historiographical self-reflexivity have frequently coalesced around the term 'historical consciousness' (*Geschichtsbewusstsein*) scholars working in and about Germany have spent more time exploring the concept than their colleagues abroad. As a result, we can tap into an extensive body of writings on the subject which is often compatible with parallel explorations of heritage and collective memory in the Anglo-American context, although the German discourse distinguishes itself through its unabashed Enlightenment optimism about the possibility of analysing collective memories objectively and influencing the formation of future historical consciousness.[6]

In the context of West German efforts to come to terms with the Nazi past, Karl-Ernst Jeismann has provided a formulaic definition of historical consciousness that has become the main reference for all discussions about the topic since the 1970s. In his assessment the faculty of historical consciousness integrates interpretations of the past, perceptions of the present and expectations for the future into a single coherent interpretive framework.[7] This definition obviously raises as many questions as it answers and in the 1980s and 1990s German scholars developed more rigorous and extensive theoretical models pertaining to the acquisition and characteristics of historical consciousness. We will focus on two of these contributions: the theoretical insights of the historian and philosopher of history Jörn Rüsen and the writings of the social psychologist Jürgen Straub. Both have developed far-reaching explorations of the concept of historical consciousness that have recently been translated into English and have begun to play an important role in the field of collective memory studies.

In 1983 Jörn Rüsen proposed an ambitious model of historical consciousness that shares Jeismann's didactic concerns but is designed to cover all phylogentic and ontogenic stages of human development. Rüsen identifies four types of human historical consciousness that often coexist in everyday life but have developed successively in the course of human history. The most basic type, the traditional historical consciousness, focuses on founding acts and rituals which represent the common origins of a group, produce a strong sense of continuity between past and present, and justify a seemingly immutable set of moral values. In the second stage of development groups and individuals perceive the past in more abstract but not necessarily more flexible terms. From the vantage point of an exemplary historical consciousness concrete historical events and processes represent a much smaller set of underlying rules for temporal change and principles of moral conduct. The third type of consciousness, the critical type, regards both traditional and exemplary perceptions of the past with great scepticism. Collectives whose members embrace this critical perspective seek to deconstruct any sense of continuity between past and present and identify with counter-narratives which call into question the validity of historical precedents and universal rules.[8]

Rüsen emphasises that the first three types of consciousness are essentially static; from the traditional, exemplary and critical perspectives, past and present are interpreted within stable transhistorically valid parameters which reflect some collective Ur-event, timeless laws of human conduct, or their absolute negation. Only the last and most advanced type of historical consciousness, which Rüsen calls the 'genetic type', can perceive and process change on the level of historical events *and* on the level of the interpretive strategies which we employ to make sense of the past. This most complex way of interpreting the past for the first time allows human beings to develop historical identities and moral values that include the possibility, even necessity, of their transformation within a process of communication over time and space. Collectives with genetic types of historical consciousness have an exceptional ability to acknowledge and embrace otherness, for instance, through the idea of universal human rights. For Rüsen, the genetic type is a thoroughly modern phenomenon which, postmodern scepticism notwithstanding, exemplifies the possibility of progress in history and historical consciousness.[9]

Rüsen highlights three characteristics of historical consciousness that are particularly important for our purposes. In his assessment, historical consciousness always takes the linguistic form of narrative and therefore requires for its development narrative competence and narrative media. In addition, historical consciousness is the prerequisite for and is inextricably intertwined with moral judgement and moral action because it mediates between our values and our behaviour towards others. Finally, historical consciousness is a faculty we use constantly; it 'serves as a key orientational element, giving practical life a temporal frame and matrix'.[10]

Rüsen's refreshingly optimistic and extensive engagement with the question of historical consciousness has not remained unchallenged. Postmodern-inclined critics, for example, reject his optimistic view of narrative which they perceive as a negative cultural force with dubious ideological and normalising effects.[11] But even academics who are much more sympathetic to Rüsen's point of view take issue with his emphasis on the moral function of historical thought. For the cultural psychologist Jürgen Straub, Rüsen's model fails to grasp the specificity of historical consciousness as an essential form of human intelligence, which Straub seeks to conceptualise as a fourth type of human rationality next to theoretical and practical reason and aesthetic judgement. In pursuit of this goal Straub has developed preliminary thoughts towards a comprehensive psychology of the historical construction of meaning which offer another excellent vantage point for a critical look into the future of historical consciousness.[12]

Straub stresses the important psychological and social functions of historical consciousness. Thinking and acting historically means acknowledging and coming to terms with the constant changes of human existence in an effort to avoid the adverse emotional and psychological consequences that the realisation of this existential instability entails. Historical consciousness accomplishes this important task by constructing relations of continuity and discontinuity, of identity and difference, between historical events and by presenting past, present and future as part of a complex but meaningfully structured world. This seemingly contradictory process of synthesising heterogeneity, which conceptualises history 'as the unity of its differences', can be accomplished only through narrative.[13] Only narrative is a flexible yet sturdy enough hermeneutic tool to acknowledge difference and sublate it within consistent overarching interpretive frameworks which are psychologically and politically useful.

For Straub, history and historical consciousness are not reflections of any natural past, although past acts of interpretation and symbolic mediation inform our historical narratives. History always belongs to the present and 'acknowledges no temporal limits: everything that has been, is, or could be, might be its material'.[14] Despite this flexibility, individuals cannot invent history at will because they and their narratives are always subject to the existing rules of plausibility. In fact, Straub conceptualises historical consciousness very much like a collective memory. Although historical consciousness is in many ways linked to autobiographical memory, historical narratives can only function as carriers of historical consciousness if they successfully reflect the identity of a social group. In addition, Straub insists on another interesting qualification in his definition of historical consciousness which highlights his Kantian agenda. He argues that historical consciousness is a rational cognitive faculty, it is 'a rationally oriented ability to construct history as well as to justify action historically'.[15]

For a critical observer of the contemporary cultural scene many elements in Rüsen's model and Straub's theoretical remarks may appear questionable. Is it really possible to reduce all forms of historical consciousness to four ideal types? In what precise sense of the word can we characterise contemporary historical culture as an expression of reason? Are there no forms of critical historical consciousness that exist outside of narrative? These are valid, obvious questions even if one does not subscribe to a postmodern point of view. Unfortunately, a close look at the imminent utopia of an interactive historical culture does not settle the discussions between the contemporaries of Habermas, the grandchildren of Kant, and their postmodern critics. Instead of confirming or alleviating our fears about narrative, reason and typological classifications, a critical analysis of video-game culture calls into question one of the keys axioms that Enlightenment theorists of history and their opponents hold in common. We have long assumed that the values and vectors of historical culture and historical consciousness are collectively produced invented traditions even if that assumption has led to very different conclusions about the political purposes and self-critical potential of these traditions. Now we might have to realise that historical consciousnesses can be invented and reproduced independently of any social context. In the past, the smallest unit of historical consciousness was a group of two individuals; in the future that smallest unit will be only one person and a computer. That seemingly small adjustment in scale will have radical consequences for the evolution of human consciousness, including historical consciousness.

Video-game culture: presence and immersion

From books to television and video games, media have undergone 'an evolution of make-belief'.[16] Books provided narrative interpretations of the world, television added visual simulation, and video games offer for the first time the opportunity to interact with alternate universes and change essential characteristics of cultural products in the process of their consumption. But the triumph of interactive media has been handicapped by the games' lack of visual sophistication. Television has for many years retained a simulative edge over video games because it delivered more compelling images of real and imagined worlds than interactive media. If we trust the assessment of experts, that is changing as I write these lines: a new generation of video-game graphics will seamlessly integrate animation and documentation and thus attain an unprecedented level of visual realism.[17] As a result, video games now outperform all other media and cultural products in the competition for consumer attention. The seductive combination of interactivity with realistic images, sound and haptic input appears irresistible. Among the many statistics one could quote in this context, the following might suffice: games are displacing television as leisure activity;[18] game sales have surpassed Hollywood box-office receipts;[19] and in Germany and the USA, children and adolescents use computers predominantly for playing video games.[20]

As we reach the often anticipated but hitherto rarely reached utopia of the blending of real and represented worlds, scholars are struggling to develop new terms to understand the computer media revolution. One of the most promising of the new concepts is the notion of presence, which is paradoxically defined as the perception of non-mediation on the part of the media consumer.[21] The concept of presence is dynamic and multidimensional; it incorporates all aspects of media use and focuses on the feelings of video gamers which might change rapidly as a result of exposure to different types of virtual play and different social settings. In essence, the cognitive social construct of presence is triggered by a very productive interaction between media biography and media technology. The intense perception of realism involved in this experience depends on how consumer expectations about realistic representations are matched by current communication technology.[22] In this spiral of hope and delivery, the devil is in the details. It is not sufficient for media to be interactive; they also have to offer a speed and range of interactivity that correspond to the consumers' desires about their interactive experience.[23] In the same vein, it is not sufficient for video games to appeal to all senses; they have to provide the right mix of specific sensory input, for instance by simulating binocular disparity or by using the latest advances in neurological research for the imitation of realistic engine vibrations.[24] The virtual world has to present a manageable challenge, neither too slow nor too fast in its response to player input and appealing to all senses without overwhelming the player.[25]

The secret is to attain an equilibrium equidistant from boredom and alienation. The right media package delivered at the right time to the right people is supposed to transpose the gamer into the famous state of flow in which he is sufficiently challenged to be engrossed in the game without being overwhelmed by the tasks presented on the screen.[26] The condition is also described by the more technical term 'immersion', defined as a psychological state in which the gamer is effectively isolated from all other virtual or non-virtual stimuli surrounding him.[27] Immersion takes place within evolutionary boundaries but it is not necessarily easily induced.[28] For the video-game industry, the gamer represents a moving target. He might acquire new skills or forget old ones or change his aesthetic preferences, for instance, as a result of communication with peers. Consequently, the media packages are constantly updated and recalibrated, although within fairly narrow limits. Since it is so difficult to hit the target by designing a completely new game, game developers tend to replicate the structure and content of past commercial successes, updated by new technology.[29] As a result, mainstream gaming culture features a fairly narrow range of genres, content and aesthetics.[30] The limits of interactive media have not yet been rigorously tested – to the chagrin of media scholars who would love to receive more data for empirical research and theoretical enquiry.

Immersion is best conceptualised as occurring on a scale of varying intensity and within a wide range of media settings and should be carefully historicised. The introduction of new media has always triggered intense anxiety about their powerful negative effects on society.[31] The fears which accompanied the rise of radio, film and television might have been linked to waves of popular immersion into the new media because the experience as well as the fears seemed to have subsided once the new technology settled into routines of consumption and lost its simulative edge for most listeners/viewers. The experience of immersion should also be related to different stages of human development, which helps us understand why very traditional media settings, such as television, may have intense immersive effects on some viewers. Young children, for example, might feel transposed into the scenes they witness on TV and might suffer harmful psychological consequences precisely because they cannot yet differentiate between the virtual and the real even when dealing with such a relatively old technology as television.[32]

Placing the rise of interactive media within its larger historical and ontogenetic contexts highlights several important characteristics of the new media. Today's video games seem particularly appealing to adolescents because the existing game formats are well suited to help them meet their specific developmental needs.[33] Some researchers have therefore concluded that keeping youths away from Game-Boy, joystick and mouse might border on parental neglect.[34] But video games have already left the ghetto of adolescence – in 2004 the average age of gamers was thirty-three – because the members of Generation X, the first generation to play widely and consistently, are moving up in age and because video games increasingly feature ontogenetically adult formats, for instance by including complex narrative structures which are particularly appealing to post-adolescent consumers.[35] Therefore, it seems very unlikely that the wave of immersive experiences that has accompanied the introduction of interactive media will subside fairly soon, as has been the case after the introduction of non-interactive media. The immersive effects will persist not because interactive media mark such a radical departure from traditional linear media (which they certainly do) but because multi-sensory interactivity approaches the sensory and cognitive limits of the human species that are unlikely to change any time soon. Video games do not just feel like they require our complete attention, a feeling gamers probably share with the first generation of movie-goers; the games actually approach the thresholds of human data absorption and reaction speed and therefore promise long periods of immersive entertainment.

The experiences of immersion and involvement, which transport the gamer into a virtual space, may have intriguing consequences for the development of individual and collective identities and memories. In addition to perceiving virtual objects like real objects, video-game players can develop feelings of spatial presence towards figures in the game. Depending on the sophistication of the virtual environment the perception of co-presence with others may even rise to the level of a sense of access to other intelligent beings and a feeling of mutual awareness and recognition between players and figures.[36] For many gamers, the experience of co-presence and the chance of developing a sense of intimacy and community with others represent the *raison d'être* of their gaming activities. That applies in particular to fans of massively multiplayer online games (MMOG), who enter large, detailed and con-tinuously existing virtual environments for extended periods of time and might form strong ties to other players which often lead to other contact through email and telephone or even face-to-face meetings.[37] But MMOGs are only the tip of the iceberg. In contrast to popular perceptions of video games as a pastime for lonely, socially inept nerds, most video-game playing is pursued as an intensely social activity organised in complex, layered networks of symbolic exchange. Friends and strangers meet off- and online to explore virtual worlds, compete and co-operate with each other, and discuss their virtual adventures.[38]

Until recently, emotionally satisfying relations in virtual environments have been primarily conducted between avatars – figures in the game that are directly controlled by players. Through their virtual representatives, gamers can display the degree of social competency and spontaneity that is essential for a fully developed sense of social co-presence. But advances in artificial intelligence increasingly blur the line between avatars and computer-controlled agents which (or perhaps better *who*) engage in sophisticated verbal and non-verbal exchanges with avatars and may appear authentic, especially to players who are used to interacting with virtual figures of various sophistication.[39] The exchange with a virtual environment that effectively simulates body movements and offers the opportunity to manipulate inert objects and build extensive social networks allows players to develop a new self-consciousness. As Biocca has argued, this virtual self-presence involves at least three different levels and bodies: the player's actual body, her virtual body and her mental models of herself.[40] As these bodies and mental images interact with each other the self can assume different, more or less integrated and persistent real and virtual identities, each with its own history and social grounding.[41] In fact, the virtual side of things might easily appear more real and more desirable – for two important reasons. Within the game environment players have a control over their lives and relations that they never have in real life.[42] In addition, again in contrast to real life, they are both participants and eyewitnesses of their virtual exploits since they watch themselves fight, negotiate and collaborate with others on the screen.[43] As a result of this dual vision and unprecedented sense of power, they may develop particularly strong affinities and attachments to their socially constructed virtual lives, identities and memories. We should therefore not be surprised if the collective memories which have been constructed within, or in communications about, virtual worlds assume a psychological and social persistence that exceeds the staying-power of conventional collective memories which have been adopted by families, professions and other groups as a result of personal contact and the use of traditional media. Since all collective memories are fictions, the media and social forums which deliver these fictions in the most attractive formats should easily outperform less appealing outlets. Memories of virtual worlds and virtual interactions will become our most cherished memories and therefore our most powerful and real memories.[44] This does not mean that virtual and real worlds will seamlessly merge, that consumers will not be able to differentiate between the two at the point of consumption. But with hindsight the difference will indeed evaporate and the virtual world, experienced with the intense pleasure of controlled interactivity, will become the memory of choice.

Games and narrative

Scholars of interactive media have traditionally assumed that video games are essentially a non-narrative medium because for many years interactivity and narrative linearity could not be reconciled with each other. In the past, game designers seemed to have had two options. If their product featured the kind of well-crafted, detailed and suspenseful storyline that readers and viewers enjoy in books, film and television, they had to limit interactive choices severely in order to protect the integrity of the story and deliver it to the consumer in one attractive, coherent package. Alternatively, if they increased the interactive choices of their game it made little sense to spend the time developing a complex narrative structure because their customers would pick the narrative apart in the process of playing the game and never find, let alone come to appreciate, the well-designed overarching story.[45] The development of the video-game industry seemed to confirm this perception. Consumers put a premium on interactivity and showed little interest in narrative complexity. As a result, a separation of labour emerged between different media formats. Traditional linear media continued to meet society's narrative needs whereas video games satisfied the new hunger for interactivity, especially among younger generations.

But in recent years we have come to realise that the incompatibility between narrative and interactivity occurred during a phase of transition from old to new media. Technological innovations and the gradual dis-appearance of the generational divide between users and non-users of video games have turned the design of interactive narrative games into a lucrative business.[46] The dilemma was not solved by offering the player a choice of many different narratives which exist side by side in the virtual game world and take the player on a variety of linear journeys to different endpoints. Instead, successful interactive games define the basic elements and rules of the story in such a way that the player can take different turns at any corner in the virtual world and create his own narrative universe. The game does not feature any rigid, overarching storyline or storylines but a vast variety of plot options which, according to the desire of the player, can assume a different narrative form every time the game is played. Far from undermining interactivity, these emergent narratives enhance attachment to the virtual world because they cast the player into the roles of creator and witness of her own narrative worlds and thus intensify the experience of presence.[47]

As this brief survey of the study of narrative in video games indicates, communication scholars rightly emphasise that traditional and interactive media offer very different narrative products. Books and films generally present one linear storyline that cannot be altered by their consumers, whereas the latest generation of video games offers sophisticated emergent narrative that may assume a radically different form and structure every time the game is played. This differentiation is certainly important but it should not tempt us into constructing false dichotomies. Just because traditional media deliver stable, coherent and linear narratives at the point of dis-tribution, this does not mean that these linear stories are reproduced at the point of reception. We know of many examples that show how consumers selectively absorb events, figures or plot structures from linear media like films and books, subsequently integrate them into a different narrative context, and in the process radically alter the political, ethical or aesthetic impetus of the original media story. Consequently, if we focus on the con-struction of narrative at the point of reception, traditional and interactive media differ only in degrees; both are used very selectively, although video games, at least in theory, can offer substantially more narrative flexibility and diversity than their predecessors.

Invented communities and the limits of historical taste

But interactive media mark a more radical departure from the past in another respect, and that innovation is particularly important for the construction of collective memories and identities. Every person can already create their own private historical narratives but they will soon also be able to invent a whole community of virtual fellow-travellers with whom to share these narratives. Thus a single person can invent a whole historical culture consisting of a past, various interpretations of that past, and a social community that believes and cherishes those interpretations and turns them into a vibrant, lived historical consciousness. Moreover, it will be possible to reinvent and recalibrate these cultures and communities any time one turns on the computer. The construction and deconstruction of invented traditions and collective memories will be accelerated to unprecedented speeds.

MMOGs are currently the only virtual environments that can reliably give players the feeling that they are part of a larger social network. Some theorists have therefore celebrated MMOGs as the realisation of Habermas's utopia of communicative action.[48] But MMOGs are just an intermediate phase in the evolution of virtual sociability. Players will always appreciate and demand the illusion of being part of a social community but in the future that illusion will be easily produced by software programs, and players will no longer have any way of knowing if they are really communicating with other individuals or if they are simply cavorting with figments of their own and their computer's imagination.[49] As avatars and non-player characters (NPCs) become indistinguishable for the average player it will no longer be possible (and perhaps not even desirable) to find out to what extent the virtual community, with which one identifies and whose collective memories one shares, is controlled by humans or computers.

So why have we not already entered this radical postmodern nirvana of virtual remembrance? Some reasons have already been mentioned. Video games have not yet taken a radical narrative and NPC turn because the technology is still in its infancy and because older generations, who are the primary consumers of narrative media and have not been raised in an interactive environment, find it difficult to make the transition at this point in their lives. But there are other, political factors which explain why interactive media have not yet begun to offer the full range of alternate worlds that we would expect to see. The video-game industry is dominated by US companies which steer a particularly conservative course and hesitate to produce anything which might give offence to the political and media establishment in the United States, even if that decision prevents them from taking advantage of fabulous profit opportunities. Pornography represents the best example for this self-censorship.[50] There is a lot of money to be made for the company that launches the first state-of-the-art pornographic video game but none of the mainstream contenders has dared to take on that challenge for fear that they would be targeted by the US religious right. History is a somewhat less controversial but also risky terrain. What would happen if Rockstar were to put out a game on the Civil War or the Second World War that featured the full counter-factual potential of interactive technology, including the options of reversing the abolition of slavery and calling into question the occurrence of the Holocaust?[51] These examples of unsavoury revisionism explain why the existing Second World War games like the 'Wolfenstein' series rarely stray from the safe path of blood and gore and US heroism.[52] But the attempt to keep the genie in the bottle and interactive entertainment technology within the limits of the historical taste of the US mainstream will fail sooner rather than later. Video-game technology is rapidly spreading around the globe and many players have developed programming skills that match the expertise of highly paid professionals.[53] *Jihad: The Video Game*, if it does not already exist, is just around the corner.

Conclusion

It might be important to emphasise again in what respects interactive historical cultures will be very similar to linear historical cultures. Video games offer fabulous opportunities for counter-factual historical exploration but that is not a new phenomenon. Twentieth-century historical culture already displayed a great fondness for counter-factual scenarios which pursued such important questions as how history might have changed if Hitler had survived the war and/or the Nazis had won it.[54] In the future, however, one will not need to seek out subcultural communities to indulge one's counter-factual inclinations; counter-factuals may be experienced in real and/or simulated social settings and in the privacy of one's own software program.

Interactive media will not necessarily have more influence over collective memories than traditional media had in the past. The visual culture of the twentieth century already determined the moral orientation of our historical consciousness at the expense of other sources of historical wisdom, like friends and family members. Research has shown, for example, that Germans born in the 1980s systematically misremembered the stories that their grandparents told about life in the Third Reich. The younger generations reinvented their grandparents' testimony according to the moral compass provided by the Federal Republic's official memory culture which the adolescents had encountered in textbooks and the visual media. In this editing process the grandparents were recast in the roles of resisters and victims of the Nazi regime even if their testimony blatantly contradicted their grandchildren's benign versions of their life histories.[55] In the future, however, the memories of family members will not be recalibrated according to the moral demands of a centralised, politically correct elite culture but according to the values and imperatives of a very local, yet very powerful, virtual community which exists only on the young generation's servers and hard drives.

Temporary experiences of presence and immersion notwithstanding, most people can differentiate between media experiences, both interactive and linear, and real-life experiences, but they lose that ability with hindsight – especially, but not exclusively, with regard to virtual experiences. In October 2006 the *New York Times* reported that companies like SONY BMG, Sun Microsystems, Adidas/Reebok and Nissan are invading the virtual world by buying shops and advertising space in the video-game environment *Second Life*, which is populated by the avatars of a million subscribers. The companies as well as the subscribers pay real dollars to the game's owner Linden Labs for their virtual selling and shopping privileges. These activities have attracted the attention of the US Congress, which plans to tax virtual monetary transactions and have led to the foundation of a *Second Life* Liberation Army which opposes the commercialisation of the virtual world, stages virtual attacks on *Second Life* consumer outlets, and demands voting rights for avatars on the board of Linden Labs.[56] These dizzying interactions and exchanges demonstrate how much the virtual and the real world are already integrated. We might still be able to keep the two apart in everyday life but will we really be able to remember accurately where we first saw an ad for the latest Nissan automobile or where we watched that fabulously authentic colour footage of Hitler's suicide in the bunker? The advertisement executives who are experts in invading people's memory and laying the seeds for the shopping decisions of tomorrow were among the first to realise that they have to follow consumers into the virtual world. Anybody who wants to shape the collective memories of the future should heed their advice and compete for the privilege to build the monuments, museums and historical media in the virtual worlds of *Second Life* and its competitors.

It might be difficult to abandon the utopian enquiry into virtual worlds and its exciting theoretical implications but we should return, at least for a moment, to our less exciting concerns about the historical consciousness of today. What can we tell enlightenment optimists like Rüsen and Straub after our excursus into the academic world of video-game research? The publications neither prove nor disprove the assertion that historical consciousness exists only in and through narrative, although they confirm that narrative innovation will play a decisive role in the next generation of video games. The scholarship on interactive media also does not offer any conclusive insights into ethics of future historical cultures, although it is difficult to imagine that they will not have a strong moral, even moralistic dimension. After reviewing the literature it appears more difficult to accommodate Straub's demand that historical consciousness should be conceptualised as rational cognitive faculty; that suggestion seems to imply that most of today's historical culture, linear or interactive, does not rise to the standard of representing a historical consciousness. But the research on interactive media focuses critical attention on the terms of the definition of historical consciousness that have largely been taken for granted, such as communication, community and collective. In the age of interactive media the social construct 'historical consciousness' will take on a radically different quality because we will experience community in different ways. Video games produce the uncanny ability to communicate with oneself while creating the impression that there is a real other involved in that communication. Inscribed into the new media is a persistent simulation of collectivity which will permit us to reproduce collective memories without friction, resistance or the occasional reality-check that tended to intrude into our private worlds and memories in the age of linear, centralised media. As a result, collective memories and historical consciousness as we perceive of them today might simply cease to exist.

Expressed in Rüsen's terms, interactive media can take on the appearance of a sophisticated genetic historical consciousness while systematically undermining the very possibility of such a genetic identity. According to the logic of Rüsen's model, that means nothing less than the return to static modes of consciousness in a period when our historical culture looks more diverse than ever. But then, I have always had the suspicion that the fourth stage of Rüsen's model was a utopian vision dressed up as realistic analysis, a vision we have failed to realise in the second half of the twentieth century and that will be even more difficult to attain in the virtual cultures of the future.

Notes

1 Krishan Kumar, 'Aspects of Western Utopian Tradition', in Jörn Rüsen, Michael Fehr and Thomas Rieger (eds), *Thinking Utopia: Steps into Other Worlds* (New York: Berghahn, 2005): 17–31, 18.

2 P. Vorderer, 'Interactive Entertainment and beyond', in D. Zillmann and P. Vorderer (eds), *Media Entertainment: The Psychology of Its Appeal* (Mahwah: Lawrence Erlbaum, 2000): 21–36; T. Grodal, 'Video Games and the Pleasures of Control', in Zillmann and Vorderer, *Media Entertainment*, pp. 197–214.

3 See in this context the contributions in Ned Lebow, Wulf Kansteiner and Claudio Fogu (eds), *The Politics of Memory in Postwar Europe* (Durham, NC: Duke University Press, 2006).

4 Stefan Berger, *The Search for Normality: National Identity and Historical Consciousness in Germany since 1800* (Providence, RI: Berghahn, 1997).

5 Wulf Kansteiner, *In Pursuit of German Memory: History, Television, and Politics after Auschwitz* (Athens: Ohio University Press, 2006).

6 See in this context the remarks of Peter Seixas, 'Introduction', in Seixas (ed.), *Theorizing Historical Consciousness* (Toronto: University of Toronto Press, 2004): 3–20, especially 5–8.

7 Karl-Ernst Jeismann, *Geschichte als Horizont der Gegenwart: Über den Zusammenhang von Vergangenheitsbedeutung, Gegenwartsverständnis und Zukunftsperspektive* (Paderborn: Schöningh, 1988).

8 Jörn Rüsen, 'Historical Consciousness: Narrative Structure, Moral Function, and Ontogenetic Development', in Seixas (ed.), *Theorizing Historical Consciousness*, pp. 63–85; originally published in *History and Memory* 1 (1989): 35–60; see also Rüsen's *History: Narration, Interpretation, Orientation* (New York: Berghahn, 2005) and his *Geschichtsbewusstsein: psychologische Grundlagen, Entwicklungskonzepte, empirische Befunde* (Cologne: Böhlau, 2001).

9 Rüsen, 'Historical Consciousness', pp. 71–6.

10 Ibid., p. 67.

11 See, for example, the critical exchange between Rüsen and Roger Simon documented in Seixas, *Theorizing Historical Consciousness*, pp. 202–11.

12 Jürgen Straub, 'Telling Stories, Making History: Toward a Narrative Psychology of the Historical Construction of Meaning', in Straub (ed.), *Narration, Identity and Historical Consciousness* (Berghahn: New York: 2005): 44–98.

13 Ibid., p. 52.

14 Ibid., p. 46.

15 Ibid., p. 50.

16 Ute Ritterfeld and Rene Weber, 'Video Games for Entertainment and Education', in Peter Vorderer and Jennings Bryant (eds), *Playing Video Games: Motives, Responses, and Consequences* (Mahwah: Lawrence Erlbaum, 2006): 399–413, especially 401.

17 C. A. Anderson, J. B. Funk and M. D. Griffiths, 'Contemporary Issues in Adolescent Video Game Playing', *Journal of Adolescence* 1 (2004): 1–3.
18 N. Yee, 'MMORPG Hours vs. TV Hours'. Available at: <http://www.nickyee.com/daedalus/archives/000891.php>.
19 T. Brahe, 'The Mainstream is Coming, the Mainstream is Coming'. Available at: <http://www.escapistmagazine.com/issue/1/14>.
20 Maria Salisch, Caroline Oppl and Astrid Kristen, 'What Attracts Children?', in Vorderer and Bryant, *Playing Video Games*, pp. 147–63.
21 M. Lombard and T. Ditton, 'At the Heart of It All: The Concept of Presence', *Journal of Computer Mediated Communication* 3/2 (September 1997). See also C. Klimmt and Peter Vorderer, 'Media Psychology "Is Not Yet There": Introducing Theories on Media Entertainment to the Presence Debate', in *Presence: Teleoperators and Virtual Environments* 12/4 (2003): 346–59; and Alison McMahan, 'Immersion, Engagement, and Presence: A Method for Analyzing 3-D Video Games', in Mark Wolf and Bernard Perron (eds), *The Video Game Reader* (New York: Routledge, 2003): 67–86; for applications of the concept of presence in historical theory see the forum on presence in *History and Theory* 45 (2006): 305–61.
22 M. A. Shapiro and T. M. Chock, 'Psychological Processes in Perceiving Reality', *Media Psychology* 5/2 (2003): 163–98; Ron Tamborini and Paul Skalski, 'The Role of Presence in the Experience of Electronic Games', in Vorderer and Bryant, *Playing Video Games*, pp. 225–40.
23 J. Steuer, 'Defining Virtual Reality: Dimensions Determining Telepresence', *Journal of Communication* 42/4 (1992): 73–93.
24 C. Heeter, 'Being There: The Subjective Experience of Presence', *Presence: Teleoperators and Virtual Environments* 1/4 (1992): 262–71.
25 C. Klimmt, 'Dimensions and Determinants of the Enjoyment of Playing Video Games', in M. Copier and J. Raessens (eds), *Level up: Digital Games Research Conference* (Utrecht: Faculty of Arts, 2003): 246–57.
26 M. Csikszentmihalyi, *Beyond Boredom and Anxiety: Experiencing Flow in Work and Play* (New York: Jossey-Bass, 2000); M. Slater and S. Wilbur, 'A Framework for Immersive Virtual Environments (FIVE): Speculations on the Role of Presence in Virtual Environments', *Presence: Teleoperators and Virtual Environments* 6/6 (1997): 603–16.
27 F. Biocca and B. Delaney, 'Immersive Virtual Reality Technology', in F. Biocca and M. R. Levy, *Communication in the Age of Virtual Reality* (Hillsdale: Lawrence Erlbaum, 1995): 57–124; B. G. Witmer and M. J. Singer, 'Measuring Presence in Virtual Environments', *Teleoperators and Virtual Environments* 7 (1998): 225–40.
28 B. Reeves and C. Nass, *The Media Equation: How People Treat Computers, Television and New Media like Real People and Places* (Stanford: CSLI, 1996).
29 Stephen Kline, Nick Dyer-Witheford and Greig de Peuter, *Digital Play: The Interaction of Technology, Culture, and Marketing* (Montreal: McGill University Press, 2003).
30 For a survey of computer-game genres, see Barry Smith, 'The (Computer) Games People Play: An Overview of Popular Game Content', in Vorderer and Bryant, *Playing Video Games*, pp. 43–56.
31 Dmitri Williams, 'A Brief Social History of Game Play', in Vorderer and Bryant, *Playing Video Games*, pp. 197–212.
32 A. C. Huston and J. C. Wright, 'Mass Media and Children's Development', in I. E. Sigel and K. A. Renninger (eds), *Handbook of Child Psychology*, vol. 4 (New York: Wiley, 1998): 999–1058.
33 K. Subrahmanyam *et al.*, 'The Impact of Computer Use on Children's and

Adolescents' Development', *Journal of Applied Developmental Psychology* 22 (2001): 7–30.

34 Kevin Durkin, 'Game Playing and Adolescents' Development', in Vorderer and Bryant, *Playing Video Games*, pp. 415–28.

35 Entertainment Software Association, *Essential Facts about the Computer and Video Game Industry*, 2006, available at: <http://www.theesa.com/index.php>; Dmitri Williams, 'The Video Game Lightning Rod', *Information, Communication, and Society* 6/4 (2003): 523–50.

36 K. M. Lee, 'Presence, Explicated', *Communication Theory* 14/1 (2004): 27–50.

37 Eliane Chan and Peter Vorderer, 'Massively Multiplayer Online Games', in Vorderer and Bryant, *Playing Video Games*, pp. 77–88; R. Schroeder, *The Social Life of Avatars: Presence and Interaction in Shared Virtual Environments* (London: Springer, 2002); M. D. Griffiths, M. N. O. Davies and D. Chappell, 'Online Computer Gaming: A Comparison of Adolescent and Adult Gamers', *Journal of Adolescence* 27 (2003): 87–96.

38 Peter Vorderer and U. Ritterfeld, 'Children's Future Programing and Media Use between Entertainment and Education', in E. L. Palmer and B. Young (eds), *The Faces of Televisual Media: Teaching, Violence, and Selling to Children* (Mahwah: Lawrence Erlbaum, 2003): 241–62.

39 F. Biocca, C. Harms and J. K. Burgeon, 'Toward a More Robust Theory and Measure of Social Presence: Review and Suggested Criteria', *Presence: Teleoperators and Virtual Environments* 12/5 (2003): 456–80.

40 F. Biocca, 'The Cyborg's Dilemma: Progressive Embodiment in Virtual Environments', *Journal of Computer Mediated Communication* 3/2 (September 1997).

41 It is interesting to note, however, that most players forgo the option of playing with multiple characters and prefer instead to focus on only one or two avatars; see Ann-Sofie Axelsson and Tim Regan, 'Playing Online', in Vorderer and Bryant, *Playing Video Games*, pp. 291–306 and compare to Miroslaw Filiciak, 'Hyperidentities: Postmodern Identity Patterns in Massively Multiplayer Online Role-Playing Games', in Wolf and Perron, *The Video Game Reader*, pp. 87–102.

42 Barry Smith, 'The (Computer) Games People Play: An Overview of Popular Game Content', in Vorderer and Bryant, *Playing Video Games*, pp. 43–56; Silvia Knobloch, *Schicksal spielen: Interaktive Unterhaltung aus persönlichkeitspsychologischer und handlungtheoretischer Sicht* (München: Reinhard Fischer, 2000).

43 Peter Vorderer, 'Interactive Entertainment and Beyond', in Zillmann and Vorderer, *Media Entertainment*, pp. 21–36.

44 For the same reason video games are fabulous didactic tools since they meld learning, identity and memory in particularly effective ways; see James Paul Gee, *What Video Games Have to Teach Us about Learning and Literacy* (New York: Palgrave Macmillan, 2003); P. Johnson, *Everything Bad is Good for You* (New York: Penguin, 2005); and C. Nelson, *Attention and Memory: An Integrated Framework* (New York: Oxford University Press, 1995). Consider in this context also the persistence of virtual diaspora communities which migrate to other virtual environments when their games close and maintain social cohesion and a collective memory of their former existence and expulsion in the new game context; see Celia Peirce, 'Productive Play: Game Culture From the Bottom UP', *Games and Culture* 1/1 (2006): 17–24.

45 Michael Sellers, 'Designing the Experience of Interactive Play', in Vorderer and Bryant, *Playing Video Games*, pp. 9–22.

46 Kwan Min Lee, Namkee Park and Seung-A Jin, 'Narrative and Interactivity in Computer Games', in Vorderer and Bryant, *Playing Video Games*, pp. 259–74;

Mark Wolf, 'Narrative in the Video Game', in Wolf (ed.), *The Medium of the Video Game* (Austin: University of Texas Press, 2001): 93–112.

47 H. Jenkins, 'Game Design as Narrative Architecture', in N. Wardrip-Fruin and P. Harrington, *First Person* (Cambridge, Mass.: MIT Press, 2004): 118–30.

48 B. Wellman and M. Guillia, 'Net Surfers Don't Ride Alone: Virtual Communities as Communities', in Wellman (ed.), *Networks in the Global Village* (Boulder: Westview, 1999); and P. E. Howard, L. Rainie and S. Jones, 'Days and Nights on the Internet: The Impact of a Diffusing Technology', *American Behavioral Scientist* 45/3 (2001): 383–404.

49 Michael Shapiro, Jorge Pena-Herborn and Jeffrey Hancock, 'Realism, Imagination, and Narrative Video Games', in Vorderer and Bryant, *Playing Video Games*, pp. 275–89.

50 Christopher Klug and Jesse Schell, 'Why People Play Games: An Industry Perspective', in Vorderer and Bryant, *Playing Video Games*, pp. 91–100. Consider in the context the debate in 2005 about the hidden sex scenes in *Grand Theft Auto: San Andreas*; see Seth Schiesel, '"Bully" looks to beat the "Grand Theft Auto" rap', *New York Times*, 11 August 2006.

51 The limits of historical taste are inadvertently highlighted in Barry Atkins, *More Than a Game: The Computer Game as Fictional Form* (Manchester: Manchester University Press, 2003). Atkins, in many ways favourably inclined towards computer games, is quite squeamish about the limited counter-factual options of a game like *Close Combat: A Bridge too Far*.

52 See the excellent list of Second World War video games at: <http://en.wikipedia.org/wiki/List_of_World_War_II_video_games>.

53 Hacking video-game software and adding new code is a popular pastime among players. Some classical games like *Doom* have been specifically designed with rewriting options in mind. See Henry Lowood, 'A Brief Biography of Computer Games', in Vorderer and Bryant, *Playing Video Games*, pp. 25–41.

54 Gavriel Rosenfeld, *The World Hitler Never Made: Alternate History and the Memory of Nazism* (Cambridge: Cambridge University Press, 2005). For counter-factual and vicarious experiences through video games, see Christopher Klug and Jesse Schell, 'Why People Play Games: An Industry Perspective', in Vorderer and Bryant, *Playing Video Games*, pp. 91–100.

55 Harald Welzer, Sabine Moller and Karoline Tschuggnall, *'Opa war kein Nazi': Nationalsozialismus und Holocaust im Familiengedächtnis* (Frankfurt: Fischer, 2002).

56 Richard Siklos, 'A Virtual World but Real Money: Corporate Marketers Find Much to Like in a Digital Utopia', *New York Times*, 19 October 2006.

11 Being an improper historian

Ann Rigney

I

Some ten years ago, Lynn Hunt, influential spokesman for the 'cultural turn' in historical studies, noted that scholars from various fields in the humanities were finding new common ground:

> Are we on the verge of a more general cultural studies that will replace the separate compartments of *history, literature, art history* and the like? Yes and no. Yes, we are all borrowing from each other more and more explicitly. Engravings are no longer just illustrations but also evidence for historical arguments. Police reports, memoirs, conduct books, and autopsy reports are not just historical sources but also models, influences, and sources for 'literary' texts. But no, we are not all reading our documents in the same way: *historians* ask different questions from their colleagues in other fields, and even when they use the same sources, they use them somewhat differently.[1]

Reading Hunt's vision of a 'general cultural studies' as a 'colleague from another field' (I work in a department of literary studies and was also trained in such a department), I was surprised. Not by the idea that there have been lots of exciting exchanges across traditional disciplinary boundaries in the last decades and that scholars working within the human sciences have been converging on particular issues and sharing theoretical wares: these are undeniable (and welcome) developments which are still ongoing. What is surprising rather is the fact that even as Hunt looks forward to a redrawing of the traditional divisions between 'history, literature, [and] art history', her pen slips back into the familiar groove of the bipartisan divide between 'historians' and 'their colleagues in other fields'. The implication is that scholars can approach the same documents in different ways depending on what they want to know, but that 'historians' as a group collectively do things that are different from all of their colleagues elsewhere. In Hunt's view of things (and I use it here simply *à titre d'exemple* to illustrate a more general attitude), there is a critical divide within the human sciences, located between 'history' and other studies of culture.[2] There are the 'historians' and there are those other scholars who do comparable things without being real historians themselves (like citizens of Hong Kong who are British nationals but not British enough to have the right to live in Britain). This difference between proper historians and 'improper' historians seems to be grounded in the idea that whereas 'art' is the object of art history, and literature is the object of literary history, 'history' *tout court* must be where the real historians are at.

History *tout court*? What could that be? One of the difficulties in trying to project a future for 'history' – the assignment of this essay – is that there is in fact no such thing as 'history', as such. Whether the word is used to cover the object of historical study or the study itself, it has arguably passed its sell-by date as an all-encompassing enabling concept that provides a foundation for a particular type of academic practice or disciplinary formation. If 'history', as such, is interpreted to mean the object of historical study then it corresponds to so much that it becomes vacuous or mystical in its scale (everything that has ever occurred; the sublime totality of everything that has happened or ever will). If it is taken to mean the historical study of the human world, it is potentially a transdiscipline that extends to all the humanities and, as such, may not automatically be located in any particular disciplinary formation (e.g., departments of history).

In practice, of course, people rarely talk about 'history', as such (except perhaps in journals devoted to the philosophy of history). In practice, we never deal with some pure, distilled form of history but with 'historical accounts of x, y, z' which claim, with more or less ambition, to be a part of the greater whole of 'history in general'. Think of histories of politics, societies, particular periods and regimes, behaviours, ways of thinking, cultures, media, sexuality, and so on. Think of the plethora of new topics of historical enquiry in the field of cultural history that emerged in the various waves of 'new histories' that hit the twentieth century. The proliferation of new topics involved a degree of specialisation that, according to some, has led to an unwelcome fragmentation within the academic historical profession and made it all the more difficult to conceive of history in general. As a result of this expansionism, 'history' ends up in the paradoxical state of being potentially 'about everything', while at the same time being governed, both in theory and in institutional practice, by the ethos of a rather exclusive club whose members are committed to the integrated study of history 'itself' *as distinct from* variant studies concerned with such epiphenomena as literature, media, art and so on. Where exactly does theme become variation? Are not all of us who are working in the human sciences doing (some form of) history, even if we do not do it all of the time?

Working in the field of literary and cultural studies, my professional commitment is to a greater understanding of how the textual medium works, and has worked in particular instances, in constructing our views of the world. A large part of my research involves looking at the way particular ways of writing and representing evolved in the course of time, or how particular narratives *made sense* at a given period, in relation to earlier forms of writing, other media practices, technological and social developments, intellectual movements, and so on. The primary focus is on the mediatisation of experience through language and through historically variable poetical forms, but this study of textual culture inevitably touches on other aspects of cultural, social and economic life. The fascinating thing about imaginative literature is that it provides a laboratory where historically variable ways of seeing the world are expressed through the prism of poetical forms in such a way that they are made uniquely observable both for contemporaries and later historians (think, for example, of Heinrich Mann's portrait of Wilhelminian Germany in his novel *Der Untertan*, 1916). The study of literary phenomena involves particular expertise in textual analysis and specific knowledge of the history of poetics. Nevertheless, to see the historical study of art as perpetually falling 'outside the pale' of history because it takes textual or visual culture as its primary object, rather than political culture, economics or military matters, is odd (to say the least), even if it can be explained both by the ongoing desire among historians to find *the* variant of history in which all the rest can be anchored (literature has never been a serious candidate in this regard) and by the fact that studying literature or any other form of art from a historical perspective poses particular challenges.[3]

Much has been written on these challenges, indeed on the question of whether it is even possible to deal historically with literary works since they are often still culturally active, both for the individual historian and for the wider world to which he or she belongs. Suffice it here to point to the fact that artistic products have a double relation to time and hence confuse both linear chronology and a clear-cut distance between past object and present interests: works of art, be these verbal or visual, are rooted in one historical context and at the same time may continue to be interesting and pleasurable in themselves for those studying them in the present day. Certainly this interference between aesthetic power and historical vision means that the historicising study of texts and other media poses different sorts of epistemological problems than other fields of research. But the same point *mutatis mutandis* could arguably also be made about socio-economic history or political history, which also differ from each other. There is no such thing as a normal historian. All history is hyphenated and all of it is complicated. The presumed unity of 'history' as an academic practice (which brings together political and economic historians but excludes literary and media specialists) may simply come down to a matter of disciplinary formation, of 'who you go to lunch with' and 'what books you read in your first year', rather than of a theoretically defensible distinctiveness.

Everything I have said so far might be dismissed as mere squabbling about nomenclature or as resentment on the part of someone left out of the club and coming to this 'manifesto for history' from an institutionally eccentric position. But hair-splitting on the difference between 'proper' historians and their hyphenated counterparts in other departments cuts to the heart of a theoretical issue: how to deal with 'variations on history'? Rather than continue to expand the notion of 'history as such' so that it has to shoulder an ever-greater thematic and institutional burden, and rather than continue to search for the thematic or methodological essence of history 'proper', I believe we should accept variation as an inherent part of historical practice and turn our attention to the ways in which different historical practices, both within the academy and *extra-muros*, relate to each other and to other cultural practices. The challenge at the present time is to find a fruitful way of imagining the border-crossings between adjacent territories, rather than to reinforce the security wall between 'true' history and mutant, secondary forms. So I propose dropping the idea that there is only one road to viewing the world historically, and that that road is the one travelled by 'proper historians' working in history departments. As the saying goes, mutation is not a bug, it is a feature.

In what follows I take the bug's-eye view from literary studies in order to reflect on the variation *within* that conceptual umbrella called 'history', not merely in the range of topics open to historical enquiry (from politics and economics to sexuality and literature), but in the nature of the practice itself.

II

The bug's-eye view from literary studies starts from the principle that it is useless to theorise 'history' in a disembodied way. As the many discussions of narrative and representation in the last decades have shown, knowledge of the past is always embedded in particular cultural practices and does not exist outside of them (it is my professional deformation, of course, to home in on the world in terms of cultural practices, but the fact that this is a partial view does not detract from its heuristic power). From the cultural studies perspective, the practice of academic historiography (including its literary, art-historical and socio-economic variants) can be seen as a subset of the many 'historical' or 'mnemonic practices' that occur in society.[4] By 'mnemonic practice', I mean publicly expressed reflection on specific differences between the present and the past. This reflection may take the form of extensive archival investigation followed by systematic analysis, interpretation in the light of a particular theory, and publication in a scholarly journal (all the attributes of academic scholarship). But it may also take the form of a commemorative ceremony in which the war dead are recollected in a ritualistic way, with a view to advancing social cohesion rather than scholarly debate. As the term 'practice' itself suggests, my starting point is the way we actively engage with the past using various media and methods, rather than some abstract notion of 'history' as a sleeping-beauty object waiting for the professional kiss to arouse it.

It follows from this that academic historical practices, while they have distinctive features, represent the professional and disciplined variant of other mnemonic practices (and as I suggested earlier there are considerable differences in focus and method *within* academic historiography itself). The idea of mnemonic practices allows us to move beyond the persistent but unfruitful opposition between 'history' and 'memory', or historiography and remembrance, that has dogged theoretical debates. More importantly, it allows us to differentiate between the various functions of these historical practices in a more nuanced and empirically based way, for example taking on board the fact that academic, disciplined history (including its many specialisms) is the variant with the most social prestige and cultural authority (feeding directly into the educational system), while it scores less high on popularity than, for example, television documentaries or novels. Dropping the *cordon sanitaire* around 'history itself', then, does not mean capitulating to uniformity. Rather it allows one to conceive of 'historical practice' in a pluralist and multidimensional way. The cultural work that goes by the name of 'history' involves various institutions, genres, media and aspects – topics, methods, modes of presentation, social reach and circulation – that together form a matrix.[5] The fact that academic historiography is the variant with the greatest claim to offer historical knowledge according to scholarly norms, rather than mere opinion or storytelling, does not detract from this basic point.

Having admitted that historical practice is made up of its variants, the question arises if these variants also represent alternatives for each other. More specifically, to what extent are extramural variations on historical practice alternatives for academic historiography? To what extent are mnemonic practices themselves caught up in other sorts of practice of a political or aesthetic nature, and to what extent are they alternatives for these? In short: which crossovers occur between historical practices and other cultural practices? The basic issue can be illustrated by reference, for example, to the phenomenon of 'defamiliarisation', as described by the Russian Formalists at the beginning of the twentieth century: the idea that the essence of art lies in our being compelled by the particular experience of the work of art to look at what is familiar from an unfamiliar point of view. To the extent that historical consciousness involves a defamiliarisation of the present in the light of the knowledge that things were once different, it has been seen as analogous to aesthetic experience in the sense that both the aesthetic and the historical open up a critical distance in relation to the present.[6] To the extent that both aesthetic experience and historical consciousness involve defamiliarisation they too are analogous to the investigation of other cultures: hence the oft-quoted adage that 'the past is a foreign country, they do things differently there' or the connection made by Victor Segalen between 'temporal' and 'spatial' forms of exoticism.[7] Having established such analogies, the key question then becomes to what extent they may be equivalent: when are aesthetic, historical and intercultural defamiliarisation effective alternatives for each other and when are they indispensable in their own specific form? The question is not merely of theoretical interest but has implications, among other things, for the design of educational programmes or ceremonial events, and the cognitive, ethical and socialising aims which are at stake in them.

Whatever answer one gives in particular cases, the question itself opens the possibility that historians may not have to do everything themselves. It means that functions traditionally attributed to academic history may also be achieved through other means, some of which have nothing to do with the study of the past, and that the 'historian' may not bear responsibility for all aspects of education and socialisation (as he or she may have done in the nineteenth century). The task of the professional historian can be defined in less all-encompassing terms, but also more specifically profiled in relation to alternative cultural practices – including literary ones.

III

Until fairly recently, discussion of non-academic histories was dictated by the belief that they were at best weakened or secondary versions of the real thing; at worst, agents of corruption. Discussions of fiction in particular have been foreshortened by the inability to think beyond the salient fact that novels are unreliable as sources of specific information about the past because creative writers, unlike professional historians, do not first have to do any archival homework and are free to make up whatever they like and say it in whatever way they choose. By now, however, it is possible to see novels in other terms than merely as a corrupted form of 'history itself' and as having an active role to play, in the production of historical consciousness if not in the transmission of specific knowledge of historical particulars.

To begin with, works written in an earlier period, and having a continued appeal at a later point in time, can provide an imaginative bridge to the past. Thus Laclos's *Liaisons dangereuses* (1782) can still command attention, and those reading it today engage in a historical practice in the sense that they re-enact specifically eighteenth-century points of view as the novel unfolds in the course of several hundred pages. That the latter-day reader's interpretations of specific points may differ from those of Laclos's contemporaries does not detract from the basic fact: it would be difficult to get closer to an imaginative re-enactment of an earlier world-view than through the intimacy of reading. I deliberately use 're-enactment' here to emphasise the parallels between reading and other performances of the past, as in battle re-enactments or contemporary museums where the emphasis lies on 'history through experience'. Latter-day readers 'perform' earlier texts in appropriating them for their own intellectual enlightenment or aesthetic enjoyment. As reader you are lured by the literary qualities of the text (the rattling good tale, the evocations of scenes, etc.) to think along with someone from an earlier period and to act out a script which, because it was formulated for another generation, will also be defamiliarising in spots. Aesthetic and historical defamiliarisation may thus converge in such a way that readers can pursue a 'dialogue' with the text to the point where, as Hans-Georg Gadamer has put it, a 'fusion of historical horizons' takes place in which readers re-calibrate their own view of the world in light of the alterity of the world expressed through the text.[8] In this way, 'performing' literary texts from an earlier period provides a type of historical experience that is qualitatively different from that offered by a retrospective, historiographical account of the same period from a present-day viewpoint.

But narrative fiction also plays a more direct role in mnemonic practice. The examples are legion: plays, operas, novels, films, television series and graphic novels which are 'historical', not in being 'from the past', but in providing latter-day representations of the past in the form of a story which is 'based' on real events, but has also been subjected to manipulation and transformation at the hands of an artist aspiring to critical or commercial success. Critics of historical fiction argue that such hybrid narratives are worse than no history at all since they offer a fast-food version of haute cuisine that whets and then immediately sates the historical appetite, giving an *ersatz* view of the past and commodifying it in the form of a pleasurable story. If works of 'historical fiction' have since the time of *Waverley* (1815) thus regularly aroused the ire of the 'proper historians' and continue to be a thorn in the flesh of historical purists, their popularity has continued unabated. The popular blockbuster is merely the hamburger variant of fiction, however, and in recent discussions more positive functions for narrative fiction in the production of historical consciousness have also been discerned. Let me recall some of them.

To begin with, fiction may serve as a 'stepping stone' that motivates people to find out more. By embodying situations and events in individual characters and presenting them in the form of narratives, fiction-makers give people at least a basic idea of a particular period and, with the help of their pleasure in the story for its own sake and their empathy for characters, channel their interest towards finding out more about specific historical phenomena.[9] Those who have found themselves reaching for the encyclopedia after reading a novel or viewing a film will recognise the mechanism. Second, and more importantly, fiction can function as a 'catalyst' in relation to other historical practices by foregrounding topics that have been ignored for one reason or another, and finding ways to express them. Novelists, film-makers and visual artists thus put topics on the historical agenda which are socially relevant but about which not much is yet known or for which little archival evidence is as yet available. In this way, artists help keep historical horizons open and, by experimenting with new discursive models, provide alternative models for making the past intelligible and observable.[10] Finally, fiction-makers may contribute to a critical reflection on mnemonic practices, including those of the academy. In artistic fictions (by which I mean complex novels like W. G. Sebald's *Austerlitz*, 2001, rather than blockbusters like

Dan Brown's *The Da Vinci Code*, 2003), 'immersivity' (the characteristic of getting lost in a story) and 'interactivity' (reflection on the constructed-ness of the story) are combined in such a way that the awareness of a specific past is linked with reflection on the ways in which we can or cannot make sense of it. In such cases, the defamiliarisation characteristic of aesthetic experience can be said to serve the interest of critical reflection on the act of remembrance itself.

Much more could be said about the varieties of narrative fiction and how these relate to other types of artistic practice, on the one hand, and to other forms of historical practice (historiography, museums) on the other. The actual role of particular fictions in promoting historical consciousness (or in cutting it off) would have to be decided on a case-to-case basis and in light of the particular audience that is reached. Enough has been said, however, to allow the basic theoretical point: namely, that outside the realm of academic history per se there are varieties of historical practice that are not merely failed versions of 'disciplined history' (they may also be this, of course), but something of a different order. These differences relate both to the topics treated and to the type of relation established to the past, and the specific combinations of pleasure, cognition, empathy, reflection that the particular medium or genre brings into play. The list of possibilities grows as new technologies, genres and aesthetic forms are invented. As a number of studies of digital gaming have pointed out, the new medium of interactive fiction allows participants to replay historical scenarios in a counter-factual way and, as such, they have the potential to heighten the players' awareness of the complexity that produces particular outcomes.[11]

Where traditionally thinking about historical practice has been focused on epistemological matters relating to representation (does a particular narrative offer an adequate account of the world?), the approach through 'undisciplined', artistic variants like the novel points to the fact that what we lump together as 'history' in fact involves various different activities that may not be subsumed in any single performance. Providing information and interpretation is only one part of the story, along with stimulating interest, experimenting with different representational forms, sharpening people's historical consciousness, and reflecting critically on historical practice itself. Acknowledging the role of 'undisciplined' variants also points to the fact that performance, re-enactment, identification, pleasure and interactivity provide alternative models for thinking about how people relate to the past.

Does this mean that academic historians should themselves write novels, design computer games, or experiment with graphic novels?

IV

The short answer is no, because historians do not have to do everything themselves. The long answer says that it is time to move theoretical discus-sions of historical representation beyond its traditional focus on individual works and to focus on the circulation of knowledge and representations through the culture at large.

Theoretical discussions about the relations between historiography and art have generally focused on the issue of how to incorporate the 'best practices' from the realm of literature and the other arts into the work of historians; as Hayden White has consistently argued, rethinking the way we write history, and extending the repertoire of forms of expression in use, is an integral part of our scholarly work, even if it is not our core business.[12] This realisation has led to various forms of experimentation with alternative ways of writing history (witness, for example, many of the contributions to the journal *Rethinking History*) and conceiving of research.

What is needed at this point, however, is not more reflection on how professional historical practice can be transformed from within, but a greater understanding of the cultural mechanisms by which it intersects with other cultural practices. The interesting question is no longer 'How far can historians go in incorporating aesthetic models into their own practice or extending their activities to other fields?' but 'How are they to talk to their neighbours?' How can a fruitful interaction between various practices be achieved without all differences being obliterated? This means thinking of historical practice in modular terms, as a series of 'hinges' between different elements, rather than as something homogeneous or continuous.

Here the view from cultural studies, and specifically the view of culture associated with the 'new historicism', is useful. Where traditionally the focus in cultural analysis was on the individual artefact, attention has shifted in recent years to the cultural life of particular stories, how they persist and are transformed as they circulate among different groups and are taken up and echoed in other media and other discursive fields. In this sense, cultural practice is always on the move, defined less by its stable points (works) than by its dynamics (the circulation of ideas and forms of expression). Variation is the key to all of this, the cultural equivalent of biodiversity. That historians should be inspired by artists and vice versa is thus part and parcel of the normal trafficking between various cultural domains. Cultural practices evolve and are constantly changing both by borrowing from each other and by hitting off each other in a critical way.[13]

This principle can be applied to the way we deal with variations within academic historical practice, where fundamental differences can become the source of new discussions, rather than a symptom of decline. It can also be applied to the relations between academic practice and some of the other historical practices mentioned earlier. The development of a 'general cultural studies', as indicated at the beginning of this piece, should help us in forming a clearer picture of the relations of different cultural practices, how they complement, stimulate, mimic, derive from each other and how they circulate among different groups. The idea that historical representations are not produced once and for all but are things which circulate and are transformed provides a new basis for defining the specific goal of 'disciplined' historical practice as distinct from the alternatives with which at some levels it intersects.

At the risk of sounding retrograde and overly modest: the core business of academic historical practice (in which I include all branches of cultural studies) lies in presenting information about things that actually occurred in the world and interpreting that information in a publicly accessible form (those forms may be inspired by artistic practices, but experimenting with them is not what historians are there for in the first instance). The challenge for professional historians is to ensure that their insights play into public discussions down the line, that their critical voice is heard in regard to illusions about the past, and that they help others to make informed judgements. This is not a call for a new generation of Malvolios out to spoil everybody else's fun or their cherished illusions. Rather, it is a proposal to think creatively of new ways to link up historiographical discourse with other forms of expression in various public domains, through co-operation with novelists and television programme-makers, but also through the intensification of internet links to reliable scholarly sources, for example from the internet movie database to relevant historical sources.

The key issue is not so much whether academic historians should be doing something radically different from what they are already doing, but rather, whether their knowledge and expertise can be brought into circulation in a multimedial world which is not at the academic historian's bidding and where blockbuster fiction has arguably as much power as academic history to shape widely held views of the past (or in seducing people into forgetting history altogether). How are informed judgements about the past to be brought into circulation and made to intersect critically with other, less well-formed or downright erroneous or mythical views? How is the cultural authority of the academic historian (of politics, of culture, of literature) to be valorised in a world where so much emphasis is placed on the do-it-yourself, perform-it-yourself, approach to the past? And where the internet provides a forum for quality information alongside an immensely powerful instrument for the proliferation of errors. Identifying these as core issues provides an exercise in modesty at the same time as an enormous challenge.

Putting things in this way is not an attempt to reassert the primacy of academic work over all other forms of history. This would be as quixotic as the Republic of Ireland declaring jurisdiction over the British Isles. Besides, it would ignore the real achievements of the last decades in broadening our understanding of the range of mnemonic practices and the variety of ways with which people can engage with the past or with other forms of alterity. Precisely because of this variety, it is all the more important to focus on the specific contribution of historians to the circulation of knowledge without falling back into a splendid isolation.

Notes

1 Lynn Hunt, 'The Objects of History: A Reply to Philip Stewart', *Journal of Modern History* 66 (1994): 539–46, quote on 546; my emphasis.
2 See also, for example, the distinction made by F. R. Ankersmit between 'historians of literature' and 'ordinary historians' in 'An Appeal from the New to the Old Historicists', *History and Theory* 42 (May 2003): 253–70, especially 270.
3 For a brief account of traditional discussions on the relation between aestheticising and historicising approaches to textual culture, see Lee Patterson, 'Literary History', in Frank Lentricchia and Thomas McLaughlin (eds), *Critical Terms for Literary Study*, 2nd edn (Chicago: Chicago University Press, 1995): 250–62. These discussions have taken a new turn in 'New Historicism'; see Catherine Gallagher and Stephen Greenblatt, *Practicing New Historicism* (Chicago: University of Chicago Press, 2001). For a balanced account of the points of convergence as well as differences between New Historicism and cultural history (as practised in history departments), see Sarah Maza, 'Stephen Greenblatt, New Historicism, and Cultural History, or, What We Talk about when We Talk about Interdisciplinarity', *Modern Intellectual History* 1:2 (2004): 249–65.
4 Jeffrey K. Olick and Joyce Robbins, 'Social Memory Studies: From "Collective Memory" to the Historical Sociology of Mnemonic Practices', *Annual Review of Sociology* 24 (1998): 105–40.
5 Jörn Rüsen, 'Disziplinäre Matrix', in Stefan Jordan (ed.), *Lexikon Geschichtswissenschaft: Hundert Grundbegriffe* (Stuttgart: Reclam, 2002): 61–4.
6 On the principle of defamiliarisation, see Victor Shklovksy, 'Art as Technique' [1917], in L. T. Lemon and M. J. Reis, *Russian Formalist Criticism: Four Essays* (Lincoln: University of Nebraska Press, 1965): 3–24; Carlo Ginzburg, 'Making Things Strange: The Prehistory of a Literary Device', *Representations* 56 (1996): 8–28. See also *Poetics Today* special issue, 'Estrangement Revisited', 26:4 (2005).
7 Victor Segalen, *Essai sur l'exotisme: une esthétique du divers* (Paris: Fata Morgana, 1978).
8 Hans-Georg Gadamer, *Wahrheit und Methode: Grundzüge einer philosophischen Hermeneutik*, 2 vols. [1960–86] (Tübingen: Mohr, 1990–3).
9 For more on these points, see Ann Rigney, *Imperfect Histories: The Elusive Past and the Legacy of Romantic Historicism* (Ithaca: Cornell University Press, 2001): 13–58 and 'Fiction and the Circulation of National Histories' (forthcoming).
10 See, for example, the special issue of *Rethinking History* 6 (2002) on the graphic novel as a medium of historical expression.
11 Willliam Uricchio, 'Simulation, History and Computer Games', in Joost Raessens and Jeffrey Goldstein (eds), *Handbook of Computer Game Studies* (Cambridge, Mass.: MIT Press, 2005): 327–38.
12 White points out that historians remained stuck for far too long in the realist aesthetics of the nineteenth century and should have been more responsive to the alternatives thrown up by modern art: *Figural Realism: Studies in the Mimesis Effect* (Baltimore: Johns Hopkins University Press, 1999).
13 For a brief account of this circulation model of culture, see Stephen Greenblatt, 'Culture', in Lentricchia and McLaughlin, *Critical Terms for Literary Study*, pp. 225–31.

12 Resisting apocalypse and rethinking history

Dominick LaCapra

The temptation in relating history and critical theory, especially via a manifesto, is to participate in a cultural and intellectual tendency that has been pronounced in the West since Romanticism: radically to question everything established – to be outrageous, radically transgressive, sublimely transcendent, even terroristic – and then leave any putting together of the pieces to unspecified others.[1] This seemingly irrepressible apocalyptic urge follows in its own exorbitant way the logic of the antidote: one fights a dubious constellation of forces by taking an extract of them and turning it back on the criticised object. The difficulty comes when one believes that the proper dosage is itself an overwhelming or excessive one, that the answer to a perceived excess (of staid research, of piling up facts to no end, of complacent style, of contextualising to the point of objectifying and neutralising the other) is to overdose on the antidote (Theory, Experience, Discourse, [Bio]Power-Everywhere, Violence-Everywhere, Experimental Writing, Disjunction, Sublimity, Shock Therapy).[2] The difficulty is that one extreme is not an alternative to another. At best, it obscures as much as it illuminates. At worst, it is locked in the same repetitive cycle as its opposite number, threatens to become all too predictable, and offers little promise of effective change.

The alternative to the apocalyptic Big Bang in historiography is not business as usual or a sober, complacent return to the tried-and-true which one recommends to students as a premature path to ancestral wisdom. The problem is to intervene in the discipline in informed and cogent but flexible, non-codifiable ways that address its current configuration and try to point it in more desirable directions, and to do so in a manner that has an eye for the dimensions of historiography that are not confined to the present but themselves have a longer history and a possible future in that they continue to pose, in different ways, thought-provoking questions over time. Indeed, such an intervention should also be mindful of the interaction between the historical and transhistorical forces that affect the historian – forces that question the possibilities of the historical enterprise and indicate the manner in which the historian, like others, is internally challenged by what has been figured in terms of the 'transhistorically' (or structurally) traumatic, the dangerous supplement, the 'extimate' other, the disorientingly uncanny – that which leaves residues and remainders that set limits to a history of meaning in that they cannot be fully mastered or integrated meaningfully into a histori- cised narrative or interpretive account.[3] Here one may define the desirable intervention, including the manifesto itself, as an essayistic attempt (essai) to make manifest, hence available for critical enquiry, the often unexamined assumptions informing a practice.[4] In this essayistic sense, the manifesto is neither an exploding linguistic bomb nor a sun-clear exposition of *the* historian's craft (*'le métier de l'historien'* in the celebrated phrase of Marc Bloch). It is rather the historian's fallible entry into critical dialogic exchange with other voices both in historiography and across the disciplines.[5] Indeed, one hopes the day is long past when one believed one could, however unassumingly, legislate for an entire discipline.

What I have expressed thus far indicates my belief that history should be engaged in a sustained, mutually questioning and self-questioning interchange with critical theory and that historians should read demanding, often difficult theoretical texts and enquire into their bearing for historical enquiry and the very understanding of historiography and historicity. One can provide no definitive list of such theoretical texts. The 'canon' changes as much as the objects of historical investigation, and at the present time its constitu- ents increasingly include the works of non-Western thinkers and theorists as well as those of more familiar figures, many of whom themselves put forth, with greater or lesser critical insight, considerations bearing on the problem of Western 'ethnocentrism', including ethnocentric conceptions of history and historiography. (Here the title of Dipesh Chakrabarty's book, *Provincial- izing Europe*, is emblematic of the reorientation of much recent historical thought.)[6] A mutually interrogative interaction between history and critical theory allows historians to enter into a larger, mutable discursive arena in the humanities and social sciences. Such a view of history is bound up with the conviction that the student of history will have to combine the traditional skills of the historian with the acuity of a critical analyst and close, self- questioning reader of demanding texts. Thus s/he would have the ability to do archivally based research requiring a painstaking concern for accuracy, lucidity and specific detail. S/he would also have a knowledge of critical and social-scientific theories that s/he is able not only to analyse and situate con- textually but deploy and put to the test in her or his own work in a careful, selective, thought-provoking manner.

Such efforts would give rise to a newer breed of historian, already in the making, who would have a solid grounding in historiography and empirical research as well as a thoroughgoing, critically informed grasp of recent theoretical developments – historians who can bring theory to the archives and subject them to a newer kind of *Quellenkritik* that is not restricted to such necessary activities as authenticating and dating documents. The very conception of the archive would be rethought to allow both for critical enquiry into the constitution or construction of traditional archives of unpublished sources and for the expansion of the concept of the archive itself to include, for example, philosophical and rhetorical traditions often harbouring unexamined or concealed dimensions, whether in unpublished material or not. Most importantly, one or another critical theory (Foucauldian genealogy, Derridean deconstruction, Frankfurt school *Kritik*, Freudian or Lacanian psychoanalysis) would not simply be 'applied' to historical material that is reprocessed unilaterally in its terms. Indeed, aspects of a critical theory might well be subject to criticism and reconceptualisation. As a result there would be a mutually thought-provoking relation between historical research and critical theory that could not be reduced to rules of method or research paradigms but rather would sensitise the historian to otherwise avoided or underconceptualised issues and enable him or her to explore questions of cross-disciplinary significance. (Here theory would be contrasted not with practice but with critically unself-reflective practices and assumptions.) In order to bring about a mutually thought-provoking relation between history and theory, the historian would have to become an informed and reflective critical theorist and the critical theorist a thinker who is concerned with the way history tests theory and does not simply illustrate abstract theses or disintegrate into an irrelevant array of incontinent contingencies or idiosyncratic particularities.

In line with these considerations, I would make a distinction between two approaches to historiography that themselves represent complementary extremes which have tempted historians in the recent past.[7] The first is quite familiar and might be termed a 'documentary' or 'self-sufficient' research model, of which positivism is the extreme form. On this first approach, gathering evidence and making referential statements in the form of truth-claims based on that evidence constitute necessary and sufficient conditions of historiography. The second (seemingly more 'theoretical') approach, which also has become familiar even though it is less prevalent than the first, is nevertheless the latter's negative mirror image. I am referring to radical constructivism (sometimes conflated with postmodernism).[8] For it, referential statements making truth-claims apply at best only to events and are of restricted, perhaps even marginal significance. By contrast, essential are performative, figurative, aesthetic, rhetorical, ideological, ethical and political factors (the list varies with author and text) that 'construct' structures – stories, plots, arguments, interpretations, explanations – in which referential statements are embedded and take on meaning and significance. As shall become evident, my own view falls at neither extreme represented by these two approaches. But the point is not to postulate a *juste milieu* between the extremes. Nor is it to resort to a tweaked objectivism or a concession-riddled radical constructivism. It is rather to articulate problems and relations in a significantly different manner.[9]

In a documentary or self-sufficient research model, priority is given to research based on primary (preferably archival) documents that enable one to derive authenticated facts about the past which may be recounted in a narrative (the more 'artistic' approach) or employed in a mode of analysis which puts forth testable hypotheses (the more 'social-scientific' approach).[10] Even on the 'artistic' approach, for which the primary if not sole form of valid historiography is translating archives into heavily documented or 'thick' narrative (and/or description), the very process of translation – how one gets from archive to narrative – as well as the constitution of the archive itself may not be explicitly understood and interrogated as problems. Indeed, on this model, there is a sense in which writing (or the signifying practice in general, including reading) is not a problem. Writing is subordinated to content in the form of facts, their narration, or their description and analysis. It is thus reduced to writing up the results of research (a frequently invoked phrase), and style is limited to a restricted notion of mellifluous, immediately readable or accessible, well-crafted prose in which form ideally has no significant effect on content. In other words, writing (or signification in general, for example the image or the film) is a medium for expressing a content, and its ideal goal is to be transparent to content or an open window on the past – with figures of rhetoric serving only an instrumental role in illustrating what could be expressed without significant loss in purely literal terms.

In its more extreme forms, a documentary or self-sufficient research model *may* bring with it a stress on quantitative methods (prominent in cliometrics and during a phase of the *Annales* school), but it generally *does* involve the following features, which add further dimensions to a predominantly, if not exclusively, referential or constative use of language that conveys truth-claims based on evidence:

- a strict separation or binary opposition between subject and object;
- a tendency to conflate objectivity with objectivism or the objectification of the other that is addressed only in the form of third-person referential statements, direct quotations, and summaries or paraphrases;[11]
- an identification of historical understanding with causal explanation or, especially more recently, with the fullest possible contextualisation of the other (especially in the form of thick description or narration);
- a construction of the object or artefact solely as document, source or evidence ('text' is taboo);
- an aversion to theory or an acquaintance with certain of its forms only to the extent that one is thereby able both to ward them off in a way that seems not to be utterly uninformed and (at times deceptively) to disavow positivism and narrow empiricism as things of the past;[12]
- a denial of transference or the problem of the implication of the observer in the object of observation or representation;
- a tendency to avoid or smooth over traumatic dimensions of history, typical of extreme events, at least by focusing on normalising processes (for example, bureaucratisation or modernisation), resorting to neutralising techniques of representation (series of facts, dates, statistics,

graphs), employing the same unmodulated style whatever the object of discourse, and relying on what has been termed 'narrative fetishism';[13]

- an exclusion or downplaying of a dialogic, responsive relation to the other (or artefact) recognised as having a voice or perspective that may question the observer or even place him or her in question by generating problems about his or her assumptions, affective investments and values;
- a form of disciplinary identity politics that rigidly polices the borders of historiography, excludes unprofessionalised 'aliens', defines the *métier* of the historian in overly one-dimensional or insufficiently dialo-gised or self-critical terms, and inhibits interaction (including interaction internalised in the historian's own practice) with humanistic and critical-theoretical disciplines as well as with problems agitating the larger public sphere.

In general one might say that a self-sufficient research paradigm and, in even more pronounced form, its positivistic extreme confine historiography to a narrowly craft-like practice, learned by emulating exemplars and based exclusively on constative or referential statements involving truth-claims (by preference based on archival research) made by an observer about a sharply differentiated object of research.[14]

I referred to the second position in historiography as radical construc-tivism. It has received its most articulate defence in *dimensions* of the complex work of such important figures as Hayden White and Frank Ankersmit, who accept the distinction between historical and fictional statements on the level of reference to events but question it on more essential structural (or interpretive) levels.[15] For them, there is an identity or fundamental similarity between historiography and fiction, literature or the aesthetic on structural levels, and their emphasis is on the rhetorical nature, 'literariness', figurality or even fictionality of structures in all these areas.[16] To quote Ankersmit:

> All that is essential and interesting in the writing of history (both in theory and practice) is not to be found at the level of individual state-ments, but at that of the politics adopted by historians when they select the statements that individuate their 'picture of the past' . . . Saying *true* things about the past is easy – anybody can do that – but saying *right* things about the past is difficult. That truly [*sic*] requires historical insight and originality.[17]

(The obvious follow-up question is whether saying the 'right' things itself involves truth-claims, including claims on structural and interpretive levels which may in some differential sense involve 'politics' but are not reducible to it. For example, I pay attention to scapegoating and quasi-sacrificial dimensions of processes, including the Nazi genocide, and I oppose them politically, but the latter is not the only or even the essential reason for the former.) In any event, in radical constructivism (as in the documentary model), the subject is sharply differentiated from the object in a manner that disavows transferential implication and gives inadequate attention to the role of immanent critique. And rhetoric (or figuration) may itself be understood in insufficiently differentiated terms as it applies to different fields, areas, texts or dimensions of texts. (For example, it is not surprising to learn that Primo Levi makes use of figurative language. The specific question is how the figurative and the literal, the hyperbolic and the understated, the affectively charged and the coolly analytic interact in his different texts as compared with those of others addressing comparable problems, such as Jean Améry and Giorgio Agamben.)[18] In comparison with a documentary or restricted research model, radical constructivism's significant twist (or reversal of the binary relation) is that the disimplicated subject, in full creative, existential freedom, presumably imposes meaning and, on epistemological and even political levels, constructs or fashions the object *ex nihilo* in a radical break with the past that brings with it a sublime elevation of the human subject to the quasi-transcendental heights of an 'endower' of meaning, with the simultaneous reduction of the object or other to raw material or unprocessed record.[19]

How may one negotiate between the extremes of a self-sufficient research paradigm (if not a born-again positivism) and radical constructivism without relying on a complacent, mix-and-match *juste milieu* but rather by rearticulating problems in significantly different ways? This is, I think, the issue for historiographical thought at the present time to which I would like to make a few contributions that do not pretend to be exhaustive.

I would begin by observing that there are elements of a research paradigm which, extricated from a self-sufficient, autonomous framework, I (along with the overwhelming majority of historians) find indispensable, including the importance of contextualisation, factual knowledge, extensive research, footnoting, familiarity with often valuable past contributions to the discipline, and the idea that historiography necessarily involves truth-claims based on evidence – or what might be called an irreducible 'aboutness' – not only on the level of directly referential or factual statements about events but, however problematically, on more structural and comprehensive levels, such as narration, interpretation and analysis. But I think that one has to rethink and resituate these features in a manner not accommodated by their insufficiently questioned role in a self-sufficient research paradigm.

Constructivists are of assistance in this process of rethinking and rearticulation, but they become misleadingly extreme when they take the valid notion that there are structural similarities between historiography and art or literature and exaggerate it, at times to the point of identity, hence downplaying the role (as well as the difficulty) of research and truth-claims in historiography. They may also divert attention from, or limit understanding of, the distinctive ways truth-claims may apply to art or literature. For example, a work of art (as well as the generically mixed 'docudrama') may be justifiably criticised if it distorts history in an epistemologically, ethically and politically dubious manner, for example by negating, marginalising or obfuscating the historical importance and genocidal nature of the Holocaust, as does Edgar Reitz in *Heimat*.[20] Art or literature may also provide both documentable and more or less speculative insight into historical processes, notably on the level of experience, or even offer a reading of the times, for example by examining the post-traumatic residues of extreme events that may even be transmitted across generations, as does Toni Morrison in *Beloved*.[21] To be sure, truth-claims are neither the only nor always the most important consideration in art and its analysis. Of obvious importance are poetic, rhetorical and performative dimensions of art which not only mark but make differences historically (dimensions that are differentially at play in historical writing as well). And truth-claims are indeed claims, but the difficulty in substantiating and validating them or specifying and qualifying them to indicate their approximate weight in accounting for processes, especially on structural, explanatory and interpretive levels, is not a reason for being dismissive about them or downgrading their importance. In different but related ways, truth-claims are relevant not only to historiography but to works of art on the level of their general structures or procedures of emplotment – which may offer significant insights (or, at times, oversights), suggesting lines of enquiry for the work of historians (for example, with respect to post-traumatic symptoms and transgenerational processes of 'possession' or haunting). Truth-claims are also pertinent on the level of justifiable questions addressed to art on the basis of historical knowledge and research combined with more specifically aesthetic questions concerning framing, genre, mode, voice and so forth. (For example, how accurate – and how well framed – is the representation of the Polish population in Claude Lanzmann's *Shoah* or of the camps in Roberto Benigni's *Life Is Beautiful*?) In brief, the interaction, mutual implication and at times interrogative relation between historiography and art (including fiction) is more complicated than is suggested by either a radical-constructivist conflation or a self-sufficient historicist binary opposition between the two, a point that is becoming increasingly forceful in recent attempts to reconceptualise the study of art and culture.[22]

One might also make explicit what is often assumed in White: narrativisation is closest to fictionalisation in the sense of a dubious departure from, or distortion of, historical reality when it conveys relatively unproblematic closure (or what Frank Kermode terms 'a sense of an ending').[23] Indeed, a critique of narrative, such as Roland Barthes' or Sande Cohen's, becomes more understandable when it is addressed to conventional or formulaic narrative involving closure (including narrative fetishism).[24] Moreover, White defends what he sees as modernist (or Ankersmit as postmodernist) narrative and argues that historiography would do well to emulate its resistance to closure and its experimentalism in general rather than rely on nineteenth-century realism in its putative modes of representation and emplotment. Hans Kellner has attempted to show how Fernand Braudel's study of the

Mediterranean at the time of Philip II does just that by enacting a satiric and carnivalesque interaction of various levels of meaning, interpretation and explanation.[25] In any case, recent critiques of narrative are most convincing when applied to conventional narratives (or the conventional dimension of narrative) seeking resonant closure, and claims about the possible role of 'figural realism' and experimental narrative with respect to historiography are often thought-provoking and well worth careful attention.[26]

One way to see experimental narratives is to understand them as exploring the intricate relations between acting out (or compulsively repeating) traumatic events and their intensely 'cathected' or emotionally invested remainders, and attempting to work them over and through, towards less constraining alternatives that provide openings to possible, and possibly more desirable, futures. (Indeed, the recent rise of trauma studies is remarkable, and it is beginning to have its impact in historiography, including forms of resistance.) Various modes of signification may even be seen as providing relatively safe (if at times unsettling, even uncanny) havens for exploring the complex relations among responses to trauma, at least if one does not misleadingly postulate a direct, unmediated passage from art to life. Some of the most powerful forms of modern art and writing, as well as some of the most compelling forms of criticism (including forms of deconstruction), often seem to figure extreme, jarring, at times opaque event and experience through traumatic or post-traumatic writing in closest proximity to trauma. (It would seem evident that important figures may be seen, with nuanced differences, in this light – say, Virginia Woolf, Samuel Beckett or Paul Celan. Beckett, for example, might even be read as staging the plight of the *Muselmann*, the most abject victim in the camps with his problematic relation to everyman, in a series of insistently minimalist, disconcerting, sometimes terrorised figures.)

At times the compelling feeling of keeping faith with trauma and its victims may lead to a seemingly possessed, even compulsive preoccupation with aporia, an endlessly melancholic, impossible mourning, and a resistance to working through. I think that, at least on a certain level, one is involved here in more or less secularised displacements of the sacred and its paradoxes. The hiddenness, death or absence of a radically transcendent divinity or of absolute foundations (figured in Lacan as the missed encounter with non-symbolisable Real) makes of existence a fundamentally traumatic scene in which anxiety threatens to colour, and perhaps confuse, all relations. There has even been an important tendency in modern culture and thought to convert trauma into the occasion for sublimity (or *jouissance*), to transvalue it into a test of the self or the group and a quasi-transcendental entry into the extraordinary. In the sublime, the excess (of affect, or disorientation, even of violence) attendant on trauma becomes an uncanny source of elation or ecstasy. Even extremely destructive events, such as the Holocaust or the dropping of atomic bombs on Hiroshima and Nagasaki (or recently the suicide bombing of the Twin Towers), may become occasions of negative sublimity or displaced sacralisation.[27] They may also give rise to what may be termed founding or foundational traumas – traumas that are commemorated and paradoxically become the valorised or intensely cathected basis of identity for an individual or a group rather than events that unsettlingly pose the problematic question of identity.[28]

I would simply refer here to a rather blatant and controversial aestheticised sublimation (or rendering sublime) of the traumatic. Shortly after 9/11, the composer Karl-Heinz Stockhausen stated, and in a sense bore witness to his own experience, of the attack on the World Trade Center:

> The greatest work of art imaginable for the whole cosmos. Minds achieving something in an act that we couldn't even dream of in music, people rehearsing like mad for 10 years, preparing fanatically for a concert, and then dying, just imagine what happened there. You have people who are that focused on a performance and then 5,000 people are dispatched to the afterlife, in a single moment. I couldn't do that. By comparison, we composers are nothing. Artists, too, sometimes try to go beyond the limits of what is feasible and conceivable, so that we wake up, so that we open ourselves to another world.[29]

Fortunately, the actual number of those killed was lower, and Stockhausen later retracted his comment. But the fact that the comment expressed his more immediate response is noteworthy. I would add parenthetically that Zizek, always ready to shock, commends the 'element of truth' in Stockhausen's statement which he rather projectively finds in the perception of 'the collapse of the WTC towers as the climactic conclusion of twentieth-century art's "passion for the Real" – the "terrorists" themselves did not do it primarily to provoke real material damage, but for *the spectacular effect of it*'.[30] Would it be banal (or insufficiently 'hip') to point out that this perception (or act of projective identification) would come as small comfort to those who do not find, in an aestheticised passion for the Real, an acceptable socio-political analysis of, or response to, the suicide bombings, including the real suffering they caused or helped to occasion (including, as Zizek himself observes, through their manipulative use as a pretext for a 'war on terror')?

Recently prominent is a genre that brings up the issue of memory and is neither history nor fiction but may play a role in both: the testimony. In the testimony one bears witness to one's experience of events. And an obvious difficulty – or a difficulty that should be obvious – arises when a fictional testimony passes itself off as historically true rather than framing itself as fiction that makes qualified, limited truth-claims about experience. (This difficulty arose in accentuated form in the well-known case of Binjamin Wilkomirski.[31]) Affect-laden, at times traumatic experience in general has a problematic relation to empirical events – a relation mediated by memory, its variations over time, and the role in shaping or even transforming memory of both historical works and fictional genres current in one's society and culture (the film, the docudrama, the novel and so forth). In her *Era of the Witness*, Annette Wieviorka provides a concise history of witnessing and testimony since the Second World War in which she tries to avoid the simple dismissal of testimony by such historians as Raul Hilberg and Lucy Dawidowicz and instead to offer a critical approach to the use of testimonies by historians.[32] In her last chapter on the trial of Maurice Papon, however, she is particularly vexed by the way historians have been called on at trials paradoxically to bear witness to history. She is even more concerned by the spread of witnessing and testimony to the second and third generations who somehow bear witness to experiences they have not directly had. She nevertheless recounts the plight of the hidden child, Esther Fogiel, whose parents were deported and whose foster parents, with whom the fleeing parents had placed the child, became brutal towards her once they learned of the parents' fate. She was raped, shunned and made to sleep in the husband's bed. The family was in fact a *ménage à trois* since the wife's lover was also part of the group. Wieviorka writes of the young Esther: 'Her only tie of affection was to a small dog. One night she heard its groans and, at daybreak, found the dog hanging above her bed. "I see it still", she stated' (p. 147). Even critics of the trial, such as Bertrand Poirot-Delpech and Éric Conan, for whom 'a trial for national memory' did not serve history and instead bred confusion, found value in the proceeding if it brought some consolation to this woman, served to lend weight and legitimation to the testimony of victims, and answered 'the victims' need to find the origin of their pain' (citing Conan, pp. 148).

Yet Wieviorka herself has certain reservations: 'Reading or hearing the voices of these "hidden children", one learns about the violence inflicted by certain traumas and their irreparable character. But does one learn history? The repercussions of an event inform us about the power of that event but do not account for what the event was.' And in her concluding lines she states: 'Historians have but one obligation, to follow their profession . . . Because when traces fade with time, what remains is the written record of events in history, which is the only future of the past' (p. 149). It is significant that this conclusion tends to run counter to the entire argumentative movement of the book which neither conflates nor dichotomises between history and memory, written document and testimony, but attempts to trace critically their complex interactions. And what is at issue is precisely the definition of the historical profession. Even Wieviorka's very critical treatment of Daniel Jonah Goldhagen's *Hitler's Willing Executioners: Ordinary Germans and the Holocaust* serves to bring out norms of historical enquiry by indicating how Goldhagen transgressed those norms (norms requiring that one not play to the emotions, not judge actors in the past, but instead seek to strike the appropriate tone, especially with respect to highly charged issues (pp. 93–4).[33] As she puts it: 'Daniel Goldhagen's work pulverized the universally established criteria for the academic writing of history' (p. 90). I would add that even the historian who avoids normative judgements about the past and its actors must make them on a meta-level that defines a more or less flexible conception of historical enquiry which brings with it institutional rewards and sanctions. How one defines 'proper' or at least acceptable history was centrally at issue in the Goldhagen controversy as well as in the earlier case of David Abraham, and it had major consequences for the professional life of both these young scholars. Moreover, one may note with respect to Wieviorka's own query about what the voices of 'hidden children' bring to history that the power or effects of an event are also parts of history, as is the poorly understood process of intergenerational transmission of traumatic or post-traumatic symptoms. In a sense, these processes may not directly relate to the events of the Shoah, but they are indeed basic elements of its after-effects and after-life that have a crucial bearing on the present and future. A more cogent conclusion to Wieviorka's excellent study might have been that her account of the vicissitudes of testimony and witnessing leaves one with the question of how to come to terms with and work through the past, including centrally how empathy and unsettlement provoked by testimonies are to be combined with resistance to a cult of intimacy, a memorialisation of memory, a confusion of compassion or empathy with identification, and an impairment of the critical perspective necessary for writing history.

Working through, which may occur in narrative but also in other genres (the essay, the poem, ritual, dance, music and so forth), is an articulatory practice: to the extent one works through trauma (as well as transferential relations in general), one is able to distinguish between past and present and to recall in memory that something happened to one (or one's people) back then, while realising that one is living here and now with openings to the future. An attempt to work over and through problems may also enable a differential approach to the aesthetic of the sublime that neither dismisses it nor remains uncritically within its frame of reference. Such an attempt does not signal total critical distance, full emancipation or complete mastery of problems, including one's sometimes haunting implication in, if not possession by, the past. Nor does it imply that there is a pure opposition between past and present or that acting out – whether for the traumatised or for those empathetically relating to them – can be fully transcended towards a state of closure or full ego-identity (as a professional historian or in terms of any other delimited identity). And it should not induce the dubious pathologisation of acting out (or other psychic processes) in a manner that occludes or encrypts normative judgements that should be made explicit and subject to argument. But it does mean that processes of articulation crucial to working through may counteract the symptomatic force of acting out and the repetition compulsion whereby the past not only haunts but intrusively erupts in the present and is compulsively relived or re-enacted, however inappropriate its scenarios may be to current conditions and however much it may be conducive to endless cycles of violence. Such processes may also enable victims not to be overwhelmed or even crushed by a single identity that pre-empts all others and blocks access to possible futures.

Processes of working through, including mourning and modes of critical thought and practice, involve the possibility of making distinctions or developing specific articulations that are recognised as problematic but still function as limits, necessary bases of judgement, and possibly desirable resistances to confusion, rant and the obliteration or blurring of all distinctions. (The latter states may indeed occur in trauma or in acting out post-traumatic conditions.) Working through also highlights the point that a truth-claim is precisely that – a claim that may be more or less validated but not an unproblematic assertion of truth. In any event, necessary for a critical historiography (but of course not exclusive to it) are the problems of differential analysis (involving problematic distinctions), specificity, judgement and articulation, which are also key components of working through problems, including divisive, highly charged aspects of the past.

Truth-claims are at issue in differential ways at all levels of historical discourse. Such claims are the vehicle of a pathos (at times approaching a pathology) that warrants recognition, and they are perhaps best understood as conveying a regulative ideal. This does not imply that truth-claims, however significant, exhaust historical discourse or that one may convert them into the idea that one is simply telling the truth about history. Moreover, truth-claims have a differential purchase in different dimensions of historiography, typically with the strongest role, as radical constructivists have intimated, with respect to propositions stating facts about events. Their role is different and more contestable on complex, interpretive levels that may be especially prominent in intellectual and cultural history but are also at issue in other areas. For example, what relative weight should one give, in interpreting the Nazi genocide, to the 'machinery of destruction' and bureaucratisation in relation to what Saul Friedlander has termed 'redemptive anti-Semitism', possibly (in my judgement) involving, at least in certain 'elite' perpetrators, a quasi-sacrificial scapegoat mechanism (even, at times, an aesthetic of the sublime) in ridding the *Volksgemeinschaft* of a putatively polluting Jewish presence? Or, to change registers, take the prevalent interpretation of Hegel's *Phenomenology of Mind* as a philosophical *Bildungsroman* and the related argument by Friedrich Kittler that Hegel's *Phenomenology* should be considered as the philosophical completion of the discourse network of 1800.[34] There are in a sense truth-claims involved here that may to some extent be substantiated, but the interpretation and argument at issue go beyond truth-claims and offer insight that, however illuminating or thought provoking, must remain in certain respects speculative and contestable. The same might be said concerning my comment about Beckett and the *Muselmann* or about the contentions that Flaubert's *Sentimental Education* is a *Bildungsroman* with the *Bildung* left out, that his *Bouvard and Pécuchet* can be read as a parodic inversion of (or even an obscene double already within) Hegel's *Phenomenology*, or that the trial of Flaubert in the case of *Madame Bovary*, the transcript of which is typically appended at the novel's end (at least in French editions), seems almost to become a part of the novel in its misprisions, indirections and self-imploding banalities.[35] In any event, it should be evident that one cannot affirm a conventional stereotype of transparent representation or even a self-sufficient research paradigm as a one-size-fits-all model of historiography or historical understanding.

There is a crucial sense in which one begins investigation already inserted in an ongoing historical process, a positioning towards which one may attempt to acquire some transformative perspective or critical purchase. A crucial aspect of this positioning is the problem of the implication of the observer in the observed, what in psychoanalytic terms is treated as transference. Transference indicates that one begins enquiry *in medias res* (or in a middle-voiced 'position') which one engages in various ways. In historiography there are transferential relations between enquirers (especially pronounced in the relations between professor and graduate student and at times between the scholar and his or her critics) and between enquirers and the past, its figures and processes. The basic sense of transference I would stress is the tendency to repeat or re-enact performatively, in one's own discourse or relations, processes active in the object of study or critique. I think transference in this sense occurs willy-nilly, and the problem is how one comes to terms with it in ways involving various combinations, more or less subtle variations, and hybridised forms of acting out, working over, and working through. Indeed, to the extent one does not explicitly engage transferential implication and the problem of repetition, one tends blindly to act them out, often becoming involved in performative contradictions.

Such blind repetitions and performative contradictions abounded in the affectively charged controversy surrounding David Abraham's *The Collapse of the Weimar Republic: Political Economy and Crisis*.[36] A typical charge against Abraham was his use of structural explanation or interpretation that went beyond any possible empirical substantiation. Yet those levelling the charge (such as Gerald Feldman and Ulrich Nocken) at times accused Abraham of conscious fabrication or lying, a charge that itself went beyond available evidence and could not be substantiated. A piquant version of performative contradiction appears when Richard Evans resorts to utterly speculative psychoanalysis in asserting that 'while Abraham did not deliberately falsify evidence . . . he *subconsciously* molded the evidence gathered in his research notes in order to fit the interpretation he had worked out beforehand'.[37] Possibly. But how could Evans know, or substantiate such a claim? I would speculate that Abraham was a suitable scapegoat (ultimately drummed out of the profession), as well as an object of disavowed projective identification, because he not only made many unacceptable errors (sloppy note-taking, seemingly defective knowledge of a foreign language, conflating paraphrases with direct quotations, misattributing statements) but also embodied anxieties (could I possibly have fallen prey to such errors myself?) that are especially acute in the context of a documentary or restricted research model, especially when the latter is taken to fundamentalist extremes. His work was also uncomfortably situated on the threshold between a faulted example of that documentary model and a form of radical constructivism.[38]

Historiography may, within limits, participate in the complex, self-questioning process of working through the past, especially on collective levels, notably in its effort critically to examine and monitor memory, counteract compulsive repetition, recapture unrealised possibilities in the past, and open possible – and possibly more desirable – futures.[39] The norm of objectivity itself need not be conflated with one-dimensional objectification of the other but instead understood as requiring checks and resistances to full identification. Objectivity in this sense is one important goal of meticulous research, contextualisation and the attempt to be as attentive as possible to the voices of others whose alterity is recognised, including the possibility that those one studies may challenge one's own assumptions and judgements. One need not blame the victim (or the intimate of a victim) possessed by the past and unable to get beyond it to any viable extent, or ignore the importance of empathic unsettlement in responding to victims and extreme situations, in order to question the idea that it is desirable simply to identify with the victim, or to become a surrogate victim, and to write (or perform, at times histrionically) in that incorporated or appropriated, 'traumatised' voice (a tendency prominent in certain forms of affective or performative writing and response).[40] Indeed, the question is whether and to what extent too insistent an empathic orientation, especially when it prompts transferential acting out and identification, may bring a corresponding shortfall in critical acuity as well as a resistance to working through problems that may require socio-political criticism and change.[41] The challenge, at least for historical understanding, is how to strive for an empathic or compassionate response that neither entails a sacrifice of analytic and critical ability nor induces a presumption to speak in the other's voice or to take her or his place. The difference or singularity of the other implies that one may speak or write not for but with respect to (and, if warranted, with respect for) the other. Empathy in this sense is a form of virtual – not vicarious – experience in which emotional response comes with the possibility of critical judgement and the realisation that the experience of the other is not one's own.[42]

Hence a concern, both historical and ethico-political, with victims and at times traumatising processes of victimisation, which unfortunately have had a disproportionate place in history, does not imply subscribing to an indiscriminately generalised 'victimology', a conflation of history and trauma, or a self-defeating competition for first place in victimhood. Nor should it be made to obscure the significance of more 'everyday' or ordinary problems in history, including less dramatic forms of violence related to structures of poverty or oppression. Yet a crucial question is whether historiography in its own way may help, not speciously to heal, but to come to terms with the wounds and scars of the past in an attempt to open more desirable possibilities in the present and future. Such a coming-to-terms would seek knowledge whose truth-claims are not one-dimensionally objectifying or narrowly cognitive but involve affect and may empathetically expose the self to a possibly disorienting unsettlement which should not be glorified or fixated on but addressed in a manner that strives to be cognitively and ethically responsible as well as open to the experience of others and the challenge of utopian aspiration. The horizon of this approach is a reconceptualisation of relations among research, theory and practice in a manner that may dispel or at least disrupt the mutually reinforcing moods of highly 'theorised' if despairing disempowerment or abjection and blank or empty utopianism, which seem so prevalent recently in the academy as well as in intellectual circles.[43] In undertaking such reconceptualisation, one may bring historiography itself into closer and more critical contact not only with other disciplines but with a larger public sphere, its problems and its possibilities.

Notes

1 For a critical investigation of related tendencies, see my *History in Transit: Experience, Identity, Critical Theory* (Ithaca: Cornell University Press, 2004). See also Frank Lentriccia and Jody McAuliffe, *Crimes of Art and Terror* (Chicago: University of Chicago Press, 2003) and James Berger, *After the End: Representations of Post-apocalypse* (Minneapolis: University of Minnesota Press, 1999).

2 Slavoj Zizek's work is filled with arresting and thought-provoking insights. Yet he has been important in disseminating the idea that the truly radical and creatively disruptive response to excess is to enter fully into the excess and drive it to the self-imploding or explosive limit – the limit of fantasy, of totalising yet aporetic knowledge, of the traumatic real. This seems to be the Zizekian 'ethic' as well as his notion of 'traversing the fantasy' – a far cry from an effort to work through problems. See, for example, *Welcome to the Desert of the Real* (London: Verso, 2002). For one of the better-argued defences of Zizek's perspective, see Paul Eisenstein, *Traumatic Encounters: Holocaust Representation and the Hegelian Subject* (Albany: State University Press of New York, 2003). On these issues, see my *Writing History, Writing Trauma* (Baltimore: Johns Hopkins University Press, 2001) with which Eisenstein fruitfully engages, although he mistakenly sees my approach simply as a historicising contextualism. See also my *Representing the Holocaust: History, Theory Trauma* (Ithaca: Cornell University Press, 1994), especially the discussion of Jean-François Lyotard (pp. 96–9), *History and Memory after Auschwitz* (Ithaca: Cornell University Press, 1998), and *History and Reading: Tocqueville, Foucault, French Studies* (Toronto: University of Toronto Press, 2000).

3 In Lacan the extimate is the anxiety-producing, traumatising, constitutive other that is within the self or the psyche and related to unconscious processes of compulsive repetition, for example those operative in a scapegoat mechanism whereby one attempts to localise, externalise and exorcise the threatening other by projecting it on to victimised outsiders.

4 On the essay see especially Theodor Adorno, 'The Essay as Form', in *Notes to Literature*, vol. 1, trans. Shierry Weber Nicholsen [1958] (New York: Columbia University Press, 1991): 3–23: 'The essay is what it was from the beginning, the critical form par excellence; as immanent critique of intellectual constructions, as a confrontation of what they are with their concept, it is critique of ideology' (p. 18).

5 For a useful critical analysis of recent tendencies in the historical profession, see Elizabeth A. Clark, *History, Theory, Text: Historians and the Linguistic Turn* (Cambridge, Mass.: Harvard University Press, 2004).

6 *Provincializing Europe: Postcolonial Thought and Historical Difference* (Princeton: Princeton University Press, 2000). See also the engaged and engaging discussion in Robert J. C. Young, *Postcolonialism: A Very Short Introduction* (Oxford: Oxford University Press, 2003).

7 Certain points made in the ensuing discussion are further developed in my recent books, notably *Writing History, Writing Trauma* and *History in Transit*. See also my 'Tropisms of Intellectual History', *Rethinking History* 8 (2004): 499–529, and the responses to it in the same volume by Ernst van Alphen, Carolyn J. Dean, Allan Megill and Michael Roth.

8 I am criticising only radical constructivism. Various constructivisms, prominently including social constructivism, have done much useful work in the critique of essentialism and any framework relying on unexamined assumptions. But the dubious dimensions of radical constructivism may be signalled without denying the 'constructed' dimensions of social or cultural phenomena.

9 On the history of these issues, see Peter Novick, *That Noble Dream: The 'Objectivity Question' and the American Historical Profession* (Cambridge: Cambridge University Press, 1988). For a discussion that includes an attempt to reconceptualise the problem of objectivity in normative terms, see Thomas Haskell, 'Objectivity Is Not Neutrality', in Brian Fay, Philip Pomper and Richard T. Vann (eds), *History and Theory: Contemporary Readings* (Malden, Mass.: Blackwell, 1998): 299–319. See also Chris Lorenz's essay in the same volume, 'Historical Knowledge and Historical Reality: A Plea for "Internal Realism"' (pp. 342–76), and the contributions to Keith Jenkins (ed.), *The Postmodern History Reader* (New York: Routledge, 1997).

10 Despite what many see as the recent rise of cultural history and the relative decline of social history, the social-scientific approach is important for many historians but today not much discussed by philosophers treating historiography (for example, both Chris Lorenz in the analytic tradition and Paul Ricoeur in the continental tradition) who tend to follow Hayden White, even when they criticise him, by focusing on narrative.

11 In Kantian terms, extreme objectification treats the other not as an end but as a means.

12 In a review of Isabel V. Hull's important book *Absolute Destruction: Military Culture and the Practices of War in Imperial Germany* (Ithaca: Cornell University Press, 2005), V. R. Berghahn, in no-nonsense fashion, sees fit to compliment the author for 'an introduction that is striking for its concise statement of her purposes and unencumbered by lengthy methodological and historiographical discussions' (*American Historical Review* 110 (2005): 1269).

13 See Eric Santner, 'History beyond the Pleasure Principle: Some Thoughts on the Representation of Trauma', in Saul Friedlander (ed.), *Probing the Limits of Representation: Nazism and the 'Final Solution'* (Cambridge, Mass.: Harvard University Press, 1992): 143–54. Santner writes: 'By narrative fetishism I mean the construction and deployment of a narrative consciously or unconsciously designed to expunge the traces of the trauma or loss that called the narrative into being in the first place' (p. 144). Through narrative fetishism, one disavows the very need for processes of working through the past, including mourning its losses.

14 History conceived in restricted terms as a craft is constituted as antipathetic to critical theory and related forms of critical self-reflection, including the type of psychoanalysis understood not as psychohistory or psychobiography but as critical theory and directed particularly at the relation between the historian and

the past or the object of study. For a recent instance of the many collections of essays that by and large confine historiography to a documentary or restricted research model, see David Cannadine (ed.), *What Is History Now?* (London: Palgrave Macmillan, 2002).

15 Compare Hayden White, 'The Politics of Historical Interpretation: Discipline and De-sublimation', included in *The Content of the Form: Narrative Discourse and Historical Interpretation* (Baltimore: Johns Hopkins University Press, 1987): ch. 3. See also Chris Lorenz's 'Can History Be True? Narrativism, Positivism, and the "Metaphorical Turn"', *History and Theory* 37 (1998): 309–29. Lorenz's carefully argued essay nevertheless includes a very limited if not dismissive treatment of fiction understood as the opposite of history.

16 These tendencies in no sense exhaust the important, provocative contributions of either White or Ankersmit whose own later work at times render them problematic. See, for example, White's *Figural Realism: Studies in the Mimesis Effect* (Baltimore: Johns Hopkins University Press, 1999): chs. 1 and 2. It would take an entire essay to trace the varying relations among the logical, the aesthetic, the political, the ethical and the sublime in Ankersmit's conception of historical representation and what he terms 'narrative substances'. For a sympathetic account of his recent turn to the 'experiential sublime', see Martin Jay, *Songs of Experience: Modern American and European Variations on a Universal Theme* (Berkeley: University of California Press, 2005): 255–60.

17 "Reply to Professor Zagorin", in Fay, Pomper, and Vann, *History and Theory*, p. 209.

18 See the discussion of Levi's figural language in Hayden White, 'Figural Realism in Witness Literature', *Parallax* 30 (2004): 113–24. In this article, White notes what is often obscured in his earlier work (but noted in *Figural Realism*, p. 22): that rhetoricity, figuration and even 'literariness' are not the same thing as fictionality (p. 116).

19 On this score, Hayden White has been consistent over time since the publication of *Metahistory* (Baltimore: Johns Hopkins University Press, 1973). As he puts it in a sympathetic review of Alun Munslow's *The New History*, 'I believe stories exist only in language or discourse, not in real events or processes. By narrativisation, story order is imposed upon historical events and processes, thereby giving them narrative meaning (*Rethinking History* 9 (2005): 137n.). A key problem in such formulations is a form of thought that overly simplifies relations through a reliance on unexamined analytic dichotomies or binary oppositions, bringing about a radically constructivist understanding of human will and assertion. One need not believe that events or processes possess the 'story order' of the so-called traditional narrative to observe that the very dichotomisation or dissociation between event or process and meaning or narrative, with events reduced to meaningless raw material, and meaning or story order (the two often seen as identical in White) construed as the imposition or endowment of the historian as creative subject, is based on altogether dubious, yet interestingly symptomatic, assumptions. A starting point for a different view might be the argument that narrative undercuts the fact/fiction, event/structure and figurality/literality binaries. And a crucial consideration would be the way an anthropocentric radical constructivism (is there any other?) perhaps unintentionally repeats the traditional philosophical and theological division between human and other-than-human animal, typically eventuating in the exclusion and even scapegoating of the latter.

20 See the discussion of dubious dimensions in the work of Reitz as well as of Hans Jürgen Syberberg in Eric Santner, *Stranded Objects: Mourning, Memory, and Film in Postwar Germany* (Ithaca: Cornell University Press, 1990).

21 See the reading of *Beloved* in Berger, *After the End*, ch. 6 as well as in Satya

Mohanty, *Literary Realism and the Claims of History* (Ithaca: Cornell University Press, 1997).

22 This perspective has informed my own approach to problems. See especially my *'Madame Bovary' on Trial* (Ithaca: Cornell University Press, 1982) or my discussion of Claude Lanzmann's *Shoah* in *History and Memory after Auschwitz*, ch. 4. For an early attempt to rethink French studies in a manner relating history and art, see Maurice Crubellier, *Histoire Culturelle de la France XIXe–XXe siècle* (Paris: A. Colin, 1974). For a recent attempt, see Kristin Ross, *Fast Cars, Clean Bodies: Decolonization and the Reordering of French Culture* (Cambridge, Mass.: MIT Press, 1995) as well as the review of Richard Kuisel that goes beyond the critical analysis of difficulties in Ross's discussion to a disciplinarily narrow, dismissive response to the book, culminating in the legislative injunction: 'Historians can ignore this book' (*American Historical Review* 101 (1996): 859). See also the final chapter of my *History and Reading* as well as the contributions to *Rethinking History* 9: 2/3 (2005) on 'History, Fiction, and Historical Fiction'. Benigni's misty, air-brushed rendition of camp life might have been more acceptable had the framing voice-over of the son, concerning the protective fantasies of his father, been more than a stereotype-laden, pasted-on cellophane wrapper (with a fleeting initial reference to a fable full of wonder and sorrow and an equally fleeting concluding reference to the father's gift and sacrifice made good by a mother-and-child reunion, facilitated by an American soldier in the 'winning' tank and culminating in the son's triumphal cry – 'we won!' – echoed by the mother). The point in responding to Benigni's film is not whether humour in general is 'appropriate' with respect to the Shoah but rather the pertinence of Benigni's extremely benign, far-from-gallows, even narratively fetishistic humour which seems out of keeping and ineffective with respect to the problems he engages.

23 *The Sense of an Ending: Studies in the Theory of Fiction* (New York: Oxford University Press, 1967).

24 See the Barthes-inspired analysis in Sande Cohen, *Historical Culture: On the Recoding of an Academic Discipline* (Berkeley: University of California Press, 1986) as well as White's discussion in *Figural Realism*, ch. 1.

25 'Disorderly Conduct: Braudel's Mediterranean Satire', *History and Theory* 18 (1979): 187–222, reprinted in *Language and Historical Representation: Getting the Story Crooked* (Madison: University of Wisconsin Press, 1989): 153–89. See also Philippe Carrard, *Poetics of the New History: French Historical Discourse from Braudel to Chartier* (Baltimore: Johns Hopkins University Press, 1992).

26 One might compare figural realism, especially with respect to extreme or traumatic events, to what Michael Rothberg terms 'traumatic realism' in *Traumatic Realism: The Demands of Holocaust Representation* (Minneapolis: University of Minnesota Press, 2000).

27 For an elated response to the bombing of Hiroshima and Nagasaki, which at times resorts to a discourse of the sublime, see Georges Bataille's 1947 essay, 'Concerning the Accounts Given by the Residents of Hiroshima', in Cathy Caruth (ed.), *Trauma: Explorations in Memory* (Baltimore: Johns Hopkins University Press, 1995): 221–35. For an analysis and critique of Giorgio Agamben's turn to the sublime in his treatment of the Holocaust and, specifically, the figure of the *Muselmann* (in his *Remnants of Auschwitz*), see my *History in Transit*, ch. 4.

28 For a thought-provoking approach to these problems, see David Simpson, *9/11: The Culture of Commemoration* (Chicago: University of Chicago Press, 2006).

29 <http://www.osborne-conant.org/documentationstockhausen.htm>.

30 *Welcome to the Desert of the Real*, p. 11.

31 *Fragments: Memories of a Wartime Childhood*, trans. Carol Brown Janeway [1995] (New York: Schocken Books, 1996).

178 *Dominick LaCapra*

32 *The Era of the Witness*, trans. Jared Stark (Ithaca: Cornell University Press, 2006).

33 *Hitler's Willing Executioners* (New York: Alfred A. Knopf, 1996).

34 Friedrich Kittler, *Discourse Networks 1800/1900*, trans. Michael Metteer with Chris Cullens [1987] (Stanford: Stanford University Press, 1990): 160–73.

35 The first idea may be found in Jonathan Culler, *Flaubert: The Uses of Uncertainty* (Ithaca: Cornell University Press, 1974). The latter two ideas are my own, and the point about *Madame Bovary* is developed in more nuanced form in my '*Madame Bovary' on Trial*.

36 Princeton: Princeton University Press, 1981.

37 *In Defense of History* (New York and London: W. W. Norton, 1997): 104.

38 Although I make a specific use of his analysis, I am indebted to Peter Staudenmaier, 'Historiography and its Discontents: The David Abraham Affair and the Boundaries of Historical Scholarship', unpublished paper.

39 For extensive discussions of acting out and working through, as they apply to historiography, see especially my *Representing the Holocaust*, *Writing History, Writing Trauma* and *History in Transit*.

40 See, for example, my discussions of Claude Lanzmann in *History and Memory after Auschwitz* and of Giorgio Agamben in *History in Transit* as well as various references in *Writing History, Writing Trauma*. On the uses and abuses of an appeal to empathy, see Carolyn J. Dean, *The Fragility of Empathy after the Holocaust* (Ithaca: Cornell University Press, 2004). Dean's book is a sign that empathy or compassion may return as a concern of historians.

41 This issue arises in responses to the work of Shoshana Felman and Cathy Caruth, among others. See my discussion of Felman in *Representing the Holocaust* (pp. 116–25) and *History and Memory after Auschwitz* (pp. 111–16) and of Caruth in *Writing History, Writing Trauma* (pp. 181–5) and *History in Transit* (pp. 118–23), including, in the latter book, a discussion of Ruth Leys's harshly dismissive response to Caruth (pp. 83–93).

42 The concept of the virtual with respect to empathy or compassion has the virtue of placing in question the tendency to identify with the other and to speak in the other's voice, including taking up the role of surrogate victim. But it is not unproblematic and has echoes with respect to religious and theological traditions. As the *Oxford English Dictionary* informs readers: 'Virtualism: The Calvinist doctrine of Christ's virtual presence in the Eucharist'.

43 For analyses that address important and extremely difficult problems but often seem to go to apocalyptic extremes by averting desperation through sometimes blank utopianism, largely abstract alternatives and underspecified concepts (the global commons, singularities, absolute democracy and so forth), see Michael Hardt and Antonio Negri, *Empire* (Cambridge, Mass.: Harvard University Press, 2000) and *Multitude: War and Democracy in the Age of Empire* (New York: Penguin Press, 2004). Noteworthy in these widely read books is a present-and-future-oriented animus that pays insufficient attention to the relevance of a sustained critical dialogue with the past (reduced to nostalgia or at best to a scrapbook of examples and anecdotes, often alternating with myths or fictions and turned to when the argument falters). Also prominent is a reliance on concepts of biopower and biopolitics, despite the fact that minimal attention is paid to ecological problems and no attention at all to the claims of other-than-human animals and the rest of nature (notably with respect to factory farming and experimentation). Still, in the manner of challenging utopian thinking, Hardt and Negri offer concepts that open perspectives and demand further thought, for example, the notion of a globalised multitude as a multiplicity of different singularities.

13 Manifesto for an analytical political history

Frank Ankersmit

Burckhardt, the citizen of Basel, thought of himself as writing a more mean-ingful and usable history – history by citizens for citizens – than the ponderous volumes of the German scholar-bureaucrats of his day, even when he presented his work only in the form of lectures to his fellow citizens at Basel. His devastating comment on the *viri eruditissimi*, as he liked to call the philologists, is well known: 'In front of them a mountain of history; they dig a hole in it, create a pile of rubble and rubbish behind themselves, and die'.[1]

Introduction

When explaining the aim and purpose of the present volume, the editors urged contributors 'to describe and give a *raison d'être* for what they think history ought to be at this particular point in time, such that everything they think a historical consciousness might consist of could be realised in the future'. Self-evidently, this is the quintessential quesion to ask both his-torians themselves and philosophers of history. We can only agree here with Huizinga when writing that 'history is the mental form in which a civil-ization accounts for its past'.[2] Crucial in this definition was for Huizinga this notion of 'accounting for' (in Dutch: '*zich rekenschap afleggen van*'). He insists that this term subsumes in itself the following elements: the require-ment of the reliability ('*betrouwbaarheid*') and authenticity ('*echtheid*') of the kind of knowledge offered by the historian; and the necessity to transcend the differences between narrative, scientific and instructive history. But, above all, this 'accounting for the past' will inevitably involve an appeal to the social, political, cultural and ethical standards that are specific for the civilisation to which the historian belongs. In sum, history is never merely a passive registration of what the past has been like, as was suggested by Ranke's famous *obiter dictum* that the historian 'merely wants to show what the past actually has been like ("*er will bloss zeigen wie es eigentlich gewesen*")'.[3] History always is, and ought to be, an *interaction* between past and present.[4] It is a kind of double looking-glass in which the past is mirrored by the present and the present by the past. It follows from Huizinga's definition that the historian always has obligations towards both the past *and* the present: good and meaningful history is written in the name of the present. So, the editors' demand that the contributors to this volume should 'give a *raison d'être* for what they think history ought to be at this particular point in time' brings us to the heart of all historical writing and of what should inspire it.

Experimental history

Huizinga's musings about his definition of history is instructive for one more reason. For when explaining what this 'accounting for the past' should mean he distinguished (as we saw a moment ago) between the requirement of *Truth* (or scientific reliability) and that of *authenticity*. Surveying the preoccupations of historical theorists over the past few decades, one may say that Huizinga's distinction between Truth and authenticity spans seventy years of theoretical speculation about the nature of historical writing. It began in the 1940s with Truth: recall the writings by theorists such as Hempel, Dray, Danto and Mink on the epistemology of historical writing. Next came the 1970s; a phase which, admittedly, does not have its counterpart in Huizinga's distinction. I have in mind here how Hayden White's *Metahistory* of 1973 redirected interest from the issue of Truth to that of historiographical Form. But now we seem to have reached a third phase, one that was announced already by Huizinga's notion of authenticity.

For it may be argued that this issue of authenticity is, in fact, a kind of fusion, or synthesis of the issues of Truth and of Form, and this might explain the contemporary fascination for the issue of 'authenticity'. For, on the one hand, the notion of authenticity undeniably has the connotation of a doing justice to the past which is reminiscent of the good old issue of Truth. But, on the other hand, the issue of authenticity can also be related to Form. For the quest for authenticity is often phrased as a search for what historical Form would be best suited to achieve authenticity. Think, for example, of discussions about the formal differences between the historical text and the (historical) novel. The question then asked was: is the (traditional) Form of the historical text an obstacle to authenticity (or not) and, hence, should the historian perhaps be more open to the many different Forms of the novel in order to overcome this obstacle? For, as the argument went on, the novel's Form is far more successful for achieving authenticity than that of the historical text. Is not the novel much more successful in giving us the 'feel' of the life-world presented in it than the historical text? And, indeed, historians themselves were sometimes ready to concede as much and to experiment, therefore, with novelistic Form. Think of Simon Schama's daring and fascinating experiments in his *Dead Certainties* and *Landscape and Memory*.[5] And with regard to historical theorists think of Robert Rosenstone, who even coined the term 'experimental history' and saw authenticity as one of its main aims.

The example of Rosenstone is especially instructive here. For in his case, theory and practice are always most closely intertwined: Rosenstone theorises about experimental history, but he is very much aware that ultimately the proof of the pudding is in the eating and that each proposal for experimental history needs an example to examine what the proposal comes down to in actual, historiographical practice. We may think here of his *The Mirror in the Shrine* or *The Man Who Swam in from History* – both books of great daring, originality and intellectual beauty.[6] Or of H. U. Gumbrecht's *In 1926: Living at the Edge of Time*.[7] These books question, each in their own way, the aims, pretensions and methods of professionalised historical writing. And each of them can be seen as the practical implementation of some alternative theory of history. This is where the great value and historiographical significance of these books is to be found. But as a result of this, there will ordinarily be a kind of one-to-one relationship between theory and practice. Put differently, experimental history may itself be a historiographical genre or denote a specific class of historical writings, but the components of this class cannot be taken together in subclasses of the larger class. Each experiment is unique in its own way.

Let me elaborate on this. In Kant's ethics and in his conception of the judgement of beauty, *generalisability* always is decisive: the ethically just action is the one that can be generalised into a general law without resulting in contradictions. And with regard to beauty, if I say, 'This flower is beautiful,' the implicit claim is, according to Kant, that others will agree (though I may, in fact, be mistaken about this). If we then contrast 'ordinary' historical writing with experimental historical writing, we shall find that the former unproblematically meets the 'Kant-test' whereas the latter has no other purpose than that of *not* satisfying it. For suppose that some variant of experimental history were to be universally followed by all historians; it would then automatically no longer be *experimental* history, but would have become professional historical writing. Hence, experimental historical writing is *sui generis* the exception, to be found in the margin only, and it presupposes the existence of professional historical writing so that it can deviate from it. It is therefore openly and unashamedly elitist and finds its *raison d'être* in its necessary opposition to the accepted wisdom of '*hoi polloi*', though this is a necessary thing. For only experimental writing may make us question accepted wisdom. The disadvantage is, however, that precisely because of this, experimental historical writing almost automatically marginalises itself by its explicit resistance to being integrated into mainstream historical writing. This is its glory, but also its curse.

Historism

When thinking over the editors' challenge, I finally concluded that I would prefer to focus here on variants of historical writing trying to satisfy the more pedestrian and 'democratic' standards of the 'Kant-test', namely, variants of historical writing that are on the one hand new but that would, on the other, not automatically lose their appeal if they were to be adopted by many historians. Variants of historical writing, therefore, that one may hope will be practised by many historians – and the more the better!

So where should we look for these variants? That question is not hard to answer. For what is the most 'democratic', the most universal kind of history? What has been the common denominator in all of historical writing, of all ages, of all civilisations and of all times? Has history not been the *history of politics* since the days of Homer, since Herodotus and Thucydides? Has politics not been the backbone of history in Egypt, China and in our own civilisation down to the present day? What would be left of history if one were consistently to rob it of its political framework? The result would be a body without a skeleton, a meaningless story without intrigue; it would be the dream of a drunken man. Of course, one may do well to move away from political history as far as possible and explore the history of the basic realities of life or, at the other end of the spectrum, the history of the most abstruse speculations of philosophical and theological thought. But all these histories will never add up to something more than a pile of incoherent details if they cannot be related in some way or other to the hard rock of political history. Whether we like it or not, history is essentially the history of past politics.

Now, this relationship between history and politics cannot fail to remind us of German historism, as it has developed since the days of Leopold von Ranke. Historists such as Ranke, Droysen and Sybel were all convinced that the state is the prototypical historical agent and that grasping *its* history is conditional for all further historical understanding. When attempting to justify this focus on the (history of the) state, German historists relied on two crucial assumptions. The first was a belief in the unique individuality of typically historical phenomena, such as historical periods, cultures, the state, institutions, etc. The historists argued that the fate of such historical phenomena is always inscribed somehow into their very nature – much in the way that it is part of the Aristotelian entelechy of an acorn to grow into an oak in due time. Friedrich Meinecke, the last great historist historian, summarised it as follows:

> From whence originates our historical-political way of thinking, our capacity to recognize the individuality of supra-individual human relationships? Obviously it must have its origins in an individualism that has, in the course of time, deepened its originally superficial conception of the individual into the secular effort of achieving a return to our most primeval sources, and where the life of one's own self is still most intimately interconnected with the life of higher human relationships and organizations. Individuality, spontaneity, the effort for both self-destination and the dissemination of influence are simply everywhere around – and so it is with the state and the nation as well.[8]

Historism requires the historian to penetrate into the heart of the unique individuality of historical phenomena in order to discover there how all that had resulted from human spontaneity, the desire for self-determination and political power hang together, at the level of the individual no less than on that of other historical phenomena, such as the state.

The second historist assumption was that this will require us, above all, to focus on the (history of the) state. Historists recognised that history is the domain of large collective forces transcending the thought and the actions of the individual (i.e., the '*überindividuelle menschliche Verbände*' in the passage from Meinecke quoted above). They would have agreed in this with Adam Ferguson's argument in his *An Essay on the History of Civil Society* (1767) that mankind often stumbles 'upon establishments, which are indeed the result of human action, but not the execution of any human design'.[9] However, when taking stock of all these collective forces, the historists concluded that the *state* is the most powerful and most conspicuous of them all. Civilisations, cultures, institutions, the economy have all made immensely important contributions to the evolution of humanity – no doubt about that! And these entities have always figured prominently in their historical writing as well (as the objective historian of historical writing will have to admit). But if we are looking for those historical forces that will allow us to have the most secure grasp of the history of the West, it is the state on which we shall have to focus before all. Try to write a history of the West without reference to the state and the result will invariably be incoherent nonsense. It would be like trying to describe cars without reference to the thing you always have under the bonnet. So the entity that ought to matter most to the historian of the West will inevitably be the state, whether one likes it or not.

This also explains what conception historists had of the practical value of historical writing. For if the historian succeeded in identifying the unique individuality of the state, his or her work would be of the greatest value to the politician. For all successful political action presupposes politicians' continuous awareness of this unique individuality of the state whose future fate had placed in their hands. As Ranke put it:

> and thus it is the assignment of historical writing to bring forth the essence of the State from what has happened in the past and to make this amply known; it is, however, the statesman's assignment to elaborate in the future and to perfect what the historian has shown to have been the case in the past.[10]

So the idea is that the politician begins where the historian stops and that there should be as much continuity as possible between the actions of the former and the writings of the latter. Ignorance of this historically determined nature of the state can only lead to dreadful disasters.

The rest of the story is familiar enough. Historism, having already lost its confidence in itself because of the 'crisis of historism', was thoroughly discredited after the Second World War by guilt of association with the horrors of Hitlerism. I believe that accusation to be too silly to deserve refutation, but this is not the place to enter into it. What was decisive was that this meant the end of historism; and even though some timid attempts have been made in the last two decades to rehabilitate it, historism still is much the *nomen nefandum* that it became some fifty years ago. And this is to be deeply regretted. For even now it is the only historical theory developed by historians themselves in order to do justice to what is peculiar to history and historical writing; it is the theory that best captures the practice of the discipline; it is the only comprehensive theory accounting for all aspects and variants of historical writing which enables us to assess the aims and hopes of any new departures.

Even more so, whatever view one takes of historism, it cannot be denied that it has been the only theory to take seriously the question of the uses of history and to give to this question a coherent and well-considered answer. The result has been that since (and because of) the demise of historism, historians and historical theorists have no longer felt the obligation to ponder the question regarding what contribution to society's well-being may expected from history and historical writing. Think of all the theories of history developed since historism: none of them considered for even a moment this issue of for what we would need history. Even worse, history was often said to be a *science* like any other science, and the question of the use of science was dismissed as the banal and pedestrian obsession of the philistine (or the taxpayer).

For a new, analytical political history

So, to recap, what was lost along with historism was: (1) the self-evident predominance of political history; (2) the recognition that history should not be written for historians only, but primarily should serve a social purpose; and (3), that (1) provides the answer to (2). In this section I wish to reconsider these historist themes with the aim of developing a new variant of political history that may help us to deal more adequately with the great political problems of the present and the future.

In the previous section we found that historists believed that knowledge of the nation's past could be a useful or even indispensable guide for the politician. This seems to be a sensible idea, if only because it is in agreement with what life itself is like. For our actions should always be a more or less logical continuation of how we have acted before: a physician should act like a physician and not suddenly start playing the role of a plumber (or vice versa). Changing these roles would create an unprecedented confusion in social life – and it would be no different in politics. This was, indeed, what the historists had in mind and why they were surely right in saying that history is the politician's (and the state's) best guide. So it certainly is not my intention to attack this Rankean insight.

But consider now the argument that something, slowly and surreptitiously, has gone wrong in national politics. For example, political parties no longer function as the *trait d'union* between the state and the electorate, the state has gradually developed a private interest of its own over and against the public interest, the people then begin to distrust politics and politicians, the executive completely overpowers the legislative, the machinery of representative democracy fails to produce the results expected from it and so on. What to do in such a situation? Obviously, the Rankean recipe would make no sense here. Extrapolating the past into the present and the future would only make matters worse. So a different strategy will be needed if we wish to repair what has gone wrong, and one that the historists, with their enviable nineteenth-century optimism, had never envisaged.

Probably we would now have to begin with finding out when and where things started to go wrong, so that after having identified that point in the nation's history we could somehow undo what had happened subsequently and instead resume the nation's historical path in agreement with Ranke's recommendations. But how would we do this? Being able to do so presupposes some more or less general theories about what political parties should do in a well-functioning democracy, about how *raison d'état* relates to the national interest, about how the state can generate trust and dispel distrust in a society, about the balance of powers and so on. In short, the kind of general theories developed by political theorists such as Niccolò Machiavelli, Jean Bodin, Thomas Hobbes, John Locke, Montesquieu, *et al.* Only the ideas developed by these great political theorists from Aristotle to, say, Foucault in our own time will enable us to conceptualise our contemporary political predicaments to identify what has gone wrong and needs mending. Only these theories will give us the technical vocabulary necessary for a meaningful discussion of our contemporary political ills.

This brings me to the gist of my argument. We live at a time when we, unfortunately, have every reason to entertain the kind of worries about the future of our (representative) democracies mentioned above and we know from the horrors of the previous century what may happen if one's worst fears about politics and politicians become a reality. Of course, I do not want to suggest that a new kind of totalitarianism is awaiting us in the near future. But one need only look at the USA – the oldest democracy in the West – in order to have one's legitimate concerns about the deterioration of representative democracy into a plebiscitary democracy, or worse, into a one-party system or, even worse still, into a brutish and selfish plutocracy. And who can predict what terrible pressures will be exerted on our political systems if nature would, in the course of the present century, have its revenge on us for having so brutally mishandled it? Then the Rankean paradigm will no longer be of any use to us; instead, we will need all the resources of political thought developed in the past to rescue a minimum of freedom and democracy.

So this is my utopian ideal for future historical writing: I'm dreaming of a new variant of political history using the lessons of the great political theorists of past and present for identifying the problems and shortcomings of our contemporary political machineries and for offering suggestions as to how these may best be remedied. Such a new variant of political history could be the offspring of a marriage of political theory and political history. For though it is true that a combination of the two is conditional for the new political history I have in mind, neither of them explicitly serves this goal of identifying and curing the diseases of our contemporary democracies. The political historian may succeed in identifying these illnesses, but he or she will not be equipped to cure them. Or, worse still, he or she may say that the attempt to do so would jeopardise one's professional 'objectivity', compelling him or her merely to register. On the other hand, the political theorist or philosopher only too often withdraws behind a Rawlsian 'veil of ignorance' to be able to say anything that might contribute to a better understanding of the complexities of our contemporary political realities. Indeed, with Rawls and his many disciples working in what has recently become known as 'the Rawls industry', we completely disappear in the mist of useless speculation and complete political irrelevance. So political theory has to be informed historically if it is to be of any practical use to us. We therefore badly need this marriage of political theory and history.

It is true that political scientists or students of constitutional and administrative law sometimes succeed in combining knowledge of the details of government with that of fruitful theories of proper and responsible government. But they lack the long-term perspective that only the historian and the political theorist can bring to these issues. And that long-term perspective is absolutely indispensable here. *For big problems have long histories; and as long as we remain in the dark about these histories we shall be unable to deal with them.* Then our problems will not go away, but repeat themselves over and over again, in agreement with the old wisdom that those who do not learn from the lessons of the past will be condemned to repeat them. And we need only look at our present governments to recognise the extent to which they cannot fathom the real size and nature of their problems and so repeat endlessly the same mistakes. So this is where this new kind of political history could be history's greatest and most precious gift to humanity's future.

This new variant of political history is not descriptive in the way that other variants are. It does not begin by focusing on some part of our political past in order to describe (and interpret) what went on there. It is, instead, *analytical* in the sense that it uses the results of traditional political history for *analysing* contemporary politics – that is, for identifying the main problems and shortcomings of the existing political system – and for the formulation of suggestions for how these political ills could best be remedied. Furthermore, the instruments to be used in this analytical political history are to be found in political theory, in the history of political thought. The explanation for this is that these come closest to what may transcend the gap between past and present: these are the instruments that are absolutely indispensable if we hope to apply the lessons of the past to our contemporary social and political realities. Without these instruments, past and present will remain stubbornly incommensurable and the effort to learn from the past will then only add to the problems that we already have.

It follows that the analytical political historian should never be tempted to rely exclusively on the approaches developed by contemporary political philosophy. For this would mean denying oneself access to the wisdom of the ages; and it is precisely this wisdom from which we can expect solace for our contemporary political ills more than from anything else. History provides us with the best perspective from which to analyse our social and political problems if only because history always comprises both the past and the present (to which politicians and political scientists so often restrict their scope).[11] And this wisdom of the past is encapsulated, above all, in the political theorist's repertoire of political notions, such as sovereignty, con-stitutionalism, responsibility and accountability, trust, legality and legitimacy, political representation, civil and political liberty, the distinction between public and private law, and not in contemporary inventions such as Rawls's 'distributive principles of justice'. What does not have its roots in the twenty centuries in which our Western states developed and has been merely dreamed up by contemporary university professors for the intellectual amusement of their colleagues is to be rejected as useless and even misleading for the practice of analytical political history.

This is certainly not meant to suggest that our choice of the appropriate instruments offered by political theory should be an easy and unproblematic one. Far from it! For here we should agree with theorists emphasising that there are no timeless and eternal political problems that would have remained the same throughout the West's political history. These theorists are right about this. Each historical period has its own political parameters, its own problems, its own political vocabulary and we should agree with Pocock and Skinner that we can take nothing for granted with regard to the meaning of these terms in any of these political vocabularies.[12] Political theory must, of course, be historicised, but it by no means follows that these terms would be useless as concepts for analytical political history. On the contrary, it is precisely their wide spectrum of meanings that makes them ideally suited for the task. So the need to historicise our political vocabularies is not a handi-cap for analytical political history but a windfall blowing favourably into the sails of the analytical political historian, and that is as helpful as it is welcome! We can now fine-tune their meanings so that they can best be applied to our contemporary political realities, much in the way that we may rummage for some time in a toolbox before we have found the right instrument for doing a job. This will not always be easy and some analytical political historians will be better at this than others in the eyes of both their colleagues and the politicians and journalists of their time. Indeed, the writings by these analytical political historians will not fail to attract the attention of politicians and journalists – as I know from my own experience.

So let us rejoice in how Pocock, Skinner and others have historicised political vocabularies and let us even try to see how we can improve on their work. But, once again, to the extent that we succeed in doing so, this does not question but only adds to what we may expect from analytical political history.

An example: the re-feudalisation of the modern state

In order to illustrate my propoal for a new kind of political history I shall discuss in this section what one might appropriately call 'the re-feudalisation of the modern state'.

Feudalism

We immediately associate the term 'feudal' with the Middle Ages. However, Heinrich Mitteis has already pointed out that from a political and administrative point of view there are no radical ruptures between the late Roman Empire and the Middle Ages. For after Diocletianus had divided the Empire into two, a process of political fragmentation set in, reducing the Empire into a mosaic of local centres frequently organised around the so-called *latifundia*. The owners of these *latifundia* – who were often of senatorial rank – ruled them in much the same way as the medieval baron ruled his fief. In both cases the lord of the domain – whether senator or baron – commanded a small army of his own, had the right to raise certain taxes and appoint ecclesiastical officials, and had the right of jurisdiction over the people living on his domain. One could say, therefore, that since the beginning of the fourth century central imperial power had been delegated to the owners of the *latifundia* and that all political and juridical authority had become 'privatised' in the sense of having become their private posssession. Feudalism was, in fact, little more than the codification of the realities of the late Roman Empire into a more or less formalised system.[13]

It has taken Europe more than a millennium to shake off feudalism. France was the first country to be successsful in this, the German Empire succumbed to feudal fragmentation and England ended up somewhere between the two. Feudal elements have survived in England down to the present: for example, all landed English property is still technically a fief, a fact that never fails to provoke a kind of mollified surprise in people living on the European continent.

Absolutism and democracy

When Europe succeeded in overcoming feudalism, this was mainly thanks to absolutism. Feudal ties were always reciprocal: they tied the vassal and his lord within what we would now call a civil law contract. This changed with absolutism. The great discovery of absolutism was the notion of sovereignty defined by Jean Bodin in his *Les Six Livres de la République* (1576) as '*la puissance de faire et de casser la loi*'. The sovereign king has the right to abolish existing legislation and to create new legislation. Because of this he stands above the law himself, he is *legibus absolutus* – hence the term 'absolutism'. The civil law arrangements of feudalism were thus exchanged for the public law of the modern state. Tocqueville always liked to emphasise that the French revolutionaries took away from Louis XVI his sovereign authority in order to place it in the hands of the people, but without changing anything in the definition of sovereign power.[14] The people now gave absolute sovereignty to itself: all exercise of political power could be legitimate only on the condition that it could be reduced, via constitutionally well-defined lines, to the will of the people.

This meant the end of feudalism and the *ancien régime*. Yet even under absolutism many of the practices of feudalism managed to survive and even prosper in new, mutated variants of traditional constructions. Think, for example, of the sale of offices, such as that of judge, of tax-farmer, of postmaster or of army officer. All these offices could be bought, sold and even become hereditary. This system of the sale of offices shared with feudalism 'the idea that public office is rather a source of profit than a duty toward king or country'.[15] And in both cases what we would nowadays recognise as belonging to the domain of public law was delegate to that of private law. The practice was difficult to get rid of since it was beneficial to both the buyer and the seller of these offices. When the French king was in need of money – which was almost always the case – one invented a number of new offices, even '*des offices imaginaires*' that were sold to the highest bidder. When Louis XIV once asked his chancellor, Louis Phelypeaux de Pontchartrain, how he always succeeded in finding buyers for even the most abstruse offices, Pontchartrain answered: 'Your Majesty should not forget that he possesses one of the most marvellous privileges, namely that each time he creates an office, God will create a fool who wants to buy it.'[16]

Public and private law

If, in our eyes, this sale of offices is an absurdity, it is because we now live in a different world. In the seventeenth and eighteenth centuries the system was not considered to be particularly odd or unnatural: Barclay defended it in the seventeenth century and Montesquieu did the same a century later. The explanation is that for us, unlike our ancestors, the domains of private and of public law are crucially different. This was also the assessment of Johan Rudolf Thorbecke (1798–1874), a historian and statesman who framed the Dutch constitution of 1848 which is still now, with only minor adaptations, that nation's political foundation. For Thorbecke, the strict distinction between public and private law was the hallmark of modernity and of where the modern state differs from the feudal state and from that of the *ancien regime*:

Political right and political obligation have not been instituted for the citizen in the first place but in order to define the domain of government by the state. The contemporary system of government is founded on this strict distinction between public and private law. One returns to a previous phase, one returns to the medieval state, as soon as one confuses civil and public law, or places both on one and the same line or reduces both to one and the same principle . . . The principles that have revealed themselves with and since the French Revolution are those of centralization and of the separation of public and private law. The French Revolution was, more specifically, a struggle against the system permitting public comptencies to be private property.[17]

In short, it was only thanks to the differentiation between public and private law that the modern, liberal state in which we presently live could shake off feudalism and the *ancien régime* with its venality of offices. The essence of what happened in France in the years after 1789 (and later on the European continent) was the separation of the public and private domain; and this is where the political tradition of the continent fundamentally differs from that of the Anglo-Saxon countries where the repudiation of the *ancien régime* never was articulated as a decision of principle. This is the deepest division running between Anglo-Saxon and continental democracies and from which stem most other differences in political culture to be observed in these two variants of democracy.

Quangocratisation

From this perspective we have good reasons to be deeply worried by the contemporary fashion of privatisation and of the marketisation of public competencies. This fashion is, in fact, a return to feudalism, and a standing invitation to all those abuses of public authority condemned in the medieval state and from which we might have hoped to have emancipated ourselves for ever with the modern liberal state. This, then, is where so-called *neo-liberalism* advocating privatisation and the marketisation of the state is flatly at odds with the *liberalism proprement dit*: all that was condemned after 1789 by liberalism as the repulsive abuses of the *ancien régime* is now warmly hailed by neo-liberalism's transformation of the past into an eternal present. And people on the continent welcoming such developments are naïvely unaware that, in fact, they advocate the resurrection of a feudalism that the Anglo-Saxon countries have never completely abandoned.

No phenomenon in contemporary politics is more relevant here than that of the so-called 'quangos' (an abbreviation of quasi non-government organisations). Quangos may differ widely in size, task and legal status, but they all live in a 'no man's land' between the public and the private domain. They have recently been defined by Matthew Flinders as 'any body that spends public money to fulfil a public task but with some degree of independence from elected representatives'.[18] It should immediately be conceded that certain institutions ought to be situated in this political twilight between the public and the private. The paradigmatic example is the nation's national bank, for transforming the national bank into a commercial bank would invite it to prefer its own interests to its task of safeguarding the nation's financial system. Conversely, putting the national bank into the hands of politicians means that they may abuse it for short-term political gains. So the independence of the nation's national bank from both public and private interests is a very good thing.

However, in the past one or two decades quangos have spread over the bodies of our Western democracies – both Anglo-Saxon and continental – like an infectious disease. The no man's land between the private and the public is now no longer inhabited only by a few institutions effectively defying each attempt to assign them to either the public or the private domain. This no man's land has now been invaded by a host of institutions exercising public functions without being subject to public control. They are therefore in a position to combine the benefits of being private institutions with those of possessing delegated parts of sovereign power – a position which is a standing invitation to potential gross abuse of public money and authority. In fact, in many Western democracies substantial parts of government bureaucracies – sometimes up to a third or a half of their previous power – have been shifted into this no man's land. And this is a very bad thing indeed, for we can now read almost every day in the newspapers reports suggesting that the days of the tax-farmer have returned.

This is neither the time nor the place to give a survey of the library of books written on the phenomenon of quangos over the past couple of decades. I restrict myself to one observation of relevance in the present context: there is a striking difference between how politicians themselves look at the quangos and what more objective outsiders, such as political scientists or courts of audit, have to say about them.[19] The former is known as 'the practitioner theory' and is always full of praise for the quangos: they are said to be more efficient than government bureaucracies, they would be subject to the discipline of the market, be closer to the citizen, operate more professionally and so on. But objective outsiders rarely discover all of these benefits in quangos and tend to be far more negative about them. More specifically, they point out that quangos generate problems that are more dangerous than those they are believed to solve. These dangers are that the absence of any government interference invites quangos to privilege their own institutional private interest above the public interests that they ought to serve.

The interesting question is, then, why politicians are systematically so much more positive about quangocratisation than are objective outsiders. Two explanations can be given for this state of affairs. First, we may observe here a conflict of political discourses. On the one hand there is the political discourse of the politicians, and on the other that of the objective outsiders.

Both are *political* discourses since both deal with political phenomena, even one and the same political phenomenon, namely the quangos. If, then, both discourses allow for such very different assessments of them, we may see this as a signal that the politicians' discourse has acquired an autonomy of its own with regard to a discourse still permitting a more or less objective judgement of the quality of governance. And since discourses and interests are always most intimately interwoven, it follows that the praises sung of the quangos in the 'practitioner's theory' should be seen as a sign that the state (or government) has acquired a private interest of its own, next to all the private interests existing in civil society itself. Put differently, one not only creates in each quango another private interest – which is bad enough already – but, worse still, the quangocratisation may also infect the state (or government) itself with the virus of the private interest.

Second, it is instructive to take into account when and where quangocracy was invented and what problems it was expected to solve. It is true that there have always been quangos, but one has to look at the UK at the beginning of the 1970s to see the first real explosion of quangocracy. So why was this? The explanation is that the British government in these pre-Thatcher days found itself in a desperately weak position vis-à-vis the trade unions. The government did not wish to agree to the trade unions' demands for wage increases, but was aware that it lacked the political prestige to refuse to comply with these demands. The way out was found through quangos or, as Matthew Flinders put it:

> the answer was found in the creation of new semi-autonomous bodies with some degree of autonomy from the government. These would semi-regulate industrial relations in a voluntarist manner. For example, in 1973 the Manpower Services Commission was formed as a public agency designed to take over the administration of employment and training services directly from the Department of Employment. The body offered a solution to all sides of a dispute . . . The example of industrial relations shows that many bodies exercising some degree of autonomy were not created because governments loved quangos, but because in some policy areas they were the only option when direct intervention and regulation had failed.[20]

Hence, crucial parts of the state were privatised so that the trade unions could no longer put their fingers on them. The important lesson to be learned from this is that the following three things relate closely to each other: a weak state; the need to privatise parts of the state; and a state having developed a private interest of its own over and against the public interest. Or, to rephrase this: the state generating a private interest of its own is the typically weak state (whereas it is, paradoxically, only the strong state that can make itself wholly subservient to the public interest) and this weak state will tend to privatise parts of itself in order to defend itself against the pressures exerted on it by the forces existing in civil society. These privatised former parts of the state can now function as a kind of buffer between state and civil society.

Analytical political history

It should now be clear what all this has to do with feudalism and why quangocratisation could well be characterised as a 're-feudalisation of the modern state'. For we may observe here the return of all the old political mechanisms from which feudalism originated. In both the Middle Ages and now we find a state that is unable to deal adequately with the challenges it has to face (do not commit the mistake of confusing the large state with the strong state!). In both cases a weak state was infected by the virus of the private interest; and a most dangerous virus it is, for we know from the Middle Ages that many states succumbed to it without any hope of recovery. In both instances we may observe a fragmentation of the state. In both cases the centre delegated its former public competencies to former parts of itself that now acquired a political and juridical autonomy of their own. In both cases contracts were signed between the state and these privatised parts of its former self. Each of these contracts meant the shift of a part of the former public domain to the private domain and was, therefore, the theft of the people's sovereignty. Private law thus took the place of public law and moved government outside the range of the people's will. In both cases the state abdicated as the nation's political centre and became just one more inhabitant of civil society. In the Middle Ages this was well captured by granting to the king's great vassals the right to be called his 'pairs' (or 'peers'); that is, his equals. These vassals could truly be said to be the king's equals, because they were bound to the king not by arrangements of public law but by those of private law. Similarly, contemporary political theorists such as Helmut Willke rejoicing in the degradation of the modern state (or presenting this as a historical inevitability) always emphasise that nowadays the state has been reduced to the status of a mere '*primus inter pares*', without being aware that they are returning, with this, to the political vocabulary of feudalism.

We have no reason at all to rejoice in this return to the Middle Ages. Liberal historians have always been quite explicit about the political dangers of feudalism. As Mitteis points out: for these liberal historians, '*hatte das Lehnwezen die denkbar schlechteste Presse. Man wurde nicht müde, seinen destruktiven, zentrifugalen, staatszerstörenden Charakter hervorzuheben. Es erschien wie ein Sprengkörper, der jeden, auch den festesten Staat, in seinen Grundfesten zu erschüttern die Kraft hatte*'.[21] It may well be that in the Middle Ages there was no feasible alternative for feudalism. But in our own time we know that a complex modern society can also be governed with the instruments of representative democracy. We also know that these mechanisms can only function as long as they have their solid foundations in public law and that they will sink hopelessly when the arrangements of private law are substituted for those of public law.

And we can know all these things, and can recognise the dangers threatening our contemporary democracies, thanks to an analytical political history combining historical knowledge with the instruments of political theory, in the way this was done in this section.

Conclusion

The sad paradox about contemporary (political) historians is that they are not historists when they should be but they are historists when they should not be. Historians fail to be historists when they think about their discipline and then always conclude that historism is an odd, obsolete and wholly useless historical theory which captures little or nothing of the contemporary practice of history. As I have argued on many occasions, this belief is totally wrong: the core of the historist conception of the nature of historical writing is still as solid as it was one and a half centuries ago. Historians unable to see this invariably mistake the admittedly antiquated nineteenth-century terminology in which the theory was stated for its essence.

But all these very anti-historist historians suddenly become the ardent disciples of historism when it comes to the uses of history and to the issue of the applicability of knowledge of the past to the present. Then they suddenly begin to recite the old historist phrases of '*jede Epoche ist unmittelbar zu Gott*' and to sing the praises of the historist warning of the dangers of anachronism. This is odd. And not only odd: for because of the contemporary historian's inconsistent behaviour with regard to historism, we have now made the wisdom of the ages inaccessible (or, at least, useless) to us by simply assuming, as a matter of course, that nothing of the past could be of use to our so different present. This wisdom of the past could not have been entrusted into hands less worthy of taking charge of its treasures for the present and future than those of these anti-historist historians. It has been historians themselves who have contributed more than anybody else to the contemporary contempt of history and of historical knowledge.

But an analytical political history, as advocated in this essay, may show the historian how his or her professional knowledge of the past can be used to improve our contemporary political systems and overcome the dangers threatening our social and political future.

Burckhardt was right, then.

Notes

1 L. Gossman, *Basel in the Age of Burckhardt: A Study in Unseasonable Ideas* (Chicago and London: University of Chicago Press, 2000): 284.
2 'Geschiedenis is de geestelijke vorm waarin een cultuur zich rekenschap geeft van haar verleden'. See J. Huizinga, 'Over een definitie van het begrip geschiedenis', in idem, *Verzamelde Werken 7: Geschiedwetenschap, Hedendaagsche cultuur* (Haarlem: Tjeenk Willink, 1950): 102.

3 It may be argued that Ranke's '*zeigen*' confuses the novel with historical writing. As long as something is only 'shown', any conclusions with regard to what has been shown are left to the reader. And this is what happens in the novel, this is why the (great) novel is endlessly reinterpretable and why the (great) novel resembles life itself. The historian, on the other hand, always aims for explicitness and wishes the text to be as unambiguous and as resistant to multiple interpretations as possible. The historian is the professional 'saying that' sayer, whereas 'saying that' is always avoided in the (great) novel. See my 'Political Representation and Political Experience: An Essay on Political Psychology' (forthcoming).

4 Huizinga, 'Over een definitie', p. 100.

5 S. Schama, *Dead Certainties (Unwarranted Speculations)* (New York: Knopf, 1992) and *Landscape and Memory* (London: HarperCollins, 1995).

6 R. A. Rosenstone, *The Mirror in the Shrine: American Encounters with Meiji Japan* (Cambridge, Mass.: Harvard University Press, 1988) and *The Man Who Swam into History* (Bloomington: First Books, 2002).

7 H. U. Gumbrecht, *In 1926: Living at the Edge of Time* (Cambridge, Mass.: Harvard University Press, 1997).

8 Friedrich Meinecke, *Weltbürgertum und Nationalstaat* (München: Oldenburg Verlag, 1962): 169 (my translation).

9 A. Ferguson, *An Essay on the History of Civil Society*, ed. *Fania Oz-Salzberger* [1767] (Cambridge: Cambridge University Press, 1995): 119.

10 L. von Ranke, *De historia et politices cognatione atque discrimine oratio*, in idem, *Sämmtliche Werke: Band 24* (Leipzig: Duncker and Humblot, 1872) (my translation).

11 Think of two people, A and B: A has read only page 287 of a novel (but knows it almost by heart); B has a read all of the novel from page 1 to page 287 (but read that page only cursorily). Then ask who will understand best what happens on page 287? So it is with history – and nothing better summarises the immense importance of knowledge of the past than this little argument.

12 J. G. A. Pocock, *Politics, Language and Time: Essays on Political Thought and History* (New York: Atheneum, 1973); the impressive monument of scholarship resulting from this approach is, of course, idem, *The Machiavellian Moment in the Atlantic Tradition* (Princeton: Princeton University Press, 1975). For Skinner, see the excellent survey of his political thought by K. Palonen, *Quentin Skinner: History, Politics, Rhetoric* (Cambridge: Cambridge University Press, 2003).

13 Mitteis writes the following about the late Roman Empire:

> die Villa ist nicht nur ein Gutshof, sondern ein befestigter Herrenbesitz, aus dem der Grundherr wie an einem germanischen Adelshof, umgeben von seiner bewaffneten Gefolgschaft, ein Herrenleben führt . . . Das grundherrliche Gebiet (territorium, massa) ist von der staatlichenn Gewalt fast völlig eximiert; die Herrschaft (potestas) bildet, da die meisten potentes die Autopragie, das Recht eigner Steuer-erhebung, erlangt haben, eine fiskalische, da sie als assertores pacis die niedrige Gerichtsbarkeit ausüben, eine juridische, da sie Eigenkirchen (capellae) haben, eine kirchliche Einheit. Das alles sind Erscheinungen, die zum Feudalismus nicht mehr im wirtschaftlichen, sondern schon im politischen Sinn gerechnet werden müssen. Dieser Feudalismus ist rein zentrifugal, er wirkt lediglich zersetzend; der Staat hat kein Gegenmittel gegen die Absorption der ihm gebührenden Treupflichten durch private Grundherren, gegen die Bildung selbstständiger Machtzellen in den grossen potestates. In allen diesen Beziehungen bestand kaum ein Unterschied

zwischen Italien und den Provinzen; seit Rom nicht mehr Hauptstadt war, wurde Italien selbst zur Provinz.

H. Mitteis, Der Staat des hohen Mittelalters:
Grundlinien einer vergleichenden Verfassungsgeschichte
des Lehnzeitalters (Weimar: Böhlau Verlag, 1948): 16, 17.

14 This is, of course, the main message of Tocqueville's *L'Ancien Régime et la Révolution* (1856).
15 C. W. Swart, *The Sale of Offices in the Seventeenth Century* (Den Haag: Nijhoff, 1949): 5; see also France R. Mousnier, *La Vénalité des offices sous Henri IV et Louis XIII* (Rouen: Mauguin,1945).
16 Swart, *Sale of Offices*, p. 34.
17 J. R. Thorbecke, *Bijdrage tot de herziening der grondwet* (Leiden: Nijhoff, 1848): 82 (with thanks to Dr J. Drentje for the reference); E. Poortinga, *De scheiding tussen publiek en privaatrechtrecht bij Johan Rudolf Thorbecke (1798–1872): Theorie en toepassing* (Nijmegen: Ars Aequi, 1987). See also J. Drentje, *Thorbecke: Een filosoof in de politiek* (Amsterdam: Boom, 2004) for a brilliant account of the origins of the relevant aspects of Thorbecke's political philosophy (esp. p. 221).
18 M. V. Flinders, 'Setting the scene', in M. V. Flinders and M. J. Smith (eds), *Quangos, Accountability and Reform* (Basingstoke: Palgrave, 1999): 4. Elsewhere, Flinders says about quangos: 'they can be used to circumnavigate the democratic process and to undermine troublesome local authorities' (p. 9) and he quotes J. Stewart when writing that the quangos introduced 'a new magistracy in the sense that a non-elected elite are assuming responsibility for a large part of local governance' (p. 22).
19 S. van Thiel, *Quangocratization: Trends, Causes and Consequences* (Utrecht: Utrecht University Press, 2000): 7–15, 163–84 and *passim*.
20 M. V. Flinders, 'Why Do Governments Love Quangos?', in Flinders and Smith, *Quangos, Accountability and Reform*, p. 32.
21 Mitteis, *Staat*, p. 3.

14 Historiographical criticism

A manifesto

Ewa Domanska

The writing of history liberates us from history.
Benedetto Croce (after Goethe)

This manifesto is intended to provide a theoretical introduction to a field of historical studies situated at the nexus of the theory and history of historiography which I call 'historiographical criticism'. This notion of criticism is unrelated to the tradition of critical historical reflection, associated with scepticism about the methods of historical cognition, critique of the historical source, the separation of history from myth, and the development of methodology ancillary to history. In its attempt to approach the subject matter of historical texts as a philosophical problem, and thus to relate it to the problems of the cosmos, the world and the human being, this method draws upon nineteenth-century traditions of criticism.

The term 'historiographical criticism' is used here by analogy to 'literary criticism' as understood by its post Second World War theoreticians and practitioners in North America and France. Particularly inspiring has been the work of Northrop Frye (*Anatomy of Criticism*, 1957; *The Responsibility of the Critic*, 1976) and Roland Barthes (*Criticism and Truth*, 1966; *S/Z*, 1970). I also draw upon the notions of the cultural critics and philosophers who combine textual criticism with cultural criticism, such as Fredric Jameson (*The Political Unconscious*, 1981), Terry Eagleton (*The Function of Criticism*, 1984), Edward Said (*The World, the Text, and the Critic*, 1983) and Jacques Derrida. The background of my considerations is interdisciplinary cultural studies with its specific critique of contemporary culture and methodological eclecticism, since I consider myself a historiographical critic insofar as I consider myself a cultural critic.

Reflection on historiographical practice has occasionally used the term 'historiographical criticism'. Friedrich Schlegel embarked on an analysis of history writing in his commentary on Condorçet's *Sketch for a Historical Picture of the Progress of the Human Mind* (1795). Much later, in his *History as the Story of Liberty*, Benedetto Croce spoke of 'the criticism of historical works' but did not undertake the kind of study I propose here. Contemporary literary critics discuss the classic works of historiography written in the eighteenth, nineteenth and early twentieth centuries, assuming that with the passage of time the classical historical work enters the canon of world literature (Leo Braudy, *Narrative Form in History and Fiction*, 1970), Hayden White's *Metahistory* (1973), Lionel Gossman's *Between History and Literature* (1990), Ann Rigney's *The Rhetoric of Historical Representation* (1991) and Philippe Carrard's *Poetics of the New History* (1992) as well as the works of Susanne Gearthart and Linda Orr can be seen as examples of historiographical criticism in the broad sense of the term. None of these authors, however, conceptualises his/her work as historiographical criticism and all of them follow goals and use methods different from those I propose here. Following in White's footsteps, the works listed above discuss the ways of representing the past in terms of the discursive conventions governing texts. Thus, Rigney describes her analyses as 'the rhetoric of historical representations', whereas White and Carrard speak of 'the poetics of historical writing' rather than criticism, even though they are clearly inspired by contemporary literary criticism. The definition of 'historiographical criticism', its assumptions, goals, and methods, has not, so far, been provided.

Crisis – criticality – chance

The etymology of the words 'criticality' and 'crisis' is the same. The meaning of the Greek κρίσιμος, κρίσις, κριτεος, κριτικός (*krísimos, krísis, kriteos, kritikós*) includes judgement, assessment, evaluation and being determined. Used by Hippocrates in his medical works, the word κρίσις (*krísis*) means the turning point of the disease, the 'critical day' (Aristotle), a sudden change which determines the patient's future condition. In this sense, the word 'critical' was synonymous with crisis, meaning both the turning point and the crucial moment. Another concept can be brought into play here, namely καιρός (*kairós*), one meaning of which is critical time. Apart from that, καιρός (*kairós*) means the right time, the appropriate moment, chance or opportunity. Furthermore, crisis, the critical moment and chance are associated with becoming at a particular point in time, being-in-the-now, the present, the accumulation of moments fraught with meaning.

These etymological considerations are relevant to my argument insofar as I believe that the concept of 'historiographical criticism' as formulated here is itself the product of a critical moment in my discipline, that is, the theory and history of historiography, as well as in history as a field of study. This crisis results from the postmodern deconstruction of the fundamental categories of modern thinking. In the context of that critique, history as an academic discipline is regarded as the child of modernity and positivism, and an ideology supporting the institution of the nation state. Scholars are aware that to predict the end of the modern era is to predict the end of history as the dominant, specifically Western European, approach to the past.

Defining historiographical criticism

Historiographical criticism is an interpretative practice, a certain method of interpreting history writing, and an instrument of understanding historical studies. In this sense, historiographical criticism is a hermeneutics.

Historiographical criticism is not a theory in the positivist sense of the term.[1] Inherently open, criticism does not produce a system or model; by contrast, theory is an essentially closed structure. In a sense, theory kills criticism, limiting interpretation to a certain pattern. Nevertheless, criticism does not stand in opposition to theory but is a supratheoretical phenomenon which tests various theories and therefore can assess their usefulness for a given community. Thus, in a way, theory functions as an 'immediate metatext', but one that does not aspire to dominate other approaches.

The starting point of historiographical criticism is in the analyses of contemporary historiography, especially works representing the trends which in my *Microhistories* I called 'alternative history', pointing to their distinctiveness from traditional historiography which is grounded upon the positivist model of historical studies.[2] Thus, alternative history includes books published in the 1970s and 1980s whose authors manifest an enhanced sensitivity to the problems of the contemporary world and draw inspiration from other fields of the contemporary humanities. Their works, therefore, reflect – more directly than the works of traditional historians – the fundamental issues of the contemporary humanities, such as subjectivity, ethics and the relationship between power and knowledge. These are also the primary concerns of historiographical criticism which deals with alternative history.

The historical work which is subjected to historiographical criticism is not treated as a (positivistic) scientific study but as a literary and philosophical work. The historiographical critic is not interested in the factual content of the work or the truth value of the facts and the manner of explaining them, however important these may be. Rather, following Roland Barthes, the critic's concern is the accuracy of the critical statement, based upon 'the critic's responsibility for his/her own word'. The critic is a 'reader-writer' whose deep reading of the text deconstructs the world of the book in order to reconstruct it. Historiographical criticism does not discover meaning but creates it. Like Umberto Eco, Barthes believes in the open work which has multiple meanings. The critic chooses some of those meanings and interprets them, thereby adding, as it were, another chapter to the book and continuing the work's metaphors rather than simplifying them. The goal of criticism is not to control the text, but to liberate its meanings. Thus, historiographical criticism is not governed by a 'hermeneutics of suspicion' but a 'hermeneutics of care', where care is understood as a requisite element of criticism and at the same time as a desirable social practice which underlies criticism. Accordingly, historiographical criticism is interested in care for the future, an interest manifested in demonstrating the possible effects on reality of different conceptions of the past.

Historiographical criticism contains elements of both description and evaluation. The blurring of distinctions between the two kinds of activity indicates that every historical description involves evaluation. Historiographical criticism describes the condition of contemporary historiography, but it is not its task to compile a list of historical works which would form a canon that determines the methods of study or the style of writing about the past. Neither is its purpose to review historical works. Rather, the main function of historiographical criticism as I see it is to refresh and renew our ways of thinking about history, understood, to stress it again, as a specifically Western European approach to the past. The goal of historiographical criticism is, therefore, to offer new perspectives on history writing, its place and role at the 'critical moment' in the history of culture and the human being. Accordingly, the essential act of historiographical criticism is, to quote Frye, 'not an act of judgment but of recognition'[3] which can help us evaluate ourselves and our condition. Paraphrasing the title of Richard Rorty's book, I would say that historiographical criticism is interested in 'historiography as a mirror of culture', and above all in the human individual who looks at him/herself in this mirror and sees there a reflection of his/her face; in other words, it is interested in historiography as a critique of culture.

In the case of the theory and history of historiography, the process of creating the future to which, hopefully, historiographical criticism can contribute would involve the following strategies: historicisation of history (stressing the emergence of history as a historical fact and demonstrating its changes and transitoriness); textualisation and discursivisation of thinking about history (understanding such notions as history, science, objectivity, the state, time, space and gender as 'linguistic events' that belong to the order of discourse fostered by modern thinking rather than to reality, as such); and emphasis on history's connections with ideology and politics (following Foucault's analysis of the links between knowledge and power), where history is treated as an ideology subservient to the Western European philosophy of violence. By using the above strategies, historiographical criticism contributes to the reflection on the subject and subjectivity,[4] essential for the contemporary humanities, and joins in the so-called ethical turn which has shifted the main focus of theoretical considerations about history from epistemology to ethics.[5]

Ethics is of key importance for historiographical criticism and is not understood as a set of abstract rules but as the product of the student's own everyday experience. Historiographical criticism combines a close reading of texts with ethical reflection which reaches beyond the text. Ethics becomes the practice of care.

The methods of historiographical criticism

In its analyses of contemporary history writing, historiographical criticism favours epistemological pluralism. Its main method is, on the one hand, close reading of texts as adopted from formalism, structuralism and psycho-analysis, and, on the other, 'interpretative eclecticism'. This method clearly demonstrates that interpretation is an interdisciplinary practice grounded upon a constant transgression of the boundaries of a given discipline and the breaking of traditional interpretative frameworks. In this context eclecticism, far from being undesirable, is a prerequisite for the emergence of new ways of study and interpretation, and a potential basis for a future integration of knowledge.

Historiographical criticism provides an alternative to the conventional scientistic model of theoretical reflection. It draws inspiration not only from analytical philosophy and the philosophy of science but from a variety of disciplines, trends and approaches, such as structuralism and poststructuralism, deconstruction, semiotics, feminist epistemology, postcolonial studies, psychoanalysis, Marxism and neo-Marxism, new sociology, reflexive anthropology, etc. Such eclecticism and pluralism is grounded upon Frye's idea of 'letting the mind play freely around a subject (the object of study)'.[6]

At this point we must address the question of the limits or the frameworks of interpretation, the question of the 'ethics of analysis'. It must be stressed that endorsing the idea of multiple meanings of texts and of the impossibility of a definitive interpretation does not mean that every interpretation is equally acceptable. The student's decision to use a given theory, interpretative category, or way of thinking is related to his/her world-view, existential situation, and the choice of intellectual tradition that corresponds to his/her view of the world and the human being. On the deep level, therefore, the choice of method is an existential and ethical choice. Speaking of the limits of interpretation, I refer to Max Weber's concept of 'the ethics of responsibility'.[7] At the same time, I realise that the problem of the 'ethics of analysis' and the limits of representation is an *aporia*, touching upon the dilemma of being situated between the freedom of choice and the abstract ideals or accepted values which impose constraints on that freedom.

The functions of historiographical criticism

Historiographical criticism has three main functions: descriptive-analytical, 'prophetic' and performative. Let me examine each of these.

Descriptive and analytical function

As I have argued above, the starting point of historiographical criticism is the analysis ('close reading') of historical works and the description of the state of contemporary historiography. The historiographical critic is a 'textual psychoanalyst' who seeks the most interesting meanings in those levels of the text which Barthes termed 'the unconscious of discourse'. The critic thus has to find ways into the text, crevices leading to hidden meanings. In other words, the critic wants to discover the secret of the work. Those crevices, the hidden doors of the text, can be found in metaphors, in form, style, subject matter and its treatment, or the historian's position in his/her own narrative. A study of those characteristics can reveal the historian's assumptions which induce him or her to address a particular topic in a particular fashion.

'Prophetic' function

Historiographical criticism is related to rapid cultural change and the crisis caused, among other things, by globalisation. In view of those changes, the primary goal of historiographical criticism would be – as Frye suggested with reference to literary criticism – to identify in contemporary history writing such elements as could be deemed 'prophetic'. The historiographical critic analyses visions of the past proposed by the historian and remains aware that debates about these visions actually concern the future concept of the world and the human being. In this sense historiographical criticism is avant-garde criticism asking, 'What are the implications of historians' notions of the past and what are their possible consequences?'

In this context the historiographical critic may be dubbed 'prophetic critic' or 'herald' who does not foretell the future on the basis of some super-naturally received knowledge or his/her own superhuman powers, but who, as Deborah J. Haynes says, *forthtells* it. The critic analyses the present and the current historiographical visions of the past, indicating the potential future results of present actions and voicing the fears and hopes of the community s/he lives in.[8]

By repeating, highlighting or quoting certain ideas, motifs, symbols and metaphors that circulate in a particular community, the 'prophetic critic' becomes a vehicle of cultural memory instrumental in transcending the present stage of the community's development and extending its 'horizon of expectations'.[9] The main task of the historiographical critic is to recognise the prophetic elements in contemporary history writing, the elements that might be regarded as signs of the future. In this context historiographical criticism would function as ethical criticism on the one hand, and social and political criticism on the other, which means that it would be concerned with the present condition of the human being, society and culture, and with the present as history. Such criticism is a mode of communication, a medium of dialogue between the past and the present, the latter oriented towards the future. The critic asks, 'What happened in the past and was presented in a given way in the historical work, and remains of significance to the present and the creation of the future?'

Performative function

Historiographical criticism is performative in nature. In the present argument interpretation is conceived as a performative act since, as I have claimed, one of its goals is to participate in the change of historical consciousness; to prepare the ground for the emergence of some 'post-historical' approach to the past which would correspond to the 'horizon of expectations' of an audience living in the new millennium and a global culture. Rather than asking what a text means, historiographical criticism endows the text with agency and asks what it does. Its target audience is the younger generation, who, after this 'critical bite', will hopefully no longer perceive history in the traditional manner. The performative function of historiographical criticism is important from the pedagogical point of view insofar as it teaches students to think critically and to look for hidden assumptions underlying a given piece of writing. Historiographical criticism clearly demonstrates that different interpretative strategies produce different visions of the past and that it is impossible to write about history without adopting some ideological attitude.

Interpretations formulated by historiographical criticism will always be 'performative interpretations', to use Jacques Derrida's phrase (*Specters of Marx*, 1993). They transform what they interpret rather than merely commenting on the text or aspiring to restore it to its 'original' meaning. Therefore, as Derrida points out, the performative act of interpretation is related to Karl Marx's '11th Thesis on Feuerbach'. Historiographical criticism paraphrases that thesis, claiming that: 'historians have only described and interpreted the world in various ways; the point, however, is to realize how interpretation can change it'.[10]

Notes

1 It is often observed that the concept of literary criticism and its relation to theory is ambiguous. See Jonathan Culler, *Literary Theory: A Very Short Introduction* (Oxford: Oxford University Press, 1997); Richard Freadman, Seumas Miller, *Rethinking Theory: A Critique of Contemporary Literary Theory and an Alternative Account* (Cambridge: Cambridge University Press, 1992).

2 Ewa Domanska, *Mikrohistorie: Spotkania w mie‚dzys´wiatach* [Microhistories: Encounters in-between worlds] (Poznań: Wydawnictwo Poznańskie, 1997).

3 See Northrop Frye, 'The Responsibility of the Critic', *Modern Language Notes* 91: 5 (October 1976): 810.

4 Historiographical criticism may be said to emerge from the problem of subjectivity. The primary function of history is that of the guarantor and guard of identity. Thus, arguably, we will find history useful as long as we continue to believe that it plays a role in shaping, guaranteeing and sanctioning our identity, whether racial or ethnic, sexual or class, national, continental or global. Belief in history means belief in a coherent subject and its fixed identity. One reason for the present disbelief in the usefulness of history is the disintegration of such a stable historical subject, i.e., a subject that has gained and developed its identity by reference to tradition and to the past preserved in history.

5 See Lawrence Buell, 'In Pursuit of Ethics', *PMLA* 114: 1 (January 1999); Michael Eskin, 'The Double "Turn" to Ethics and Literature?' *Poetics Today* 25: 4 (Winter 2004); Todd F. Davis and Kenneth Womack (eds), *Mapping the Ethical Turn: A Reader in Ethics, Culture, and Literary Theory* (Charlottesville: University of Virginia Press, 2001); Robert Eaglestone, *Ethical Criticism: Reading after Levinas* (Edinburgh: Edinburgh University Press, 1997).

6   Northrop Frye, 'Polemical Introduction', in his *Anatomy of Criticism: Four Essays* (Princeton: Princeton University Press, 1973): 3.

7   Weber distinguishes two basic maxims which form the ground for any ethical action: 'ethics of conviction' (*Gesinnungsethisch*) and 'ethics of responsibility' (*Verantwortungsethisch*). The former refers to one's beliefs and focuses on maintaining them (for example, one should, at all costs, object to an unjust social order), while the latter foregrounds responsibility for one's own actions and is aware of human imperfection and its unpredictable consequences. Weber argues, however, that 'the ethics of conviction does not amount to lack of responsibility, nor does the ethics of responsibility amount to lack of convictions' and that the two cannot be reconciled (Max Weber, 'The Profession and Vocation of Politics', in *Political Writings*, ed. and trans. Peter Lassman and Roland Speirs (Cambridge: Cambridge University Press, 1994)).

8   The terms 'prophetic critic' and 'prophetic criticism' were introduced by Deborah J. Haynes in her *The Vocation of the Artist* (Cambridge: Cambridge University Press, 1997). This concept brings to mind Friedrich von Schlegel's well-known statement that 'the historian is a prophet looking backwards' (*der Historiker ist ein rückwärts gekehrter Prophet*).

9   Reinhart Koselleck, 'Space of Experience' and 'Horizon of Expectation', in his *Futures Past: On the Semantics of Historical Time*, trans. Keith Tribe (Cambridge, Mass.: MIT Press, 1985).

10 Jacques Derrida, *Specters of Marx: The State of the Debt, the Work of Mourning and the New International*, trans. Peggy Kamuf (New York and London: Routledge, 1994): 51.

15 The past of the future

From the foreign to the undiscovered country

David Lowenthal

Historians should disdain manifestos: they are contradictions in terms. To issue proclamations and thunder denunciations (from the Italian *manifestare*) is the duty of prelates and politicos. Historians who thunder risk Disraeli's taunt: manifesto writers are 'monotonous rumbling terrors'.[1] Our calling is not to moralise or preach but to discern and reveal – to make manifest what deserves being evident.

History is the most and the least evident of insights. The past is such common knowledge that it is acceptably taught by untrained amateurs rather than by accredited historians – who anyway, according to dismissive post-modernists, have no special claim to expertise.[2] Yet the past also seems an elusive will-o'-the-wisp, a limbo of mystery and confusion. Irretrievably gone, it is more an object of desire and dream or regret and recrimination than a realm of certain knowledge. We can only marvel at its traces, recall its memory and endlessly retell its history. And that history proves weird beyond imagination, alien, exotic, often incomprehensible. 'The past is a foreign country', begins L. P. Hartley's *The Go-between*. 'They do things differently there.' The dawning awareness of that difference some two centuries ago and its subsequent implications are explored in my *Past Is a Foreign Country* and, recently, by Peter Fritzsche and Frank Ankersmit.[3]

Less explored than changing views of the past are those of the future. Yet impressions of what lies ahead often mirror or transmute reactions to previous times. Since about 1750, both past and future have notably expanded in Western consciousness. Over the next two centuries, the collective annals of memory and anticipation lengthened exponentially, grew more copious and capacious, and resembled the present less and less.

Not any more. Among scholars, to be sure, past and future continue to extend in time, gain content and complexity, and seem ever more foreign. But for the lay public the past half century has reversed most of these trends. In the popular mind, both what was and what will be have shrunk, not in actual length and volume but in how these are grasped and reacted to. Nostalgia is rife and apocalyptic fears abound in mindsets that know and care about ever briefer time spans. Today's immediacy junks the past and starves the future. Disowning our Enlightenment legacy, we cease to revere ancestors or to welcome descendants. The past, formerly guide and mentor, degenerates to domesticated pet. The future, once embraced as a friend, becomes a fearsome foe.

Past and future enlarged by enlightenment and revolution

Before the late eighteenth century the past seemed much like the present. To be sure, Renaissance humanists had rediscovered an antiquity felt admirable by contrast with the subsequent Dark Ages; but people of all times and places were scrutinised and judged through a universalising lens. Memorable events marked past epochs, but private and public affairs for the most part seemed driven by immutable forces and desires. Human nature was everywhere the same, like nature undeviating in its effects.

The imagined future mirrored the past. For the Christianised West, time began with the Creation a few millennia back; time would end, replaced by eternity, with the Second Coming and Judgement Day. Most thought that momentous date no farther in the future than the Creation in the past. The terrestrial secular span elicited little curiosity about times past, whose denizens had lived much as their descendants did down to the present. And it evoked little speculation about the future, unfolding along the same preordained lines. Few expected earthly progress or improvement. Future hopes and fears, prayers and often bequests, were addressed not to this world but to Purgatory or the Paradise, remote from mundane circumstance.[4]

The lengthened and distanced past

The Age of Discovery and the Enlightenment altered both past and future lineaments; technology and the French Revolution utterly transformed them. Finding exotic peoples the world over, seeing the strangeness of past ways of life in classical texts and in newly excavated Pompeii and Herculaneum, scuttled prior convictions that behaviour was everywhere essentially similar, the path from past to present and future clear and inexorable. History, like geography, became complex and contingent.

Two sets of revolutionary events profoundly distanced the present from the newly foreign past. The guillotine and Napoleon changed so much so irrevocably that contemporary observers felt nothing could ever be the same. Indeed, to jettison obsolete tradition for rational perfection had been the revolutionaries' express intent. Those who fled Jacobin terror were trebly exiled: from home, from childhood, from customary ways. Those swept up by the Industrial Revolution were likewise distanced, from farm to factory, from country to city, from life ordered by diurnal and seasonal rhythms to one ruled by machines and clocks. Caught in the cogs of accelerating change, they were cut adrift from timeless, familiar routines. And would-be revenants to ancestral homelands found themselves lost in alien landscapes, their nostalgia incurable.

The past became not only foreign, but increasingly ancient. In Earth's features, in fossils of extinct creatures, in planetary and stellar movements, in evolutionary processes, scientists discerned lengthening reaches of terrestrial time, jettisoning biblical faith that had made the history of the Earth coterminous with that of humanity. Archbishop Ussher's 4004 BC Creation became a last-ditch stand, then a metaphorical figure, and with Gosse's *Omphalos* an anachronistic jest.[5] And to account for evolving modes of subsistence, transport, language and government, human history too had to be extended increasingly further back into the mists of what had been prehistoric.

As humanity's history lengthened and became better known, scholars grew more involved with it, even responsible for it. Computer pioneer Charles Babbage forecast a time when echoes of all deeds done, words uttered, even thoughts unvoiced would be retrieved from stones, seas and the very air – 'one vast library, on whose pages are forever written all that man has ever said or woman whispered, [where] stand forever recorded, vows unredeemed, promises unfulfilled'. A past thus known in its entirety confirmed scriptural portents of sinners haunted to the end of time.[6]

The lengthened and secularised future

As the past lengthened, so did the future. Given the antediluvian Creation, why need the last trump be imminent? Many, supposing themselves midway in time, with beginning and end equidistant, now foresaw a long road ahead. The lengthened future also became more alluring. The Enlightenment invented faith in progress. Savants saw life improving and felt confident in continuing advancement. Science increased knowledge, nature was being tamed, diseases cured, prosperity rising, civic order spreading. Salvation was no longer exclusive to the hereafter; human advance augured paradise on Earth. Only occasional setbacks delayed universal progress. But assurance of a better future did not lessen the urge to further its coming. Indeed, ardent endeavour was requisite to posterity's perfecting. Things did not improve just by themselves or by divine fiat; future well-being demanded present effort.

Zeal to perfect both nature and humanity spurred nineteenth-century stewardship. Ecology, like evolution, showed human destiny dependent on the continuing health of the commonweal, the planet, perhaps the cosmos. And heightened concern for the future in turn hinged on informed esteem for the past; for 'people will not look forward to posterity', as Edmund Burke admonished amnesiac ingrates, 'who never look backward to their ancestors'.[7]

The past amplified and attenuated

The past has continued to expand over time, over space, in content, and in controversy. Temporal horizons beyond those imagined by Jules Verne and H. G. Wells are now daily fare. Once commonly confined to 'Western civilisation', history now includes all cultures everywhere. Once limited to the annals of kingship and conquest and the deeds of great men, it increasingly focuses on the quotidian lives and aspirations of 'people without history' – previously unsung women, children, workers, the poor, the enslaved, the unlettered. Every facet of life is now historicised: a vast panoply of players, a multiform narrative embracing annals of child-rearing, cookery, commemorating, tattooing, funerary practices, music-making. Historians also conjure with kinds of evidence and modes of analysis undreamed of by their precursors.

Nature seen as history, history as nature

One notable enlargement takes all history ever farther back in hominid, terrestrial, solar and galactic time. As astronomy makes cognisant a fourteen-billion-year cosmic past; biology and archaeology lengthen human prehistory. Everything – plants, animals, continents, planets, stars and galaxies – is now historicised. And biological and stellar histories increasingly resemble human annals in complexity, contingency and unpredictability. Supposed clockwork regularity and enduring equilibria no longer differentiate natural from human history. Nature now shares humanity's unstable, turbulent, inconstant career; geologists and biologists conjure with time-bound deviations and tipping-point transformations.

Concurrently, human history is naturalised, integrated into the larger ecological saga. No longer a mere prologue to humanity's play, ongoing natural history commingles with purposive thought and action. Just as the biosphere continually alters our environments, so human ecological impacts are noted ever farther back. Genetic research links human DNA history with other species extant and extinct. Climate, soils, plants and animals, including symbiotic micro-organisms within us, continue to shape and be shaped by human destiny. Everything human is ever affected by nature; all nature is anthropogenic. These interactions require scientists to become historians, historians to learn science.[8]

That human action has long irreversibly transformed Earth, and now does so with mounting intensity, is well known among environmental scientists and historians. But it newly and increasingly alarms the wider public. With an Earth made fruitful people felt at home; an Earth despoiled and degraded is hard to acknowledge. Harder still is the knowledge that present-day impacts, unintended even more than deliberate, could be lethal for all life over aeons to come.

History popular and problematic, ancient and recent

The past, now longer, bigger, more inclusive and substantial than ever before, is perceived in myriad novel and vivid ways. But these accretions have cost the public much of what history previously promised – ordered coherence, causal continuity, consensual assurance, contextual clarity. And the newly enlarged and convoluted past arouses fears similar to those unleashed by the nineteenth-century expansion of time. Then, Earth's demonstrably awesome antiquity cast disturbing doubts on scriptural history. Today, ecological insights disconcert those who found surrogate comfort in nature's presumed constancy and regularity. Content with an Earth little disturbed by remote cosmic events, they took heart in the benign succession of seasons and in an ecological order that promised stability and equilibrium. Now, however, revelations of episodic mass extinctions, of recent and sudden reversals of oceanic currents and climatic regimes, leave nothing safe or certain any more; natural history is as upsetting as human. The new bloated past is too chaotic to comprehend, those unschooled ever less able to absorb it. History's consumers are fascinated by relics and remembrances, caught up in bygone splendours and horrors. But they cheer or jeer at pasts they understand less and less. Our collective legacy grows more bewildering than enlightening.

Sheer elongation deforms the past, inflating the very old and the very recent at the expense of stretches between. At one end we are obsessed by origins, prehistory, primordial antiquity. Primacy confers power and possession and status; knowing how something began seems to explain all. At the other end, we are engrossed in very recent times; personal recall has special salience; electronic media privilege up-to-the-minute data. Web and data bank purvey yesterday, not yesteryear. Educators follow suit: twentieth-century events, notably the adrenalin-pumping Second World War and the Holocaust, dominate curricula. Hitler overwhelms British school history.

Ancient and recent alike are sexy, accessible – and murky. Great antiquity charms *because* it is little known; the veriest tyro freely opines on prehistory, unlike classical, medieval or early modern times. On yesterday, too, any ignoramus can assert eyewitness knowledge. Yet sheer recency leaves it incoherent. Hindsight cannot assimilate what has just happened into a properly mulled chronicle. To sift and evaluate require the test of time. Hence we delay nominating to halls of fame, designating historic sites, erecting memorials and monuments. It takes two or three generations to sieve a trustworthy collective past from the muddled trauma and trivia of living memory, the nostalgia or amnesia of initial heirs. Emphasising the very recent detracts from the past's entirety. It elevates fleeting fad and fashion over enduring culture.

Recency and antiquity, alike engorged at the expense of intermediate eras, make the past in its entirety harder to grasp. Starts and ends are mythic, befuddled, inscrutable: 'In the beginning . . . they lived happily ever after.' What comes first and last is literally unhinged – nothing prior attaches to the primordial, nothing links beyond the latest, itself soon engulfed by the present.

The eviscerated past

Popular media further narrow the past by privileging action over reflection, empathetic bonding over critical distance, discrete events over continuity, individual over collective experience, kaleidoscopic imprint over patterned palimpsest. To be sure, historical ignorance is lamented by every passing generation.[9] What is new is *acceptance* of ignorance; being uninformed is no impediment to nostalgia. In some previous epochs oblivion was accounted a blessing: to heal Civil War wounds, seventeenth-century English parliaments enacted Acts of Oblivion; French revolutionists deemed it desirable to expunge all memory of the past; pioneers exhorted Americans never to look back. Today the past is not shrugged off or deemed valueless. Only *knowledge* of the past is eschewed, while empathetic feeling is exalted. For that, being ill-informed or even uninformed is a positive aid.

The result is the loss of an enduring social framework grounded in shared cultural references. Like ignorance, the fading away of familiar terms of discourse is a complaint recurrently voiced. But today's media and schooling lend the charge new cogency. Once-memorable people, events and idioms ebb ever sooner into oblivion.[10] For those devoid of history, temporal depth conveys no meaning. A confrontation in Paris left Alethea Hayter fearful that historical consciousness would soon 'be not merely eclipsed but extinguished'. An Anglophone visitor at Sainte Chapelle asked her what the place was about:

> 'Well, it was built by Saint Louis . . .' 'Saint Louis?' was her puzzled reply . . . 'Yes, it was built by a king of France who went on a crusade . . .' 'Crusade?' she asked, bewildered. Despairingly I persevered. 'Yes, he went on a journey to the Mediterranean, and brought back a sacred relic, the Crown of Thorns . . .' 'Crown of Thorns?' she queried, still more at sea. At that point I gave up; I felt unable to insert any idea of the significance of the Sainte Chapelle into a mind which had been given no context of European history or Christian belief at all.[11]

The erosion of canonical names and dates precludes fellowship with any past. 'Our entire collective subjective history . . . is encoded in print,' notes Sven Birkerts. Hence the shift from print to visually oriented electronic culture 'has rendered a vast part of our cultural heritage utterly alien'.[12] The lack of any frame of reference leaves today's children bereft of a crucial arc of connectedness. To be sure, some communal references persist: mass-media consumers share extensive sports, music and fashion repertoires. But that store of data is trivial, inchoate and ephemeral; it nourishes no discourse beyond its own short-lived icons; it links its devotees with only a very recent past; its substance is too thin to support a meaningful social fabric. It does not compensate for 'the loss of the historical frame of reference, the amputation of the time dimension from our culture'. To be 'in the swim' is not equivalent to 'being in the culture'.[13]

Some contend that the ease and speed of modern information retrieval makes cultural memory redundant – why store in the mind names and dates readily found on the internet? But references at our fingertips are not the same as having them in our head. To converse, to compare, to contrast, even to consult an encyclopedia requires a stock of common knowledge not merely on tap but ingrained in communal awareness.

For historians, the past grows ever more foreign. But the public at large cannot bear so alien a past, and strenuously domesticate it, imputing present-day aims and deeds to folk of earlier times. In popular media, at historic sites and museums, human nature remains constant, people unchanged from age to age. Legends of origin and endurance, of victory or calamity, project the present back, the past forward. The past ceases to be a foreign country, instead becoming our sanitised own.[14]

The future fearsome, shrunken, forsaken

The repute of the future, like that of the past, has radically changed over the past half century. But it has gone the opposite way. Fifty years ago modernists banned the past and welcomed the future; now, yesterday is our solace for a fearsome tomorrow. Once friendly and familiar, the future has become not just foreign but frighteningly alien.

The collapse of future hope is recent. At the end of the Second World War many looked ahead with optimism, for themselves and for the world. To be sure, evil abounded – war, poverty, racism, pestilence, hunger were rife; resource scarcity loomed. But these ills seemed curable. Science, technology and global peace held huge promise. Neither Hiroshima nor the Holocaust extinguished sanguine expectations. The next half century largely quenched such hopes. Mistrusted for its betrayals, the future became attenuated, eclipsed, forsaken. No longer fondly envisaged by fictional time travellers, it featured instead as fascist nightmare: Orwell's 'boot stamping on a human face – for ever'. We hand down a depleted if not incinerated planet under totalitarian diktat or reduced by greed and improvidence to savagery and misery, and a dysfunctional social order seemingly bent on collective suicide. Doomsayers a generation ago felt the 1970s a decade of Despair, foresaw the 1980s as one of Desperation, the 1990s of Catastrophe, the twenty-first century the era of Annihilation. We seem almost fated to fulfil their forecast.[15]

Habitual parlance, to be sure, still plugs a bright tomorrow. Forward-looking glee suffuses feel-good hype – therapeutic, commercial, political. Every website, campaign flyer, estate agent's leaflet, healthcare ad promises perfection for us and our offspring for generations to come. Oil producers and forestry firms trumpet devotion to the clean, green world far ahead.

'We're developing the cures of the future,' boasts a pharmaceutical firm; 'we'll care for your great-great-grandchildren'. Politicians intone similar commitments. 'Let us build a better world for our children and grandchildren,' exhorts President Bush. For the Disney empire as for the President, ' "educating future generations" is a [vital] part of the official corporate rhetoric'. The American International Group is the 'financial organization to choose for your Great-Great-Great-Great-Great-Grandchild', but this seven-generation pledge is mocked by the indictment of its CEO.[16] ' "Our children – the future" is a slogan that makes its appearance only when its effectiveness can no longer be taken for granted.'[17]

Future rhetoric flies in the face of mounting neglect. Far from facing what lies ahead, we ignore it as risky, if not ruinous, instead lingering in present comforts or retreating to the safety of the past. And no wonder! For the same voices that soothe us with future dreams flood us with portents of disaster. Alongside pie-in-the-sky assurances of rejuvenated skin and flesh, revived fortunes and psyches, come doom-laden warnings of imperilled life and limb, home and workplace, land and sea and air.

Modernist confidence, post-war angst

Only recently the future was a modernist utopia. Science, social engineering and giddy speed begat cornucopian prophecies. Disney's 'Tomorrowland', a high-tech urban image of 1956, looked as designed by Le Corbusier.[18] The archetypal future was 'a city of gleaming, tightly clustered towers, with helicopters fluttering about their heads and monorails snaking around their feet . . . under a vast transparent dome', wrote modernist guru Reyner Banham; life there would be 'unmitigated bliss'.[19]

Already fading in the 1960s, that future was a thing of the past by the 1980s. High-tech gave way to hand-lettered preachments extolling pastoral virtues, with 'windmills and families holding hands'. Banham was bemused. 'What kind of future is that? Where's your white heat of technology? Where's your computer typefaces? . . . Where's that homely old future we all grew up with?'[20] It was shunted aside by the more homely past. As 'glittering streets in the sky' turned into jerry-built, crime-filled high-rise slums, 'Tomorrowland' morphed into 'Celebration', small-town homes with lawns, white picket fences, a recycling plant down the road. Heritage, roots and historic preservation assuaged present sorrows and future perils. The nostalgised past became the foreign country with the fastest-growing tourist trade of all.[21]

From upbeat post-war prognoses, confidence plummeted to all-time lows. The future is commonly seen as grim, if not calamitous. End-time preachers herald the horrors limned in the Book of Revelation. Worse still, it is our fault.[22] Early Christian Armageddon was foreordained. But today's envisioned endings stem from our own follies – squandering resources, eroding nature's fabric, polluting the planet beyond recovery, perfecting weapons that invite mass annihilation by any nation or cult with a grievance, if not by accident.

'Will the world survive the machinations of a technologically very knowledgeable, very depressed Luddite?' A savant underscores the 'finite probability that this may cause the end of [our] part of the universe'.[23]

Compare the current mood with that just after Hiroshima and Nagasaki. The human race then seemed likely to blow itself out of existence. Nuclear imminence was vivified by the Bulletin of Atomic Scientists' minutes-to-midnight clock, radioactive horror by *On the Beach* (1957) and *The Late, Great Planet Earth* (1970). The Bomb rendered tenuous all we did and built.[24] James Clifford recalls 'the everyday fear . . . that I and everyone I knew might not survive'. Few laid future plans.[25] The writer Alan Brien's 1950s set were convinced that 'none of us would survive . . . Not only did they reject parenthood and marriage, they refused to consider taking out a mortgage or life insurance . . . A few carried their distrust of the future . . . so far as to never make appointments of any kind, even for a drink, more than a week ahead.'[26]

Or so they claimed. But few *behaved* that way. Most carried on as though they had all the time in the world – pursuing careers, marrying, buying homes, having children. 'How could any woman even think for a minute of bringing into this soon to be vaporised planet an innocent creature who would almost certainly never reach maturity?'[27] Yet many did. Indeed, birth rates burgeoned in the post-war baby boom. Surprisingly, the nuclear threat strengthened the nuclear family. Did that contradiction – denial of the immediate future coupled with continuing, even heightened, long-term commitments – mean a conflict between head and heart? Were we so habituated to nesting and begetting that instinct overrode reason? Were we enacting our ingrained upbringing, or reacting out of some obligation to replenish Earth in jeopardy? In fact, the Bomb apart, it was a time of expanded hope. We inherited a world freed from the incubus of global conflict. Science and social planning promised to banish famine, strife, poverty, ignorance. For all the annihilation brouhaha, most never truly credited it. We continued to conceive, bear and rear children. After all, reflected an old historian a generation later, 'the certainty we will all die doesn't stop us making plans for our own futures'.[28]

Dwindling prospects

The longer term well beyond their own lives engrossed my students in the early 1950s. Asked how far ahead concerned them, these eighteen- and nineteen-year-olds cared deeply about the next 150 to 200 years – when their potential grandchildren's grandchildren might be living. And one in three felt affinity with an unlimited future, as with Pat Frank's 1946 bestseller *Mr Adam*, keen 'to keep intact the thread that ties us to the hereafter'.[29]

Distant horizons are now rare. The 'future' that concerns young people polled today is tomorrow, next weekend, next year. Few envisage becoming grandparents, or even parents. Heedless of future millennia, they are reluctant to plan for their own lives, let alone for potential offspring. They hardly know how to look forward, for any sense of the future but the most grim is foreign to them. Impulse and immediacy trump progressive ideals of life as a career, a consecutive, cumulative, goal-driven enterprise.[30] 'Why bother?' ask Norwegian youths. 'Why strive to reach a future worse than what we already have?' 'Nothing prepared us', conclude assessors of eleven-year-old Australians' bleak predictions, 'for the depth of children's fear of their future'. 'Nothing [seemed] more alarming' to an American teacher 'than the impoverishment of our children's capacity to imagine the future'.[31]

These youngsters cannot be blamed. They only reflect their seniors and mentors, lampooned by Woody Allen: 'More than at any time in history, mankind faces a crossroads. One path leads to despair and utter hopeless-ness. The other, to total extinction. Let us pray we have the wisdom to choose correctly.'[32] The future is not only bleak but ever briefer. In government and industry, ten-year plans become five-, then two-. 'When I was a child', says Daniel Hillis, 'people used to talk about what would happen by the year 2000. Now, thirty years later [in 1993], they still talk about what would happen by the year 2000. The future has been shrinking by one year per year for my entire life.'[33] When 2000 arrived, the future vanished altogether.

What shrank the future? What cut planners' future in half, Hillis's yearly, my students' from two centuries to two days? The reasons are many and disheartening. Loss of faith in progress; the demise of job security; the dawning conviction, without precedent, that our children will be worse off than ourselves (a conviction they share); fear that coming calamities are unavoidable and insoluble; growing doubt that science has the skill (or statesmen the will) to cure social malaise or curb environmental ruin. Science and technology seem the 'cause, not a solution, of the ills of mankind'.[34]

The SKI syndrome

Future altruism succumbs to voracious immediate demands. 'Decade after decade', conclude American economists, echoed in Britain, 'the Nows have taken from the Laters'.[35] Advocates of intergenerational equity are derided by economists who trust market forces to guarantee future well-being, assume coming generations will be incomparably richer and more resourceful, and expect technological miracles to rid us of toxic legacies of nuclear waste, chemical pollution, lethal additives, corporate bankruptcies, government deficits and long-term debts dumped on our heirs.[36]

The costs of this mindset are manifold. Infrastructures decay for want of maintenance; fatalist apathy mounts in the face of what cannot be set right; we splurge on ourselves instead of saving for children; we even cease breeding as 'monumentally ruinous . . . Avoid childbirth if you value your wealth', advises a market analyst. Parents 'are in worse economic shape than they've ever been', judges another. 'Having a child is now the best indicator' of imminent financial exigency.[37] We are like Samuel Butler's Mr Pontifex, who enjoyed his money more than his offspring because it gave him so much less trouble.[38] Being 'less interested in offspring and willing to sacrifice for them' and no longer caring 'to leave the site of one's life in better shape than it was found' reflect 'a growing incapacity or unwillingness . . . to identify with the future'.[39] Few conjure up images of descendants enjoying their legacies.[40] A cartoon shows dismayed heirs at a reading of the deceased's will: 'Being of sound mind and body, I blew it all.' We have turned Enlightenment devotion to posterity on its head. To the SKI (Spending our Kids' Inheritance) generation, dwelling on the distant future 'bespeaks a sort of mental corruption'.[41]

Our stance augurs the depleted, congested, listless impending world of Peter Dickinson's dystopian novel, where children 'never thought about the future, or what was going to happen to them when they grew up', and 'the whole human race is thinking in shorter and shorter terms . . . You can't get a bridge built . . . You can't get a road repaired. People . . . won't invest or save'; suicide is endemic.[42] Dickinson's future seems well on the way. And as apocalypse approaches, many prefer to welcome it than to ward it off. Some even hasten its advent.

Immediacy against past and future

The new future thus resembles the new past in one major respect: its brevity. We think ahead, if at all, for times ever nearer. Any future that compels attention is our own, not our children's, much less humanity's, let alone Earth's in aeons to come. A century ago, legacies, like reputations, were handed down intact; estates were not spent, they were husbanded. 'Society was working not for the small pleasures of today,' wrote J. M. Keynes, 'but for the future security and improvement of the race.'[43] Except among environmentalists, stewardship is now passé. What lies ahead matters ever less and elicits little care. We hearken to self-help happiness sages who censure 'morbid contemplation of the past or future' and consider 'one day at a time' a moral imperative. 'Make the most of now,' exhorts a mobile-phone firm. 'It's the most precious thing in the world. It only exists for an instant. Then it's gone. So . . . squeeze every drop of enjoyment out of it.'[44]

Discarding duration, we reduce ourselves to Burke's 'flies of a summer'. And Hamlet's 'undiscover'd country from whose bourn no traveller returns' becomes more foreign than Hartley's past. 'The great problem with the future', suggests Stewart Brand, 'is that we die there. This is why it is so hard to take the future personally, especially the longer future, because that world is suffused by our absence.'[45] Yet impending mortality makes us not merely undertakers but historians and seers. Although hard-wired by our Palaeolithic heritage to think and feel no more than two or three generations ahead,[46] the durable accretions of history lengthen both our cultural memory and our future commitments. In league with the dead and the unborn we learn to transcend our selves. That great insight, outliving the self, was memorably broached by Burke, lent spiritual nous by Émile Durkheim, and advanced as imperative policy by Arthur Pigou.[47]

It is now all the more imperative. Awareness of long-term menace spurs efforts to protect the Earth by preventing catastrophe or mitigating damage centuries, even millennia, ahead. Our newly enlightened and alarmed generation 'has identified, warned about, and even suggested . . . how the distant future can cope with' threats of meteor impacts, global warming, radioactive waste disposal, and nuclear war. For this, holds a physicist, we deserve 'the everlasting gratification of future generations'.[48] Truly to merit such gratitude, these long-term risks will require more active attention than they have yet received.

'Adam and Eve', writes a columnist, 'committed a sin that had catastrophic consequences for the rest of time.' Norway's 'doomsday' seed vault at Svalbard, designed to freeze-store seeds of three million species for regeneration against agricultural catastrophe, is touted as the first practical recognition that 'science, and the moral reasoning it requires, have made humans responsible for the future in ways we have never been before'.[49] In fact, it is the second such recognition. The first was the (likely fruitless) effort to design permanent warning markers for the radioactive wastes being deeply buried at the US Waste Isolation Pilot Plant near Carlsbad, New Mexico – markers meant to be read and heeded long after our language becomes gibberish and our society extinct. 'How we present ourselves in these ancient sepulchres may be our longest-lasting legacy,' muses a physicist. 'It is sobering to reflect that distant eras may know us mostly by our waste – and by our foresight.'[50]

If they are lucky, that is. Care of the future along with concern for the past now warrant a renewed manifesto, if there is to be, as this volume's editors urge, any future of discourse at all to which historians might contribute.[51]

Notes

1 Benjamin Disraeli, speech, House of Commons, 13 February 1851.
2 Diane Ravitch, 'The Educational Backgrounds of History Teachers', in Peter N. Stearns *et al.* (eds), *Knowing, Teaching, and Learning History* (New York: New York University Press, 2000): 143–55.
3 L. P. Hartley, The Go-between (London: Hamish Hamilton, 1953); David Lowenthal, *The Past Is a Foreign Country* (Cambridge: Cambridge University Press, 1985); Peter Fritzsche, *Stranded in the Present: Modern Time and the Melancholy of History* (Cambridge, Mass.: Harvard University Press, 2004); Frank Ankersmit, *Sublime Historical Experience* (Stanford: Stanford University Press, 2005).
4 J. A. Burrow and Ian W. Wei (eds), *Medieval Futures: Attitudes to the Future in the Middle Ages* (Woodbridge: Boydell Press, 2000).
5 Martin Rudwick, *Bursting the Limits of Time: The Reconstruction of Geohistory in the Age of Revolution* (Chicago: University of Chicago Press, 2005); Philip Henry Gosse, *Omphalos: An Attempt to Untie the Geological Knot* (London:

Van Voorst, 1857); Ann Thwaite, *Glimpses of the Wonderful: The Life of Philip Henry Gosse 1810–1888* (London: Faber and Faber, 2002): 222–7.

6 *The Ninth Bridgewater Treatise*, 2nd edn [1838] (London: Frank Cass, 1967): 112–15.

7 *Reflections on the Revolution in France* [1790] (London: Dent, 1910): 31.

8 David Lowenthal, 'Environmental History: From Genesis to Apocalypse', *History Today* 51:4 (April 2001): 36–42; David Christian, *Maps of Time: An Introduction to Big History* (Berkeley: University of California Press, 2004).

9 Samuel Wineburg, *Historical Thinking and Other Unnatural Acts* (Philadelphia: Temple University Press, 2001): 32–5.

10 Elaborated in my 'Dilemmas and Delights of Learning History', in Stearns *et al.*, *Knowing, Teaching, and Learning History*, pp. 64–82, and in 'Archival Perils: An Historian's Plaint', *Archives* 31 (2006): 49–75.

11 'The Rise and Fall of Clio', *Spectator*, 18 July 1998, p. 38.

12 *The Gutenberg Elegies* (New York: Ballantyne, 1994): 19–20.

13 Ernst Gombrich, *The Tradition of General Knowledge* (London: London School of Economics, 1962): 11, 21.

14 See my 'The Timeless Past: Some Anglo-American Historical Preconceptions', *Journal of American History* 75 (1989): 1263–80, and *The Heritage Crusade and the Spoils of History* (Cambridge: Cambridge University Press, 1998).

15 George Orwell, *Nineteen Eighty-four* (Harmondsworth: Penguin, 1954): 213; Richard A. Falk, *This Endangered Planet* (New York: Random House, 1971) 420–31; Robert L. Heilbroner, *An Inquiry into the Human Prospect* (New York: Norton, 1974): 44.

16 Pfizer ad, 2003; George W. Bush, State of the Union message, 2 February 2005; David Remnick, 'Future Perfect: The Next Magic Kingdom', *New Yorker*, 20–7 October 1997, pp. 210–24, at p. 223 (Disney); AIG ad, 2005.

17 Christopher Lasch, 'The Age of Limits', in Arthur M. Melzer *et al.* (eds), *History and the Idea of Progress* (Ithaca: Cornell University Press, 1995): 227–40, at 233.

18 William Strauss and Neil Howe, *Generations: The History of America's Future, 1584 to 2069* (New York: William Morrow, 1991): 347.

19 'Come in 2001 . . .', *New Society*, 8 January 1976, pp. 62–3.

20 Ibid. See Jean Gimpel, *The End of the Future: The Waning of the High-Tech World* (Westport, Conn.: Praeger, 1995).

21 James Collard, 'Tomorrow's People', *The Times Magazine*, 27 December 2003, p. 22; Remnick, 'Future Perfect', p. 217; Lowenthal, *Past Is a Foreign Country*, p. 4.

22 Gerald Horton, 'Science and Progress Revisited', in Leo Marx and Bruce Mazlish (eds), *Progress: Fact or Illusion?* (Ann Arbor: University of Michigan Press, 1996): 9–26, at 33.

23 Luigi Luca Cavalli-Sforza, 'Are There Limits to Knowledge?', in Martin Ruegg (ed.), *Balzan Symposium 2002: Meeting the Challenges of the Future* (Florence: Leo Olschki, 2003): 57.

24 Paul Boyer, *By the Bomb's Early Light: American Thought and Culture at the Dawn of the Atomic Age* (New York: Pantheon, 1985); Frederic J. Baumgartner, *Longing for the End: A History of Millennialism in Western Civilization* (New York: St Martin's Press, 1999): 213–20; Robert Jay Lifton and Richard Falk, *Indefensible Weapons: The Political and Psychological Case against Nuclearism* (New York: Basic Books, 1982): 67–73.

25 *Routes: Travel and Translation in the Late Twentieth Century* (Cambridge, Mass.: Harvard University Press, 1997): 344.

26 'The Extended Father', in Sean French (ed)., *Fatherhood* (London: Virago, 1992): 12.

27 Ibid.

28 E. H. Carr, *What Is History?* [1961] (Cambridge: Macmillan, 1988), Preface to 1982 edn, p. xii, p. 128.

29 Boyer, *By the Bomb's Early Light*, pp. 279–80.

30 Jonas Frykman and Orvar Löfgren, *Culture Builders: A Historical Anthropology of Middle-Class Life* (New Brunswick: Rutgers University Press, 1987): 29–30; John Paul Russo, *The Future without a Past* (Columbia: University of Missouri Press, 2005): 114–15.

31 Paul Otto Brunstad, 'Longing for Belonging: Youth Culture in Norway', in Jennifer Gidley and Sohail Inayatullah (eds), *Youth Futures: Comparative Research and Transformative Visions* (Westport, Conn.: Praeger, 2002): 143–54, at 149; *Sydney Morning Herald* 1990 survey, quoted in Richard Eckersley, 'The West's Deepening Cultural Crisis', *Futurist* 27:6 (November/December 1993): 8–12; Andrew Delbanco, *The Real American Dream: A Meditation on Hope* (Cambridge, Mass.: Harvard University Press, 1999): 98.

32 'My Speech to Graduates', in his *Side Effects* (New York: Random House, 1980): 57.

33 Hillis quoted in Stewart Brand, *The Clock of the Long Now: Time and Responsibility* (New York: Basic Books, 1999): 2–3.

34 Stephen Baxter, *Deep Future* (London: Victor Gollancz, 2001): 3. On the global decline of confidence in science and government from 1973 to 2002, see National Opinion Research Center, University of Chicago, *What Do Americans Think about Issues That Shape Their Lives?* (Ithaca: New Strategic Publications, 2005): Tables 1.8–1.19, pp. 17–28.

35 Laurence J. Kotlikoff and Scott Burns, *The Coming Generational Storm* (Cambridge, Mass.: MIT Press, 2004): xvi.

36 Wilfred Beckerman and Joanna Pasek, *Justice, Posterity, and the Environment* (Oxford: Oxford University Press, 2001).

37 Antonia Senior, 'The Mother of All Mistakes', *The Times*, 19 August 2006, Money, p. 3; James Surowiecki, 'Leave No Parent Behind', *New Yorker*, 18–25 August 2003, p. 48. See Elaine Tyler May, *Barren in the Promised Land* (Cambridge, Mass.: Harvard University Press, 1995): 128–33, 207–9; Madelyn Cain, *The Childless Revolution* (Cambridge: Perseus, 2001).

38 Samuel Butler, *Ernest Pontifex, or the Way of All Flesh* [1873/1893] (London: Methuen, 1965): 20.

39 John Kotré, *Outliving the Self: Generativity and the Interpretation of Lives* (Baltimore: Johns Hopkins University Press, 1984): 1.

40 Grant McCracken, *Culture and Consumption* (Bloomington: Indiana University Press, 1988): 42–3, 50; Carole Shammas *et al.* (eds), *Inheritance in America from Colonial Times to the Present* (New Brunswick: Rutgers University Press, 1987): 211–12.

41 Garrett Hardin, 'Why Plant a Redwood Tree?' [1974], in his *Naked Emperors* (Los Altos: William Kaufman, 1982): 160–3. Diderot typified Enlightenment horror at the prospect of childlessness.

42 Peter Dickinson, *Eva* (London: Macmillan Children's, 2001): 86, 243–4.

43 John Maynard Keynes, *The Economic Consequences of the Peace* [1919], in his *Collected Writings* (Cambridge: Cambridge University Press, 1971): II: 12, 41.

44 Hugo Williams, 'Freelance', *Times Literary Supplement*, 9 December 2005, p. 14; Vodafone ad, *The Times Magazine*, 5 November 2005, p. 2.

45 *Clock of the Long Now*, p. 150.

46 Edward O. Wilson, *The Future of Life* (New York: Knopf, 2002): 40–1.

47 Burke, *Reflections on the Revolution in France*; Émile Durkheim, *The Elementary Forms of Religious Life* [1912] (New York: Free Press, 1995): 213–14, 351–2, 372, 379. Arthur Pigou, *The Economics of Welfare* [1920], 4th edn (London: Macmillan, 1952): 27ff.

48 Alvin M. Weinberg, 'Scientific Millenarianism', *Futurist* 31 (1999): 929–36.
49 James Carroll, 'Seeds of Salvation', *International Herald Tribune*, 27 June 2006, p. 7.
50 Gregory Benford, *Deep Time: How Humanity Communicates across Millennia* (New York: Avon, 1999): 36–49, 71–2, 85.
51 See my 'Stewarding the Future', *CRM: Journal of Heritage Stewardship* 2:2 (2005): 6–25.

Afterword
Manifesto time

Hayden White

The manifesto is a radical genre. It presupposes a time of crisis and that, moreover, the crisis is manifest, plain for all to see. And it usually calls for action (or in the case of religious manifestos, a change of heart) to overcome or ameliorate the situation at hand.

The time of the manifesto is the present (and the immediate future); the 'now' time (Benjamin's *Jetztzeit*) of decision. The manifesto has no interest in the past except as part of the problem to be solved. The manifesto, as Derrida reminds us in *Specters of Marx*, typically tells us that 'the time is out of joint', that it is 'high time' we set things right, and then proposes a course of action or a change of heart in order to move on to better times in the future. Derrida also notes that the paradigm of the modern manifesto is to be found in the ancient (biblical) forms of the prophecy, on the one hand, and the gospel (*evangelion*), on the other. The former, of course, promises punishment for those who, bound by the Covenant, violate its terms; it tends towards the apocalyptical. The latter proclaims the advent of a new time ('the time is fulfilled'), with a new law, and new prospects of community; it tends towards the revolutionary. The modern political manifesto may combine the two modes, mixing fire and brimstone and love and light in equal measure. The artistic manifesto – think of those of the Futurists and the Surrealists – combines threat and promise in a simulacrum of revelation. The scientific manifesto – think of Bacon, Galileo, Darwin – is a different breed: cool, calm and collected, because the scientific manifester, having a certain knowledge in hand, knows that time is on his or her side; like Galileo censored, s/he can afford to wait: '*Eppure, si muove.*'

And what of a manifesto for history? Does it make any sense to manifest for a scholarly discipline, and especially a contemplative rather than a drastic one, fixated on the past, committed to the long view, suspicious of generalisation, and hostile to every futurism? In their introduction, our editors posit a 'now' of postmodernism in the sense that 'we have come to the end of 'the experiment of modernity'' and the (failed) promise of 'human rights' communities. They presume that the deconstruction of 'the Western tradition' has pretty much demolished all of the foundationalisms on which every prior vision of the historical or historicality was based. Consequently, as they put it, 'history *per se* now wobbles'.

So, the question they put to our potential manifesters is (*manifesticamente*) 'What is to be done?' What is to be done to, for or with history? What is to be done with historical consciousness? What is to be done with all that knowledge about the past amassed by thousands of devoted historians over the last two centuries that is now so extensive, so variegated, so deeply textured that no single thinker could possibly discern its basic outline, much less master its oppressive detail? What comes 'after history' understood as a structure of knowledge whose originary impulse and achieved coherence are not so much finished as, rather, no longer meaningful to whatever it is that constitutes *our* postmodernity?

Keith Jenkins has from time to time suggested that history is a concept that has had its day, a mode of knowledge that is passé, and a relic of an earlier time. In their introduction, our editors entertain the thought that the genre of the manifesto belongs to that modernity that has now passed into 'history'. This would imply that any new manifesto for history or for anything else would have to differ from the kinds of manifesto produced in modernity. At the least, it would have to be a *postmodernist* manifesto, parody of a manifesto or, if we accept Jameson's idea of postmodernism, a 'pastiche' of other, earlier manifestos.

Above all, a postmodernist manifesto could not be a *sincere* manifesto. Rosenstone says it openly when he remarks of the editors' project that they have 'got to be kidding'. And LaCapra implies it when he sternly hopes that the time is past when any individual would try to legislate procedures for any discipline pretending to genuine scientificity. So, our reluctant manifesters edge up to the manifesto, not quite manifesting and not quite *not* manifesting.

What then? Ironic manifestos? Postmodern manifestos? This might mean that instead of pointing out what is 'manifest' in the current situation in our discipline and what must 'manifestly' be changed in it, we could expect a post-manifesto manifesto, pointing out what is not obvious in the present situation, and especially what there is in the present that really belongs to the past, what has to be *uncovered* or de-revealed as past still present in the present in order to be overcome. And when it comes to 'history', this process of uncovering and de-revealing would be carried out as much on the modernist concept of 'history' itself as on those aspects of the present that continue to haunt the living although they deserve to be laid to rest or interred or, better, archived. It is this kind of double- and triple-thinking which might account for the tone of irony that permeates this book.[1] It might also account for the recurrence of the notions of *criticism* and *critique* advanced in a number of the manifestos (specifically those of Ermarth, Domanska, Scott, Joyce, Poster and LaCapra) as a solution for the problems of history in a postmodern time.

Now, it may be that a group of professional students of history (however chosen) might not be best suited to the task of envisioning some 'history for the future'. The members of the profession who call themselves 'working historians' (as against 'non-working historians' or 'working non-historians'?)

have an in-built aversion for the kind of projective thinking that the manifesto requires. Moreover, what it means to be a professional or at least what it means to be 'disciplined' is to avoid any kind of extremist thinking. I think that Dominick LaCapra speaks as a *professional* historian when he warns against the extremism of 'radical constructionism', on the one hand, and what he calls 'the self-sufficient research paradigm', on the other. In his desire to 'resist apocalypse', however, he may be overestimating the stakes in the effort to reform or revise our discipline. As Robert Rosenstone asks, who – other than professional historians – cares about the future of professional historiography? In their increasing specialisation and remoteness from the concerns of the present, they have, as David Harlan points out, long since ceased to matter to anyone working outside their specialised fields of interest. The general public gets most of its history from the media and popular writers of biographies, battles and crime.

All this concern about any position that may go 'too far' or claim 'too much' suggests that our manifesters want to resist anything of a radical cast of mind and are satisfied to recommend cosmetic revisions, such as adding new fields of research or new forms of presentation to the established procedures and practices of 'conventional' or 'traditional' historiography. Thus, Ewa Domanska suggests that we add an equivalent of literary criticism to the way we read historiographical texts, but she does not suggest – as she has suggested in her other work – that this might require a change in the way we *write* history as well. She hopes that the historiographical critic might discern 'prophetic' moments in historical writings, moments that point to the future without prescribing the form that it might take. Mark Poster predicts that we will have to take account in some way of the media revolution and the impact of digitalised information storage and retrieval systems in the writing of history in the future. His suggestion that we might have to expand our notion of the real to include the 'virtual' is tantalising, but I was left unclear about what this new content of the historical account would imply in terms of the way in which 'history' might be presented either in writing or in images. Beverley Southgate asks that we consider taking up once more – but in a slightly different register – the old humanistic programme of studying history in order to discern 'what it means to be *human*', although it is unclear why it should be thought that historians might be better equipped to provide an answer to that question than practitioners of other disciplines. Some seventy years ago, Ortega mooted this question when he wrote that man has no nature; what he has is history. This suggests that we might be better off studying nature to discover why man has a history, rather than studying history to find out if man has a nature.

Frank Ankersmit, in what I found to be a surprising two-steps-backward-in-order-to-take-one-step-forward programme, counsels a return to the good old ways of Ranke and traditional historism, in order to restore history to its traditional task of teaching (political) philosophy by example. He asks us to utilise the 'wisdom of the past' (*sic*) in order to criticise dangerous political experiments that repeat all unknowingly certain programmes that were proven unworkable in earlier times. He cites Pollock and Skinner as pointing the way to such a programme; and this makes sense, because both are historists through and through, which means that they study texts of political philosophy, law and ethics in order to show how incomparable they are to any later (or earlier) time. Even Robert Rosenstone's seemingly 'extreme' suggestion of leaving some space in our accounts of the past for the play of the artistic imagination returns history to its *earlier* (Romanticist?) alliance with 'literature'. This suggestion is congruent with Ann Rigney's proposal for a kind of 'federalism' of the disciplines, each performing its traditionally assigned tasks in an atmosphere of mutual tolerance, exchange and civility, even though she knows that we have just passed through a sequence of 'culture wars' that have left the disciplines of the traditional humanities wounded, perhaps beyond repair.

And yet all of these reluctant manifesters indicate, more or less openly, the need for an expansion of the imagination in historical studies, if, that is, they are to be returned to the kind of relevance to the solution of *present* problems that they were once thought to have had in certain earlier times. For it takes imagination to recognise that much that went without saying in modernist times has to be revised, rejected or simply 'archived' in postmodernist times. And here the issue really has to do with whether one believes that the time in which we live is so different from what came before (or what was once thought to have come before) that a fundamental reordering of the human and social sciences is demanded.

Well, all of our manifesters appear to think that *something* has happened to Western society, to the humanities in general, and to historical studies in particular. Whether they think that what has happened amounts to a fundamental change in what Hannah Arendt called 'the human condition' is unclear. But it seems obvious that for those of us who believe we live in an epoch in which the rules of the societal game have changed, rendering our current understanding of who we are and where we are heading problematic, some sort of radical rethinking is required. Historians deal with change and should, therefore, be more receptive to the possibilities of fundamental changes in our sciences and arts than are those who think that history is always more about continuities than discontinuities. Whatever latitude there may be for a difference of opinion over details, one gross fact (yes, *fact*) stands before us with undeniable clarity: this is the population explosion, the movement of populations, and the impact of these displaced multitudes on traditional and 'modern' communities, social institutions and ideologies. As Fredric Jameson has observed, it may well be that such seemingly 'new' historical phenomena as the two world wars, the Depression, mass manufactured genocide, and atomic warfare are indeed 'commensurable', at some level, to their historical prototypes. But the sheer mass of peoples now populating the globe requires changes in our notions of that 'human nature' we are all interested in and that 'history' which formerly we thought was its creation.

So, it is not a matter of simply incorporating women, subalterns, primitives, gays, people of colour, immigrants and whatever other group now claims a place in 'our' history or rather in our (by which I mean 'Western') accounts of 'history'. It is now a matter – for us, historians – of rethinking history in terms adequate to the present age. Which means rethinking what is new and 'unheard of' in the present dispensation rather than seeking to accommodate earlier categories of explanation and presentation to what is manifestly new and different in a world seen only 'through Western eyes'. That is to say, if by history we mean not simply 'the past' but the relation between the 'present' understood as a part of 'history' and the 'past', then it is incumbent upon us to think about the possibility of the present *as* history.

But, as Keith Jenkins might ask, why history? What argues for the consignment of this task to the study of history? My answer to that question is that, after the end of religion and metaphysics, history is now all we have. Whether we like it or not, all of the human and social sciences now have their foundations in the messiness of the historical record, the debilities of the so-called historical method, and what Domanska calls the 'openness' of the historical imagination.

A number of the manifestos contained herein – those of Chakrabarty, Dening, Ermarth, LaCapra, Joyce, Harlan and Scott – deal with these kinds of considerations, which is to say, what is there about the present that requires revision or reform of the conventional historical 'apparatus' (what Althusser called the 'dispositif')? These manifesters, in general and for the most part, point us in the direction of a reformulation of historical thinking as a kind of *critique*. This seems, to me, to be the most fruitful idea emerging within these manifestos. Here critique means not only seeking to discern the limits of our current ideas about history, but the turning of a historical consciousness thus critiqued to the criticism of history's relations with the other disciplines of the human sciences and arts. Joan Scott pushes this point and invokes Foucauldian post-structuralism as a justification of it. It is not too strong to say that Foucault's idea of critique returns historical thinking to that historism from which – as Ankersmit asserts – it became detached during the time of history's service to delusionary humanism, on the one hand, and a false scientism, on the other. That is to say, insofar as critique has a meaning beyond the idea of discerning formal structures of expression, meaning and value in one's own and others' discourses and examining these for logical or artistic consistency, then this meaning is nothing other than the effort to identify the irreducible *historicity* of all things. And this means discerning the time-and-place specificity of a thing, identifying the ways in which it relates to its context or milieu, and determining the extent to which it is both enabled and hamstrung by this relationship. Above all, critique means the de-transcendentalisation of every regime of truth and knowledge, the denial of universals, substances and essences that are pressed upon us in all times and everywhere, and attention to whatever it is in a thing that makes it a singularity resistant to generalisation, abstraction and reification. In a word, critique means historicity, and historicity means attention to the evanescent immanence of everything. Not exactly a postmodernist idea, but modernist at least and radical enough – in Foucault's formulation – to be intriguing.

But by 'historism', however, we must mean the idea that, instead of there being a foundation or substance to which we can refer historical events and processes for the determination of their meaning, historical existence is itself the only foundation we have – which in turn means that, since history is a process of continual making and remaking, we have no stable or firm foundation at all. I take it that this was what Foucault had in mind when – in 'What Is Enlightenment?' – he spoke of giving 'a more positive content to what may be a philosophical ethos consisting in a critique of what we are saying, thinking, and doing, through a historical ontology of ourselves.' He goes on to say that criticism

> is no longer going to be practiced in the search for formal structures with universal value, but rather as a historical investigation into the events that have led us to constitute ourselves and to recognize ourselves as subjects of what we are doing, thinking, saying . . . In that sense, this criticism is . . . genealogical in its design and archeological in its method . . . And this critique will be genealogical in the sense that . . . it will separate out, from that contingency that has made us what we are, the possibility of no longer being, doing, or thinking what we are, do, or think.

In other words, historicisation, especially of the present, lifts the veil of its necessity, shows unacknowledged possibilities, and suggests routes of escape.

So, critique means, as Jameson says, 'Always historicize!'[2] but not in the conventional way of the professional historian, that is to say, not as a way of providing an event with a past from which it must have derived, but rather as a way of restoring events to their presents, to their living relations with their conditions of possibility. But more: it means treating the present as well as the past as history, which is to say, treating the present historically, as a condition adequate to its possibility but also as something to be gotten out of. It is this attitude towards the present as belonging to history – which is to say, as something worthy of being overcome and escaped from – that links critique to a particular kind of modernism or feeling of modernity characteristic of our time.

With the exception of Ankersmit and Southgate, our manifesters are all modernists in the sense of seeing the present age (even when they call it 'postmodernist') as offering problems, enigmas and anomalies that cannot be fruitfully confronted by any 'wisdom of the past'. Modernism, wherever it has appeared, is the conviction that today, now, or the present moment warrants study less as an outcome of some past than as a singularity that might give us notions of the kinds of knowledge we need from the past – and especially from the immediate or recent past – in order to 'get out of it' and move on to other, more creative forms of selfhood, community and rationality.

Now, this notion of escaping from the present constitutes a major difference between our postmodernist and our modernist manifesters. This split is more important than any split between progressives and conservatives could be, because, as Chakrabarty points out in his essay, it is historians of a generally 'liberal' persuasion, such as Evans, Ginsburg, Davis, Hobsbawm, Appleby and, yes, I must add, Lowenthal, Domanska, LaCapra and Southgate, among our manifesters, and countless others, persons of goodwill and generous mindedness, who continue to believe that, with just a little adjustment, the older values of objectivity, empiricism and emergent causality can still serve to make historical studies worth doing and relevant to the solution of the problems of our modernity.

But it won't work. Objective, empirical, causalistic historiography never convinced anyone of anything they did not already believe. Nor can the dissociation of the past from the present save the study of either from ideological distortion. Why? Because the dissociation of the past from the present *is* the ideological distortion which permits 'history' to be put in the service of any political cause, right, left or centre, and allows the facts to be separated from their description, on the one side, and from the events of which they are predications, on the other.

A number of our manifesters suggest that what current historiology lacks is imagination, or imaginativeness, or – to put it slightly differently – a capacity to appreciate the cognitive value of image-thinking, especially in an age of mediatisation and the elevation of the image over the word as the sign that addresses both the reason and the senses simultaneously. Mark Poster deals with this issue in his manifesto in terms of the import of the new media for the writing of history in the future. But Robert Rosenstone, Greg Dening, David Harlan, Ewa Domanska and Ann Rigney address it too, in their reflections on the relation between history and art. This is a complex issue and relates to the effort by modern historians to transform their discipline into a 'science' by isolating it from philosophical speculation (of the Hegelian sort), on the one side, and fiction (of the romance kind, *à la* Sir Walter Scott), on the other. Fear of these two heresies appears regularly throughout the history of modern historiological theory. We see it in Dominick LaCapra's desire to save history from the twin dangers of naïve positivism, which thinks that everything in the past just lies out there waiting to be found, and radical constructivism, which seems to hold that there is nothing out there, that the past has to be invented out of whole cloth (whatever that is), and that in the process 'anything goes'. LaCapra appears to be on the right track in his effort to infuse a few simple principles of psychoanalytical self-awareness into historical reflection, and he is surely right about the limitations of what he calls 'the self-sufficient research paradigm' (or what the other manifesters call 'conventional history') and 'radical constructivism'. He counsels exchange between history and critical theory, especially inasmuch as historians, in their adoption of the stance of 'objectivity', set up barriers to any consideration of their own unconscious identification with or revulsion towards their objects of study. Such is especially the case, LaCapra suggests, when it is a matter of events of the recent past that may involve guilt and responsibility for crimes and violations and in which national identities themselves are threatened by the ways in which different professions may wish to come to terms with them. LaCapra finds in the psychoanalytical conceptions of trauma, transference, acting out, working through and mourning ways of thinking about historians' relation to their objects of study – and to their colleagues in the profession who may honestly hold views that appear vile, disgusting and inhuman in the extent to which they do not accord with each individual historian's own putatively objective findings.

Of course, it is not so simple as that. As LaCapra insists, whatever else it may be, historical discourse always involves a truth-claim of some kind (or rather of many kinds) and at different levels of the discourse itself. And here critique as history and history as critique have to confront the question of whether truth is an epistemological issue, a semantic issue, or both. The idea that truth is a semantic issue is a hobby-horse of the philosopher Jerry Fodor, and I think it gives us a way of thinking about the issue of the relation between history and literature raised by a number of our manifesters.

In large part, the issue of the relation between history and literature was created by that 'post-structuralism' which, as Joan Scott and Elizabeth Ermarth argue, was a product of what some people call 'the linguistic turn' and others 'the discursive turn' in the human sciences. If, as Ermarth points out, language is a complex system of encoded signs, the elements of which bear no necessary (natural) relationship to the things in the world to which they refer, then the meanings ascribed to things and their relationships in discourses are more a function of the codes used to indicate them than of any substance or essence of which the things are different kinds of manifestations. When it comes to complex systems of signs (sequences or sets greater in extent than a simple sentence), we are engaged in the work of endowing complex bodies of phenomena with complex structures of meaning. The arbitrariness of the choice of code or codes to be used plus the inherent ambiguity of reference (in non-algorithmic discourse, in which the meanings of the unit-terms are stipulated in advance) submits the whole issue of the truth of the whole set or sequence to the domain of semantics rather than that of epistemology. It is this rather than generic difference and similarity that constitutes the disturbing similarities between some kinds of factual discourse (like histories, for example) and some kinds of fictional discourse (like novels, romances or epics). With respect to historical theory, the difference between a factual account of past events and a fictional account of them would no longer lie in the differences between their respective referents (real and imaginary, respectively) but in the differences and similarities between the codes used in each to endow those events with one kind of meaning versus another kind.

Chakrabarty raises the issue of the imagination in reference to the case of subaltern studies, which has to posit a past reality of the colonised covered over, hidden or repressed by colonial powers before it can begin the work of consciousness-raising in the present. Subaltern studies is a good example of critique-history because it must begin by dismantling the ornate cover story which blocks access to the past of India's poor and oppressed groups, and because it is directed at the task of consciousness-raising in the present and must make use of something like Vico's poetic history in order to produce what might be called not so much history but the 'history effect'. Here elements of empathy, sincerity, intuition, generosity of spirit and a sense of the possible are more important than forensic skills and dialectics. The pay-off is more likely to resemble a literary work than a conventional history.

None of our manifesters is interested, I think, in turning historians' attention to imaginary events and entities and having them write fictions rather than histories. On the contrary, most of them seem to presuppose that historical writing is better understood as a kind of discourse than a (simulated) eyewitness account of events and entities that never had the concreteness and clarity of outline with which historical writing typically endows them. In presuming that historical reflection is a discourse rather than a discipline (or, better, that the discipline of historical reflection is discursive rather than starkly constative), we can begin to see that historians might very well utilise the kinds of literary devices typically used by writers of imaginative prose (or even poetry) and, beyond that, wish to endow the events and entities they have come to know through research with the kinds of meaning in which poetic discourse has dealt since the time of the epic (if not before). Here it is a matter of summoning up before the mind's eye a complex picture or spectacle of happening that bears the truth of the kinds of meaning that everyone recognises as proper to serious poetic utterance. It is a matter of code-switching over the arc of the discourse rather than of imposing a fictional structure of meaning on real events.

Elizabeth Ermarth, Joan Scott, Ann Rigney, Robert Rosenstone, David Harlan, Ewa Domanska and Greg Dening make a point like this or at least head us in the direction of it by their examples. In all these instances, however, our manifesters raise the history–literature connection in terms of the necessity of imagination as a supplement to the analytical reason of the professional scholar. It is here that the problem of history's traditional 'others' is raised; here that the issue of the relation between the professional historian and the amateur or dilettante rears its head; and here that the subjectivity–objectivity question is (however peremptorily) laid to rest.

Modern, professional historical studies harbour a distinct suspicion of, not to say outright hostility towards (literary and visual) art – especially to modernist art (both abstract and expressionist) and its postmodernist counterparts. Why this is so would take too long to document, but in general historians do not like modernist art's abandonment of the mimetic pro-gramme and its commitment to free formal invention. Insofar, then, as there is any artistic element in professional historical discourse, it is to some version of mimetic realism that it remains wedded. This realism justifies a belief in a picture-theory of representation and the correspondence theory of truth to which most historians are committed. But modernist and postmodernist art are informed by a coherence notion of truth and to a notion of referentiality that is more performative than mimetic or constative.

Now, I take it that this is what, among other things, Greg Dening wishes to tell us in the way he has composed his (anti-)manifesto. 'I do not write fiction . . . I do not write non-fiction, either.' So what does he write? On the basis of the sample he provides, I would say – consistently with Ermarth's insistence that we look for difference and credit the negative – that Dening writes 'not non-fiction'. If this sounds enigmatic (or simply silly), I apologise; but if one examines the text Dening has so generously given us (it must have taken a lot out of him to write it), one can see that it falls outside the categories we conventionally use to classify prose work. It is imaginative (rather than imaginary); it is concrete (rich in apt figures and tropes); it is realistic (in its technical information); it is poetic (in the way it uses images that engage the bodily senses of the reader); it is referential (its objects are located in time and space that are both real and imaginary); and so on. It is not, as Ann Rigney observes in another context, a matter of a historian *becoming* a novelist or a lyric poet but rather of using all of the resources that his and his subjects' languages provide for the conjuring up of a complex image of life in the there and then of a specific reality. It at once brings closer and defamiliarises a specific group of people engaged in an epic, if not a noble (no other words seem right), enterprise. It shows an aspect of the common humanity that is worthy of being memorialised. It may not be that 'gift of the past' that Patrick Joyce celebrates but it is a gift of some kind from somewhere – the imagination of Greg Dening, I surmise.

Does Dening's gift qualify for inclusion among the works that would (*à la* Foucault) critique historiography by historicising it? Yes, but not by argument; rather indirectly and by performance. That is, inasmuch as it shows the advantage of bringing a sensibility cultivated in other disciplines (ethnography, in this case) to the work of representation. So too in its formal aspects: Dening has chosen a mode of representation that gets him beyond the subject–object split that so bothers the realists among us historians. It is often pointed out that poetic utterance is neither factual nor fictional because it suspends the referential function in order to bring attention to the power of making meaning out of sounds which, taken individually, have no meaning at all. But this does not make the discourse in which the poetic function is allowed expression either more or less subjective or objective. Because the poetic text is not making truth-claims of the kind that could be confirmed or disconfirmed by appeal to either observation or documentary evidence. It is making a meaning-claim by showing how some aspect of the real world is possible. The philosophers of critique tell us that we must be seeking 'the conditions of possibility' of anything whose reality we are trying to identify. This search can be undertaken with a variety of means, of which conceptual thought is one. But figurative thought or rather figurative thinking is another means, and poetic utterance is its instrument.

The claims of the imagination are pertinent to other issues raised by our manifesters. To Poster's prophecy that 'historians of the future will be writing a history of the virtual . . . [which] requires a fundamental rethinking of the basic constituents of historical texts, historical research procedures, theoretical frameworks, etc.' To Chakrabarty's and Joyce's recommendations for rethinking the nature of the archive that historians of the future will have to use – both the archive that has become digitalised and the archive that has been set up to obliterate memory of the victims of colonisation and imperial exploitation. To Harlan's and Rigney's defence of the dignity of the historical novel and historical film, and especially Harlan's argument that it is 'voice' we find captured in such new genres as 'the postmodern historical romance' as analysed by Amy Elias in her book *Sublime Desire: History and Post-1960s Fiction* (2001).

It is here that a second name, equal in its postmodern authority to that of Foucault, enters the picture. The name is that of W. G. Sebald, author of a number of works that occupy the *limines* between history and literature; or, if one wishes, between fact and fiction. Both Rigney and LaCapra invoke Sebald as a possible model for the kind of historical text we might wish for in the future. LaCapra notes the invention in the post-Holocaust years of the new genre of the testimony, the personal account of great, indeed monstrously criminal, events that fuse memory and history in the interest less of telling the truth about the past than of telling what it felt like to be the victim of powers answerable to no law of God, man or nature. Sebald provides a 'literary' treatment of the genre of the testimony which, by what Rigney calls its 'defamiliarising techniques', succeeds in subjecting the genre to the kind of sympathetic 'critique' to which we would wish all of our compelling cultural products to be subjected. If by 'critique' we mean identifying the conditions of possibility of a given entity's appearance in history and if we mean by 'identifying the conditions of possibility' of such an entity the detailed description of its historicity, then Sebald's *Austerlitz* (and indeed his other works, including his *Luftkrieg und Literatur* – 'The Natural History of Destruction', on the bombing of Hamburg in the Second World War) certainly qualifies for the title thereof. Indeed, it does not seem outlandish to say that postmodernist discourse theory might point the way – for our time – to the resolution of the problem of objectivity versus subjectivity in the relation of historical events, to the problem of fact versus fiction in the description of historical events, and to the conflict between explanation and narration in the representation of historical processes.

Beyond that, postmodernist experimentation in the representation of historical reality may very well get us beyond the distinction – always kind of scandalous – between the professional historian, on the one hand, and the amateur, dilettante or 'practical' student of history, on the other. No one owns the past, and no one has a monopoly on how to study it, or, for that matter, how to study the relation between past and present. As Ermarth says, we are all historians today. If we are interested in making sense of the real world, we cannot be otherwise. But we are not bound to be bound by the conventions that bind the professional historian to his or her traditional practices in the study of the past. As the Bard has Coriolanus say on the eve of his exile, 'There is a world elsewhere'.

Notes

1   There are different kinds of irony too: humorous in the case of Rosenstone, enthusiastic in the case of Dening, and bittersweet in the case of Lowenthal. And in two instances, those of Southgate and Ankersmit, there is (if I am not mistaken) a good deal of parody as well: parodies of older, premodernist programmes, humanist and historicist, respectively.
2   Fredric Jameson, *The Political Unconscious: Narrative as a Socially Symbolic Act* (Ithaca: Cornell University Press, 1980), p. 9.

Index

constructionist history 3, 46, 62, 69, 141–2, 145
constructivist 128, 165, 166, 171, 176
conventional history 52–60, 62–4, 227, 228
CPU 42
critical history xii, 24, 26, 27, 30, 35, 88–97
critical theory 24, 36–7, 40, 160–2, 174, 175, 227
Croce, B. 197
cross cultural 98–107
Culler, J. 178, 203
culture/cultural/ cultural
    history/cultural turn xi, xii, 4, 5, 8, 13, 13, 15, 17–20, 23, 28, 30, 33, 35, 39–48, 50–7, 59, 60, 62, 64–6, 67, 68, 69, 71, 74, 75, 77, 78, 83, 86, 93, 94, 97, 98–107, 108, 110, 113, 114, 119, 120, 122–4, 126, 129, 131–3, 135, 136, 138, 141–3, 146–7, 149–54, 157–60, 166, 167, 169, 171, 175, 177, 179, 182, 183, 190, 197, 200, 202, 203, 208, 209, 210–11, 215, 217, 218, 223, 230

dalits 77–80, 84, 86
Darwin, C. 56, 106, 220
database 42, 47, 48, 158
Davis, N. Z. 81, 82, 83, 86
deconstruction/deconstructionist 3–5, 8, 9, 23, 26, 36, 83, 113, 116, 134, 142, 162, 167, 198, 199, 201, 220
deconstructionist history 3, 142
Deleuze, G. 4
DeLillo, D. 109, 114, 115, 117, 129
democracy 25–6, 73, 79, 83, 85–6, 125,178, 185, 188, 190, 193
Demos, J. 110, 117, 129
Dening, G. 5, 7, 8, 98–107, 224, 226, 228, 229, 231
Derrida, J. 1, 6, 9, 23, 26, 31, 32, 34, 35, 36, 37, 38, 76, 116, 197, 203, 204, 220
dialogic xi, 5, 78, 99, 102,103, 126, 161, 164
Dickinson, P. 215, 218
Dickow, A. 26, 36
digital logic 38
discipline of history, the 19, 40, 44, 69, 77, 79, 80, 83, 88, 92, 123
discourse xii, 2–3, 5, 6–7, 16, 18, 21, 29–30, 36, 47, 60, 81, 86, 94, 106,
116, 125, 127–9, 133, 158, 160, 164, 171, 172, 176, 177, 178, 191, 192, 200, 201, 210, 216, 224, 227–30
discursive condition 8, 51, 52, 58, 60–5
Disney 45, 212, 217
Disraeli, B. 61, 205, 216
dissent/dissenters/dissenting xii, 1–3, 6
diversity xii, 1, 7, 69–70, 83, 141, 145
docudrama 165, 169
Domanska, E. 7, 8, 197–204, 221, 222, 224, 226, 228
Durkheim, E. 216, 218
DVD 46

Eaglestone, R. 203
Eagleton, T. 197
Elias, A. 115–16, 118, 126, 128, 129, 230
Eliot, T. S. 72, 76
empirical/empiricist 1–3, 5, 19–20, 22, 27, 32, 33, 35, 51–3, 55–6, 60–3, 67, 69, 78, 80, 95, 129, 133, 138, 153, 161, 163, 168, 172, 226
'end of history' 2, 73, 198
Enlightenment, The 4, 6, 24, 28, 37, 65, 72, 133, 136, 144, 154, 205–7, 215, 225
epistemological/epistemology 2–5, 20, 22, 28, 53, 83, 114, 127, 151, 156, 165, 200, 227
Ermarth, E. D. 4, 5, 6, 7, 8, 10, 20, 31, 35, 37, 50–66, 221, 224, 227, 228, 229, 231
ethics xi, xii, 5, 6, 10, 19, 22, 25, 32–7, 42, 68, 75, 89–90, 93, 141, 144, 154, 162, 165, 174, 175, 176, 179, 181, 199, 200–4, 223
Evans, R. 81, 123, 172, 226
eviscerated past, the 210–11
existential/existentialist/existentiality 12–14, 58, 125, 128, 129, 135, 165, 201
experimental history 3–4, 10, 13, 51, 55–6, 64, 124, 155–8, 160, 166–7, 178, 180–1, 220, 223, 231
fact/s 15, 16, 18, 19, 22, 26, 27–33, 47, 50–2, 57, 61, 64, 76, 80, 83, 104, 109, 117–18, 121, 123, 129, 133, 142–3, 160, 163, 165, 171, 176, 199, 223, 226, 227, 229, 230
Fanon, F. 34, 100, 106

Sceptical History
Feminist and Postmodern Approaches in Practice
Hélène Bowen Raddeker

'One of the great virtues of the book is that it uses examples from historical writing worldwide, examining global subjects . . . The book is clearly written and full of insights about a wide range of historical topics. It is a welcome handbook for both teachers and students, even for advanced historians who want to know more about postmodern theory.'

Bonnie Smith, *Rutgers University*

Sceptical History familiarises readers with the postmodern critique of history whilst also focusing upon the question of how to practise postmodernist feminist (sceptical) history.

A highly original work, this book considers major themes including cultural, class and sexual identity and 'difference', weaving them into debates on the nature and methods of history. In so doing it arrives at new ways of doing 'history and theory' that do not exclude feminist approaches or attention to non-Western history.

Hélène Bowen Raddeker's arguments extend beyond the postmodernist critique of history to other aspects of postmodernist thinking, including the postcolonial challenge to humanism and Eurocentric metanarratives of progress. Using a wide range of historical and cultural examples, she draws extensively on feminist scholarship and historiography.

Sceptical History provides an accessible guide to some of the most complex theories current today.

ISBN13: 978-0-415-34115-8 (hbk)
ISBN13: 978-0-415-34114-4 (pbk)

Available at all good bookshops
For ordering and further information please visit:
www.routledge.com

What is History For?
Beverley Southgate

'An essential read . . . this is an informed scholarly and lucidly written text on the purposes of history which also confronts the inadequate shibboleths of today's dominant 'history culture' – Professor Keith Jenkins, *University College, Chichester*

'Beverly Southgate has an elegant and open style that is an excellent vehicle for getting complex ideas across' – Professor Alun Munslow, *University of Staffordshire*

What is History For? is a timely publication that examines the purpose and point of historical studies. Recent debates on the role of the humanities and the ongoing impact of poststructuralist thought on the very nature of historical enquiry, have rendered the question of what history is for of utmost importance.

Charting the development of historical studies, Beverley Southgate examines the various uses to which history has been put. While history has often supposedly been studied 'for its own sake', Southgate argues that this seemingly innocent approach masks an inherent conservatism and exposes the ways in which history has, sometimes deliberately, sometimes inadvertently, been used for socio-political purposes. This fascinating historicisation of the study of history is unique in its focus on the future of the subject as well as its past and provides compulsive reading for students and the general reader alike.

ISBN13: 978-0-415-35098-3 (hbk)
ISBN13: 978-0-415-35099-0 (pbk)

History: What and Why?
Beverley Southgate

History: What and Why? is an introductory survey of the nature and purpose of history.

Beverley Southgate argues that the traditional model of the subject as a re-discovery of the past `as it was' has now been superseded. It has been successfully challenged by developments in other disciplines, such as linguistics, psychology and philosophy, together with the work of Marxist, feminist and post-colonial historians.

This book combines a historical perspective with a clear guide to current debates about the nature of history. It proposes a positive role for historical study in the postmodern era.

ISBN13: 987-0-415-25657-5 (hbk)
ISBN13: 978-0-415-25658-2 (pbk)

Available at all good bookshops
For ordering and further information please visit:
www.routledge.com

The Routledge Companion to Historical Studies
Alun Munslow

The Routledge Companion to Historical Studies serves as a much needed critical introduction to the key issues, historians, philosophers and theories which have prompted the rethinking of history and its practice that has gathered pace since the 1990s.

Key concepts that address both how historians work and organise the past, such as class, empiricism, agency/structure, epistemology, and hermeneutics are examined through the ideas of leading historians and philosophers such as Vico, Croce, Collingwood, Elton, Kant, Nietzsche, Derrida, and White. Many entries have been substantially updated and offer an essential analysis of the state of history thinking and practice today. Alun Munslow has added 29 new entries including Carl Becker, Frank R. Ankersmit, Richard Rorty, Jean-Francois Lyotard, Jean Baudrillard, gender, justified belief, the aesthetic turn, race, film, biography, cultural history, critical theory and experimental history.

With a revised introduction, setting out the state of the discipline of history today, as well as an extended and updated bibliography *The Routledge Companion to Historical Studies* is the essential reference work for all students of history.

ISBN13: 978-0-415-38577-0 (pbk)

Available at all good bookshops
For ordering and further information please visit:
www.routledge.com

Philosophy of History
M.C. Lemon

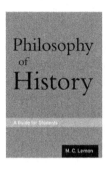

Philosophy of History is an essential introduction to a vast body of writing about history, from Classical Greece and Rome to the contemporary world. M.C. Lemon maps out key debates and central concepts of philosophy of history, placing principal thinkers in the context of their times and schools of thought.

Lemon explains the crucial differences between *speculative* philosophy as an enquiry into the course and meaning of history, and *analytic* philosophy of history as relating to the nature and methods of history as a discipline. Divided into three parts this guide provides a comprehensive study of history thought since ancient times.

ISBN13: 978-0-415-16204-3 (hbk)
ISBN13: 978-0-415-16205-0 (pbk)

Available at all good bookshops
For ordering and further information please visit:
www.routledge.com

Lightning Source UK Ltd.
Milton Keynes UK
UKOW05f2025120916

282827UK00014B/293/P